For Mike:

Not on the rocks but the stepping
stones ...

A DREAM OF WHITE HORSES

Michelangelo, Bernini and his school I understand better, those
fellows had the courage to commit a madness now and then.
William Blake

My instinct tells me that my head is an organ for burrowing, as
some creatures use their snout and forepaws, and with it I
would mine and burrow my way through these hills. *Thoreau*

DEDICATION

To my mid-wives, Linda and Grace;
Jim, Oliver, Hugh, Dave, Ben, Bob, Hamish, Stephen, Colin,
Peter, Mike, Tanky, and Haworth, on the rocks; Allen, Steve,
Irwin, Gerald, Al, Jim, Ian, Geoff, David, Terry, Robin, Phil
and Ken, on paper; Tony, John and Judy, Mary and John,
Sharon and Paul, and Clare, with homes from home;
Gloria, who gave me the room to write in;
and, in all ways, Lia my wife:
Because you were there.

EDWIN DRUMMOND

A Dream of White Horses

RECOLLECTIONS OF A
LIFE ON THE ROCKS

FOREWORD BY ALLEN STECK

DIADEM BOOKS · LONDON
1987

Published in Great Britain by
Diadem Books Ltd., London

Copyright © 1987 by Edwin Drummond

All trade enquiries to Cordee,
3a De Montfort Street, Leicester

British Library Cataloguing in Publication Data:
Drummond, Edwin
A dream of white horses.
   I. Title
   828, 91409   PR6054. k78/

   ISBN 0-906371-96-1 (UK)

Printed in Great Britain by
A. Wheaton and Co. Ltd. Exeter
and Penshurst Press, Tunbridge Wells

[4]

Contents

Foreword

by ALLEN STECK

One wonders if Drummond is a poet who climbs, or whether he is a climber who writes poetry. Possibly the former for the climber in him seems less dominant now that he has passed the magic age of forty; it does not matter, except that the mixture lends a distinctive creative force to his writing. Drummond is a Keats Prize winner (1973 and 1974) and the recipient of a National Poetry Prize (U.K.) in 1979. He has recently brought his poetry onto the stage in England where he prowls around a twenty-foot tripodal scaffolding reciting his poems, periodically shinning up one of the legs and mantelshelfing onto a tiny summit platform to deliver particularly notable passages. The performance has been given in various Universities and at the National Mountaineering Conference, where, unexpectedly, it was well received. I have not seen this, and I find it greatly amusing that an assembly of cynical climbers, not knowing what to expect, were so greatly impressed by the confidence and audacity of Drummond's performance which, by all accounts, combined athleticism with polished theatricals.

In *A Dream of White Horses* Ed Drummond, poet and climber, has assembled an intense personal story of surprising depth and honesty. It is, in fact, the most compelling autobiography written by a climber that I have seen in many years. The writing binding this complex mosaic together is rich in imagery, and though occasionally mannered and cryptic, it flows along refreshingly like a mountain stream over ribbed granite. But let there be no mistake: *A Dream of White Horses* is written by a climber specifically for climbers — admittedly a narrow audience — whose knowledge of the jargon, the agony of climbing, the names of famous climbers and their favourite cliffs is presupposed, almost excessively so. He does not at all underestimate the patience or the intellect of his readers.

I first met Drummond the writer early in 1969 when he submitted the brief story "White Elephant, White Whale" for publication in *Ascent*. We liked this brief commentary for its frankness and humility; it was an apology by a visiting English climber, for lacking the skill to make the second ascent of the North America Wall on Yosemite's El Capitan. Even though Drummond did complete a number of hard routes that season, Camp 4 residents considered him a soft-spoken, eccentric, presumptuous Englishman, more intent on notoriety than the simple, simian pleasures of climbing. When I met Drummond in person on his return from Yosemite, I recall being charmed by this eccentricity as well as his naiveté (not presumption) in thinking he could climb the N.A. Wall. It was evident that a powerful ego lay beneath his otherwise calm exterior; Drummond soon proved himself capable of big-wall routes and, ultimately, climbing the N.A. Wall, which now had become an *idée fixe* for him. 'When I am worthy of an El Capitan climb,' he wrote to me in 1971, 'I shall come back.' His two great multi-day first ascents in Northern Europe occured in the early 1970s and generated two more *Ascent* stories, "The Incubus Hills" (1971) and "Mirror, Mirror" (1973). The editors were bold enough to write on the contributors' page in the 1973 volume:

> We consider Ed the only true successor to Scotland's immortal Robin Smith as a creative climber/author. Drummond's style and goals as a climber have always seemed off-beat, out of the mainstream of British climbing. In a country of fierce little crags he has become a "big wall man" and though his climbs, like his prose, have aroused controversy, several must be recognized as masterpieces.

Fourteen years later, the statement still seems valid. The core strength of his writing lies in his startling imagery, whether simile, metaphor, or simply the choice of an evocative adjective. These images are often woven into a beautiful, lilting cadence. The ultimate effect is that Drummond magically brings you right to his stance on the cliff; you feel and see, as though his senses were yours. An extraordinary gift. But there are occasional lapses where Drummond loses discipline: stringing words together to form cryptic utterances, mentioning people's names without introduction, piling metaphors one on top of another − all of which tries our patience. His neologisms, though forced, do have a poetic charm. Here, Drummond is the custodian of peotic license, the iconoclast, ripping pages from *The Chicago Manual of Style* to insulate his bivouac hammock. There are many noteworthy elements in this *dream of white horses.* Drummond's building climbing activities are only partially revealed in "Nelson Mandela's Column", where he uses his climbing skills as social protest against apartheid in South Africa. The Statue of Liberty and Grace Cathedral were also protest climbs, but the attempt on the Transamerica Building, in San Francisco, was strictly for Drummond himself. He accomplished these illegal climbs with the knowledge that there would be consequences in the form of incarceration, forced work programmes and heavy fines, not to mention the potential groundfall. Unlike climbing a remote crag in Scotland, Drummond's building climbing is ineluctably under public scrutiny, but I must add that he undertakes these forays into sensationalism with a certain panache.

"Jimlove Menwords" a review of *Menlove* by Jim Perrin, is a serious piece in which Drummond suppresses his poetic urges and presents an extremely intellectual nineteen-page dismissal of most of Perrin's analyses concerning the life, and death (by suicide) of Menlove Edwards. The inclusion of this essay in an autobiography is startling, yet understandable, almost essential for in his discussions Drummond reveals his own philosophic nature. This essay is also important for its extensive literary merit, evidence that Drummond is able to alter his style to suit the occasion. Which he does also in "Proud" and "A Grace Period", both stories focussing on aspects of his life much less involved with climbing, though no less traumatic, and presented in a softer, more lyrical style. This happens not so much in "Proud" and its gloomy, measured glimpse into troublesome adolescence as in "A Grace Period" where his descriptive narrative of travelling through eastern Nepal while occupied with worrisome ruminations concerning his marriage, is perhaps the most graceful in this book. There is a linkage between the two essays: that problems of adolescence often persevere to haunt the adult emotional web.

"Stone" and its epilogue, "Hubris, An Open Letter to Royal Robbins" along with "The Incubus Hills," "Mirror, Mirror," and "Frankenstein and Linda" form the most powerful climbing writing in this collection. The intensity, the magnitude of the undertakings themselves (they rank among the most demanding routes in the world; Drummond's own ascents have yet to be repeated) is reflected in the audacious and innovative prose. Acquaintances of mine have characterized Drummond's ego as colossal and frightening; what they do not realize is that climbs of this nature demand such a measure of inner strength. "Stone" is the fitting culmination of this frenzy of climbing. The story of his baptism by hypothermia during the fourteen-day solo attempt of the North America Wall, his old nemesis, is perhaps Drummond's most poetic expression of a demented state of mind. What he does not say at the close of his story is that his deathly embrace with hypothermia was broken at the last moment by a timely helicopter rescue about the same time that two Japanese were found frozen to death a few feet from the rim of the Nose route. '. . . after two weeks alone an ego starts to cave in,' he writes, 'to be delivered from that oppressive igloo . . . was the high point of my life.' I sensed the subliminal suggestion of a death wish as I read these stories, but Drummond prefers to deal inferentially with this mystifying irony: there is no opening of this Pandora's box. In reality, though, Drummond is no different from all other climbers who push their audacity to the limit: are we not all moths at the flame?

ALLEN STECK
Berkeley, 1987

To Climb or Not to Climb

If climbing is speaking a fluent body language,
yesterday was all Greek
to me . . .

Feet stuttered on doorsteps of granite:
a blank face.
Tongue-tied, my fingers
let me down, looking at the ground
as if I'd forgotten my name.

Arms hung dumbfounded.
Body too English,
my head pounded
as I mantelshelfed — stiffening
like I was being searched
against a wall in Tehran.
I crammed fists into cracks
I could have laybacked,
not eyed the slack like a noose.
Refusing to move
until I was tugged.

Back? Down?
To creep to the tent,
and dream I'm in the *corps d'esprit*
as I seemed to be

once? A hermit on Vector,
depressed in the cave when it rained,
the overhang, the slab and curling lip
where I almost peeled
— lifted out like a crab — grappling —
joy in my arms, my girlfriend
asleep in the field.

Never a hard man . . .
On Dinosaur
with Bob, on the second ascent
and his first extreme,
bronze-aged by the setting sun,
the age of mammals had just begun.
Scissoring splits I clawed up Mammoth,
putting my foot in it — the haemorrhage-red sling
that Brown disparaged.
On Great Wall, itching to throw off
Pete Crew's shoes,
and wiggle up with my toes
like Wilmott tried to later.
Taking my past
so close to breaking
on Ulysses' Bow, that the armour shattered
and the arrow flew
through my thumping heart again.
Stanage: where I grasped
the meaning of leaning
from Higgar Tor and the Rasp,
up to the thin smile on another jutting jaw,
where Dave Sales sighed

his last.
As you drove me away
I felt I was being deported.

Today I got up early
and began drinking: very
black coffee.
Thinking . . .

Of weightlifting
before it's too late.
Joining my local gym,
learning to press, snatch and
update Atlas.
To winter at Joshua,
between the branching granite
and — like lemurs up their trees —
the young climbers,

letting down a rope to me
when I was sinking fast, in difficulties
they just doodled up.
A part-timer to the last,
shy of being born again
through pull-up-push-up-pain,

I could stop.
Drop the chains
of karabiners, take the long way
round Cloggy.

Clogwyn Du'r Arddu!
Centre stage, a Midsummer Night's Dream,
ten years ago . . .
The colosseum of climbers,
thrown to the lines
that silence the garrulous as well as the great.
The wind was sweeping across the drops,
the sombre hills
drummed summer thunder
while I hopped and leapt and drilled

that bolt — a ring of violence —
then left for America in the hushed silence
of rain to come.
Now the interval is over.
Though all the performers have gone
— it's winter —

knowing my lines
I've come on again from behind the scenes,
the Bottom, or Fool
of British climbing,
squinting up at Master's Wall
— the one spot of the sun still on —
asking what it all means,
before the final curtain falls.

Or will it lift again?
That is the question . . .

Between the Lines

Under Stanage, a Sunday in late September, 1985. The air is kaleidoscopic with flies, sifted from the long, rain-bent grass, by sudden sunlight and a combing wind. Through the car window the ash trees are flocks of hummingbird-green leaves; leaving. A white butterfly totters past, Icarus for a day.

I'm sitting in the back of the VW camper with my shirt off; the Californian tan gone, a paleface again. For more than a year — after being pulled off the North America Wall — across the States, through Europe — Italy, Yugoslavia, France, I've been driving, looking for you all whom I left ten years ago.

Parked here for seven days and nights now. On a quick trip to Manchester and Accrington, in a chance conversation I heard about the extermination of the trout from the rivers by acid rain: 'Though no one says anything,' he said, 'we just fish from big holes in the ground they keep stocked up.' And, sitting here, I've seen you through the windscreen in canary-yellow and goldfish-orange anoraks and cagoules — and so many more of you! — drifting across the edge in all weathers; schools of climbers and hikers and flocks of hang-gliders drawn to the long purple trench, a breakwater against the swollen Pennines. Though you didn't know I was here, watching and writing.

Last Tuesday I wandered up, with my boots dangling from one hand and an empty chalk bag from the other, to that wing of grit I clung to, uplifted, twelve years ago. Some of you were there. A little embarrassed to ask, nevertheless, you gave me a handful. I floated up, fingers white-feathering the edge of the arête, to all appearances unruffled.

'How long have you been back?' one of you asked, which made me feel less stiff. Though later, when I was working on that boulder problem I hadn't done in over a decade, I wished you'd have waved, or called that you were leaving. For I'd noticed one of you come around the corner to see what I was up to. I watched you too for a while as you walked away down the track. You didn't look back; you were looking where you were going.

Like the two quartz pebbles, not so much as blinking when I scratched my way up the face without them. And it was then, as I strolled back past, that I looked up. And realised: Well. Maybe. I went up a ways, a bit of caterpillary nonchalance — but the thoughts started pecking so I crept back to the van.

[14]

Perhaps if you'd have been there watching I would have done it. You could have given me a spot. I wouldn't have had to ask even, I mean you'd have just understood that, well, I needed . . . Wouldn't you?

I couldn't have said that ten years ago. I felt it every time though that I leafed through climbing magazines in the States, always hoping to find that you'd not forgotten. I hadn't ever been able to bring myself to tell you how much you've always meant. I just hoped or something that you'd see that I couldn't simply go on climbing and say nothing.

I'm not complaining. The strange thing is that whenever we've met, you've always been really nice; polite. Of course I did notice the funny looks you'd give each other while I expounded, especially if I had my beret on, the one with the butterfly that looks as if it's just come out of my ear. And you haven't forgotten a thing! Only the other day Caroline asked me if I still ate dates. Which made me remember that perhaps my fingers were a bit stickier after I'd munched that block I hauled up in my socks in 1967 − for the only chalk we had back then was treacly experience − and maybe that was why I chattered that the ragged crack would go free. We talked on for a while, about the children and running marathons − we both wept at the end of our one and only − and soon, both relaxed. I had a second cup of coffee and looked around. There were several photos of Nick up in the house. One, of him looking out from his belay seat beneath the roof on the Salathé, had the hint of a smile, gently nervous, encouraging and warning at the same time; which was how I remembered him looking on me as I struggled to free the last move of the great wall section of the Rimmon route in 1970. I miss him. Drowned in an avalanche in the Himalayas, his two sons see his face every day at the head of the stairs as they rush off to school. Like the sky today semaphoring sun and shadow at the same time, confusing the insects, brushing the dust from the ledges and uncurling the fingers of ferns and climbers from their respective pockets, his look made you get up. And I sensed he was closer to trusting me than you. Or . . .

Monday at Phil's: I put down the phone. I felt like I'd been beaten up. I didn't care to ask Phil if he felt I was lacking in in . . . He knows me better than that. Don't you Phil? The telephone call had been like that recurrent dream I used to have, in which I'm trying to hide in the cloakrooms at my junior school. I have no clothes on. I can feel the damp, black macintoshes. It is like being naked among a clutch of constables who haven't noticed me yet. It's not the first time that he's put me to the wall.

But I feel almost grateful to him. As if I needed to be arrested.

'That must have hurt,' he added.

I mumbled 'Yes, yes,' reassuring him I was still on the line, as if he was a beginner dentist who needed to know I had nerves − and not a judge who'd once put me away. How was he to know I had escaped?

[15]

But how much of my willingness to take it from him is due to my getting softer, especially since the baby died and the realisation was born that at times I'd driven a bulldozer over people who looked up to me, putting my foot down, revving the hyperlogical arguments that got me through a degree in Philosophy and two marriages unscathed (like bolting up a slab) and how much to the truth of what he said, and the speed at which those low blows cut through my unconditioned nether regions! — I have no way of telling.

I looked up at the mirror as if checking my x-ray. I was scarlet. When he said, 'However, I have to admit that the climbing world is a hell of a lot more colourful because of your presence,' I had to smile.

Before calling him up I'd had the idea of saying — which I dropped as soon as I heard his Harley Street-dark voice, 'May I borrow your etriers?' However, to tell him directly what I had only hinted at in my recent letter, in which, in passing, I renamed a famous national monument, would have made him feel I was even more fickle than he suspected.

'You flit across the climbing scene every few years. Are you just the court jester? A lot of climbers think you're a real publicity seeker. Any book you write must address the central question: What are you?'

' "A literary thug" David said,' said Terry, when I told him the next day, as if we three were wise mice to his big cat, and not literary men who needed to put their words where their mouths are. It was starting to come back: Sitting in Mac's car in 1967 in the back next to him. Pete was in the front, Mac at the controls of his big, breasty Volvo, and we speedboated the bumpy road after Deiniolen, going downhill fast to Anglesey. I'd neither seen nor heard of him before. He was so frontal, demanding to know what my grading system meant, that I went limp beneath the heaviest armour- plated reply I could find to prevent him pricking my bubble. My system was, as I see it now, an attempt to mathematicise our rock dance. It was spawned by that promiscuous positivism in Philosophy that set up traffic signals in the river of life we call speech, and which has constructed most climbing discourse nowadays to sound like a voice-printed bank statement, a telephone directory of names and grades and ratings.

I don't recall what I said exactly in response to his grilling; no doubt it was as noetic as a geometrical point, having position but no magnitude, and probably made as much impression in the suddenly hushed car as a pin dropped in the Padarn on a Saturday night. Clad in my shorts and knee-length socks in the back, I felt as out of place among those iconoclasts as a racehorse being driven to the dogs. So it should have come as no surprise that when we reached the foot of Mammoth, he dropped his jeans and shat in the sea. 'That offended you didn't it,' he jeered, Falstaffian, the brown clods switching back and forth while I looked — distinctly — off.

But I wonder too how many of us by now would have had our feet up by the fire, a pipe in our mouths, and Rebuffat's latest book in our hands, after a stroll along our local outcrop on a Sunday afternoon, having pointed out some unconquerables we top-roped once, were it not for him: his rhythm and force, whitewater among the type setters; in a way his faithfulness. 'Are you going to be one of these four year wonders?' he said as Mac hit the gas over the Menai Straits. The godfather of climbing's overworld, putting out contracts for Changabang, The Goblin's Eyes, Cerro Torre, Everest the cruel way, whatever was new, whatever was never.

'It may interest you to know,' he told me over the phone, 'you weren't the first climber to make an anti-Apartheid protest. We did at Birmingham, just after Mandela was imprisoned.' I'm still not sure whether to tell him or not.

But hadn't he come all the way from Manchester to the crown court in London, where we were on trial after Nelson's, to act as a character witness? With reservations: we'd been charged with having caused over five hundred pounds worth of damage to the lightning conductor — which I vehemently denied:

'Come on you know me better than that!'

'What about Linden?' he shot back. So the Defence paid his train fare.

'You should be a politician,' he said, after the charges were dismissed and he'd been listening, headmasterly his stance, as I talked to the press outside the court about South Africa and Barclays.

Still, the scepticism's not just his. I remember Geoff saying in 1978, when I called him up just before going on the Column — and bear in mind I hadn't seen or spoken to him since I left for the States in 1975 — 'We were all scared of you.' So some of it is true. And the question mark I like to think of as a halo now feels more like a crown, if not of thorns, then paper.

But I don't understand how it is that he can dash around for more than twenty years with his hands overflowing with these squiggles that mean so much to us, these words like birds that move without moving, and still say he doesn't understand poetry.

Maybe it's the poets who are to blame. Spooning the syrups and cyanides of words without attachment to a shared world, spending days and years indoors, deprived of wind, of the elements, sun on your back like a hand, rain in the face, blisters, wet sandwiches, had they become mental mercenaries, instead of nurses on a battlefield of ideas, cities, people, land? But wasn't it the climbers too? Hinging on the layback at the end of Vector for the first time — like swinging on the door of your first car — hadn't their cult of silent strength reduced their accounts to the level of arrows scratched on the rock? A lonely crowd, poets and climbers, they send publishers up the wall.

Speaking of which, I should love to get him on a climb, redskins for five days on the Salathé say, sharing the last sardines after the headwall, with the wind scrubbing the stars and our women blowing car horns from the meadow.

I've just put my shirt back on. I was getting chilled, exposed like that. Will it rain? The clouds are bruising above Bleaklow now and the ferns are running. If Neil's going to get some pictures I must call him right away. I am going to try it. I'm feeling much better now that you've read my mind. And Geoff has said he might use a photo in the magazine. Which would be good publicity for the series. Don, I want to call it. Another one of you I never met, although I felt that every new route I did, I did standing on his working class shoulders. Besides, it's always been his route too, since he made the real leap, daring to try it all those years ago. In pumps I'll bet. I was — with it being next to Goliath — thinking of calling it David. But Don is more alive.

Incidentally, I get my chair next Tuesday, all twenty feet of it. Don't laugh — at least not in the wrong places. That's something else he told me, that since I've been gone, you've become more cynical. And Dave said the same thing.

'As long as they come,' I said.

I've had to close the door. It's raining after all, and this page — no guidebook duck's back — was beginning to look sorry for itself. I'd better leave it at that for today. But I will be back, there's a lot I must tell you about now that he's got me started. Proud: the father-figure I buried when he tried to become my mother; Frankenstein — and Linda the woman who tried to love him; Grace and Makalu — where I chose not to climb . . . And then there's Nelson's. Although I'm not ready to tell you about the Statue, I've included the stone.

There's the best and the worst of me here; my ups and downs. While some of the stories bloomed off their routes — ones like Great Wall, The Incubus Hills, Mirror, Mirror — others I had to dig for . . . Routes and roots.

Now I'm going climbing. There's a lot to do: All those smooth white blackboards at Raven Tor, Dovedale, Verdun, where I never did my homework; the Valley, that mango-yellow granite and the swifts on their ecstatic elastics, stretching all the way from Africa to the warm cunnies of the cracks. The hippos of grit ruminating deep in the heather all over Yorkshire. The winter-white elephants crossing Scotland; the whale-wave at Bowden Doors in the Cheviots; the Dolomites like scapulas in the back of Italy and the Dru, God's carrot for Bonatti. The three hundred foot albatross that landed at Almscliff last winter, its wings iced, its eyes still open. The tiny Ark rammed into the hillside at Higgar Tor, which first brought me to Sheffield. The Himalayas, those big bumps on the world's skull that have

[18]

drawn some of our finest hands to feel what lies beneath the surface we will lie beneath as well. All these moutains that never move. Until we do. Feet of clay, rope of blood, eye of faith, lead on.

You will be there won't you?

PART 1

Mirror, Mirror

The Heretic

I am weary of cathedrals
– Florence, Zagreb, Pisa –
a holy tourist
offering my Nikon . . .

I need the dreaming spires
of Tissington, the Dru,
or a stint on the Ben,
to let my spirit climb

out of my mind again:
who's in or out of print,
words in stone, stained glass or ink;
another crucifixion.

A day on Cloggy would clear my head like mint.

Or Gogarth.
A new line
in Wen Zawn,
threading the old red rope
through the mind's eye once more,
while the gulls harangue
and the waves roar
at my footsoles.

Treading the hinging overhangs
like seedlings or hot coals.
Praying for holds.

Proud . . .

THE HOUSE IS TALL, damp, gloomy, old. Our breath condenses on the blanket; in the morning it's wet, white fur. There is a river a stone's throw away. It breathes on the house at night. Nazis used to live here, firing across the river at the Allies. Our first guests are huddled around the fire in the kitchen. I've come upstairs to find some photographs to show the children. They are bored with adult talk and watching the fire.

Suddenly — there he is, standing next to me: big white stomach, pudgy, drooped breasts. And that arm, bemothered around me. In Ogwen, North Wales, 1962. I am squinting at the Brownie that Elsie, out of the picture, holds, squirming to keep my shoulder out of his damp armpit. My elbow sticks surreptitiously in his ribs. I have clenched my muscles, but shame has thrown a shadow on my face and a weak smile lies in the corner of my mouth. Was it surprising I started to climb?

. . . Jim rubbed coconut oil into my hair. I was just seventeen. On that first, warm, weekend that we went to Wales, when the oil thinned in the sunlight, with my slicked-back locks I looked like Bill Haley Jr. Later, up in the clouds with Jim, on the mountain that I'd scrambled three years before on a YHA holiday, the one with two, huge, standing stones on the summit, called Adam and Eve, the oil hardened and my hair looked as if it had been dipped in meringue. What would Mavis have thought of me then?

She'd dropped me the previous year. I had only just begun to feel her. We'd been together since we were fifteen. But each time I eased my fingers in the tight white cup, I started crying, uncontrollably: 'Why! Why!' She didn't like it. Then Cook, my friend, who had a habit of making a snorking noise in his nose, now, when I asked him not to if Mavis was there, took no notice. And he started walking back to her house with us, every afternoon, both of them laughing when he did it, in spite of my stony stare.

Anyway, after the school play, *The Importance of Being Earnest* (which I was), Malcolm liked me and it was he who introduced me to Jim, 'A tremendous man' he bumped into at the restaurant where he had lunch every day; who then appeared regularly. Malcolm always had money, even enough for a large slice of torte cake from Stantons, which he would cleave with a ruler in the playground, after I got back from the outside market: 'I'm a Methodist.' I gave him an apple.

He took me home. His parents fed me, listened endlessly, and gave me

[24]

ideas. His elder, mongol, brother David, used to call me 'Cariad — dear', in Welsh. One night after a church membership class at which the minister, Ankers, said he'd spit in the face of a god who pre-ordained anyone to Hell, I decided to stop swearing. Our friendship blossomed; Mal stopped going out with girls and both of us vowed, finally, to decide to begin to try seriously starting to stop doing it (as much), soon. We started running, after the chaste Herb Elliot, who, trained on sand dunes in the torrid Aussie wilderness, left the pack standing in the Rome Olympics, like Christ, Satan. And it was only Malcolm who believed me when the other boys were jeering. I was explaining why I hadn't saved those three easy shots in the final ten minutes, that resulted in us scraping a four-all draw. When I produced the culpable pink tablets that 'the doctor gave me to stop,' and which 'slowed my reactions,' they all shut up, even Malcolm, even though he didn't and I still did: (five hours the previous night). They were Gon chilblain tablets. Anyway, I did have chilblains.

But, after meeting Jim, I did stop. For a year. And this story is about that year, from 1962 to 1963, during which, after hanging in the balance, my mental testicle finally dropped. Accompanied by Bertrand Russell and Emily Brontë, I started to climb.

'It's okay, I'm here.' I am swinging my legs, happy as a sailor on the edge of his bunk with land in sight. The slow shadow on the rocks several hundred feet below, looks up to me and waves. An hour later he poses while I snap him, pretending to push apart the two pillars. On the way down in thick cloud, he tells me he likes me the most. Back at our camp below Idwal Cottage, Elsie has prepared the usual curry. He tells her he's never felt so young. We wrestle on the grass while she watches, beaming. After dinner we pray, read the Bible and go to sleep in the back of the blue Ford Thames van, with Jim in the middle, on the double mattress they've taken off their bed. I see the grey stones grow lilac. I wake in the night feeling crushed. Jim's jammed against me. I can't move. Elsie is snoring. There wouldn't have been room for Malcolm anyway.

On Friday evenings after school I go to their house across town. Often I have to shout up to the bedroom where Jim studies the bible in the afternoon: 'I was praying, I didn't hear you knocking', he says the first time, rubbing his eyes. Elsie tells me how he often stays up until three or four, 'studying the word'. When she gets back from the Royal Hospital canteen where she supervises a twelve-hour shift five days a week, with alternate Saturday mornings, she makes a diabolical, lip-blistering, eyeball-rolling dish that makes my face stream and my tongue wag with the new vocabulary I've acquired of "God", "Love", "Sin" and "Death", from the Methodists. After dinner she sweeps up the flakes of papadum and rice grains from under the wobbly, knee-bumping table, while Jim reads "The Word"

[25]

out loud, the two of us snug on the sofa by a blazing fire I can't remember him comparing to those other, nether ones in his sermons. She washes up — in a bucket for they have no sink — with water she fetches from an outside tap. After an hour or so of Jim expounding what he was reading for the first half an hour, I find myself wondering — even though I've given up television — whether there'll be a football match on tomorrow. That isn't wrong, even though Jim doesn't play . . . We pray, Jim and I on our knees, with our elbows resting on the sofa, Elsie sitting in a chair at the table, her head lowered, propped on her hand as if she was tired. We ramble round the universe, going through a list of names and ailments that after a few weeks begins to sound like an auction and shipping forecast rolled into one: pains, mysterious swellings, engagements, broken arms, headaches, truancies, unemployment, gall stones, broken bedsprings, births, donations, the cost of coal, sneezing canaries, even stolen bicycles and snow that blew through the poorly-tiled roofs of many of the Mission's congregation, and ruined the sheet music of Sister Agatha, the pianist, are offered up for action with ululating cries of 'Praise the Lord' in Pakistani-American-Scottish accents, to the windy Midland nights; while my bum burns as I edge towards the fire away from Jim's soft thigh.

Malcolm has only come once. The second time I go alone, Jim unveils a surprise. I'm late; Elsie's already there, and as I come in the door she looks at me as if I might know something . . . We follow Jim into the cellar. There is a curtain, a dark green blanket, hanging on a string attached to two nails that have been half-hammered into the mortar between the damp, red bricks. We peep. A large, enamel bucket. 'Now you won't have to go up the garden in the rain' says Jim winking. Elsie is thrilled and busses us both on the foreheads. In the night it starts to rain, waking me. I can hear the drain-pipes tinkling . . . Then I realise the sound is coming from the cellar. Someone is using the bucket. 'Edwee?' I don't say anything. I'm asleep. Then I smell the curry — he's standing over me — I'm being tucked in. Then. I twist my face into the pillow. The stairs creak as he climbs to the bedroom. I spit and spit into the fire.

The following week I'm saved. After my testimonial at "The Mission on the Hill" Jim and Elsie had founded there in Coseley, near Dudley Zoo, my second, childhood home — she a Deep-South White, who'd missioned in Pakistan, and he the son of a former Scottish tea planter, who, he says, had married an Indian princess — he says I could be a second Billy Graham. He sends for brochures of Bible Colleges: he would pay.

Then my Father is saved. He stops behind after the service one night, following the usual call for "souls", to talk with Jim. I freeze: surely Dad doesn't? His head is bent to Jim. Jim has his arm around him, whispering in his ear. Then — their faces sort of touch. After, we have the curry: zinging

[26]

meat balls sprigged with cloves and oodles of yellow dahl, exotic yet familiar like coconutatoe. My Dad says he hasn't had a meal like that since the war.

My pocket money goes up. And Dad builds a flight of stairs for the Mission, from the windowless ground floor to the inaccessible second level. God's latest carpenter, for four winter weekends, his lean, muscular arms — African in the gloom — saw, hammer, chisel and drill a way out of the dark corner, sawdust confettied in his hair, up to where light splashes through the broken windows he will also repair: 'Elsie will have her Sunday School'.

I am going to the Mission two or three times a week; I go to Beckminster twice — once for church and once for the membership class since I can't have one without the other and if I'm not a church member I can't become a local preacher: if I can't become a local preacher?! — I screech to a halt at school, drop Maths, Physics, Chemistry and sit in on English for the last term and a half of the school year. I sell my records: Cliff, Little Richard, Buddy Holly; even Elvis, including the first 78 we ever had, Teddy Bear, that Mom got the day she forged Dad's signature, for a gramophone on hire-purchase from Curry's. She goes mad:

'You must be mad.'

'They're sinful Mother.'

'You want your head examined.'

Shortly after, Dad signs for her to go to Stafford, for 'a good rest,' Electro-shock, everyday, for two weeks; all on the National Health . . . Maybe one day my head will be examined, a special stethoscope placed against one ear, and I bet the sorbo-rubber chorus of The Jordanaires, Elvis' backing group on Teddy Bear: 'pumpada-da — pumpada-da,' will still be knocking around, long after the gospel songs have gone out the other. For I must have played with it undulating in the empty house while my parents were at work, thousands of times.

I lead prayer sessions — after the television's turned off. Twenty-three years later, it is a vision of Hell: my parents with their heads bowed in silence, seated either side of the fire, while their eldest — and "new-born" — son, brays and moos his unutterable loneliness in an archaic, cuntless, masochistic code.

At school I am getting a reputation. I denounce *Sons and Lovers* to Mr Heggs, the English teacher, having heard the previous day we would be reading it soon. Jim told me all about it. Fuscia-faced, Heggs says something to the whole class. My tongue sticks in my throat.

'He has no right to say that,' says Elsie.

'We're praying for you,' says Jim.

'I'm proud of you,' Malcolm says after church on Sunday. I feel

[27]

treeemendous. At school the next day he tells me he had one the previous night, his first in six weeks: 'I'll pray for you.'

'Stupid sods' — Cook overhears us in the changing rooms. We don't swear though. I wonder if he'll tell Mavis? I pass my driving test first time, even though, returning, I reverse onto the pavement. Jim and Elsie paid for my lessons and Jim is at the test. In his long, black macintosh, as I leave the centre, he looks like a policeman coming up to tell me I'm free: 'Another miracle,' he pronounces.

Now I'm driving, and we go to Wales every other weekend for the rest of the school year. Since we don't get back until late, Elsie, after Sunday School, now takes the service, delivers the message, cleans and locks up. Alone. Alone in the back of the van most of the time, Jim studies, sleeps and stirs the curry Elsie made for us, before she helped carry down the mattress from their bed — while me and my shadow get higher and higher on the wind-hit hills. And it must be that on one of these weekends, it happens: I fall in love. Probably on that rustic Carnedd, that from a distance looks more like a poor man's Machu Pichu.

From below, after the road climbs away from the university of Bangor and the sea, winding up the Nant Ffrancon pass, the mountain, fortressed and corniced with buttresses, ridges and spires, some days sails gilded summits like the higgledy-piggledy beginnings of millions of buildings. Tumbledown Dames I hunch around, where shafts of light brush velvet moss, plumbing cool caves while I listen to ritardandos of drips, ticking indifferently downwards; perched on grey, elephant-warm boulders, talking to myself or clinging, gargoyle-eyed, I make my first, stiff moves; the summit jigsaw of scree: slugging legs head's a punch-bag — take any more: Stop. Sit . . . Pylons, tiny eiffels at my feet, the river my shoelace.

Once, upon this time, I bring Tessa, my young Alsatian, for the weekend. We fall asleep for an hour on a ledge of heather, just under the summit. Bees murmuring about their business, she licks my face, puts her head on my chest and, only once, lifts it, to snap, apathetically, at a passing drone. There is a curl of moon over Idwal.

On another occasion, crawling, literally on my hands and knees for a good quarter mile, between the tops of Carnedds Dafydd and Llewellyn, on a wet, white carpet, the wind whipping, rain spitting in my face and the dog cowering beside me, I feel great, generous, important. The pain! The pain! So after finding our way down in the dark, following the stream, clearing its throat into Llyn Ogwen — the night crucifixed with stars, the rain dissipated, when I hear the patter of heavy feet and 'Is that Edwee?', the van warm, the curry ready to eat, I decide not to bother about the arm.

Anyway, he says he'll lend me the van whenever I want. A blast, I drive it everywhere, have my accident, take it to school everyday and really rub it in at home by parking it behind the old man's, which he's never let me drive once. While he bicycles to work because he can't afford the petrol. One day when Elsie needs to use the van and he won't let me use his, I explode: 'I am your son!', bringing him skidding across the yard in his slippers, swinging his fist over my head as I rise, simultaneously, smiling. The fist . . . trembles. And comes down, very slowly. Three days later, when he offers me his hand, I keep mine in my pocket. That night I leave home, without telling them where I'm going.

I go back, back to Wales, on a 125c.c. ex-post office motorbike that my Dad had been able to get for me from one of his friends in the GPO garage. I stay for three days, in the corner of an old, stone barn down by the river. I drink water. And sleep. On the third day, dazed, I plod the hill behind. From the ridge, my eyes climb out of my head, across the hanging valley, zig-zagging up the grassy chest of Y Foel Goch. A few, stray, wisps of snow cling like white hairs, that could easily be brushed off: 'God!'

When I get home — very nervous the whole way that the bike will break down — my Dad asks if I've learnt anything on my mountain:

'Your mother was very worried.'

'How did you know?' Has he visited Jim? He smiles ruefully. We shake hands. And it is a week before I tell Jim that I'm back. He comes straight to the point:

'You must be baptised' — I blink — 'by full immersion.'

Late April, Ogwen, Tessa howling in the back of the van; Jim escorting me, clad in my underwear, across the fields to the river. He doesn't like her, and insists that she remains locked up until the rite is over. 'The chosen speak in unknown tongues,' he says, pulling off his trousers and wading into the full length, mirror-sized hole he's broken in the ice. He beckons me. The water saws at my thighs while he does the words. Then, glimpsing her in the van window, he's pushing me. The river eats my face — down — keeping me under . . . Gurgling. Can't hear a word.

He rubs my hair, saying nothing. Perhaps he's disappointed I let out no more than air when I rose, gasping, again. I don't let him dry me there though. I peep: big as my thumb; not sticking out and not sore at all. Four months now. We walk past the barn. It's not empty: when I stick my head in the door, a couple of sheep look up as if I'd forgotten something.

Next day, Sunday, we scramble up Foel Goch. At one point, he, in an icy runnel, slips — ten — twenty — shuddering to a flop on mattress-thick turf. 'I was scared,' I tell him, holding his heels afterwards on the snowy, sloping holds, as I follow or dart to the front to pull. Clearing rubble from ledges, I remember picking up my toys and things when grandfather had to go to the commode; his patient, painful progress to the dreadful chair that was the real reason I made my friends wait outside. When we get there he is shaking

[29]

with thanks: 'I'd follow you anywhere Edwee, you're like a goat' — but I'm already off down before the arm can get to me.

The last time that I borrow the van that term, I leave it at the end of their street; well after midnight. Slipping a note through the letterbox, I lower the keys inside with a piece of string I brought along for just that purpose. Their bedroom's dark. I thank God he's not up studying.

Next morning, Malcolm and I leave for Scotland. With a Methodist group from Dudley who, every other year, spend several weeks with one in Fort William. It's after the A6 murder and even though Mal and I spend many hours brandishing our thumbprints, few drivers stop to check. We spend the night out in our new sleeping bags, still more than forty miles from Fort William, in the ferns. Around five in the morning it begins to drizzle midges. For hours, until our friends whom we telephoned the previous night come, by car, to find us, we stomp along the deserted glen wearing fungus-green sleeping bags over our heads — only our feet visible — until the midges fizzle out.

The following week, fifty of us troop up a mountain. I've never heard real, unearthly, moaning before. Wailing and wahuuing with cold when the clag clamps down, we sound Hawaiian. A man's war wound opens: guava-pink, pushing out from his stomach. And there is a great white hole where the wind roars and someone says people climb: They must be mad. Lower down, debouching out of the clouds, I hear 'The Ben'. Looking up, the sky tearing its hair, a tremendous thing is dashing its head at the ground, streams pouring down its thousand faces. I send Jim a postcard, addressing it 'Jim Proud . . .'

Little black eyes, overhung by bulging brows; wide, smooth, forehead, with one line — like a ripple, as if something has sunk in. Round, thick-skinned cheeks, minutely pocked by a severe, sub-tropical ravaging. A large head with a crop of tight, bovine curls, receding, whose gaze, twenty-three years later, seems graven, reserved, behind the twinkling eyes, for its own thoughts. He hardly ever has to shave the soft, suede-yellow skin, although he does each Sunday before church, where, when he whispers he seethes and when he speaks he booms, preaching, Doom! Doom! his right hand pounding the spittle-splashed book while the lost souls jump for joy. If he's silent he's probably praying. Even in sleep his lips move, as if more words are trying to get out. Sitting still for any length of time, his legs begin bouncing up and down like a Kentucky jockey's. When he walks he rocks from side to side, followed by small children. I love his ears: elephantinely exquisite. When we wrestle they seem made for bending. His slim, red lips are long and Elvish.

'We must come to Scotland,' I write. I hesitate: 'together'. Then, expansively, 'And find your father.' Jim was 'disowned' by his father according to Elsie, after he 'found God'. It's been weeks since I saw him. And am I looking forward to a curry!

He's there when I get back, watching television with my Mom. My heart sinks. 'He comes every day,' she says, gazing up at him, 'waiting for you.' His mouth curls into a smile.

'Welcome back son,' he whispers, following me closely upstairs. Which he does five days a week for the next two months, having obtained a job at a refrigerated meat factory in nearby Wolverhampton.

I feel like I'm being dated, dreading the sing-song knock at my door, his arms spreading as he draws me to him; the smell of pork around his mouth; the murmuring noises. His tongue starts coming out − I almost vomit. Paralysed I sit by him on the side of the bed and nod at bible college brochures showing teams of white-shirted, short-haired men looking serious.

I can't go on. I have local preacher exams in the new year and haven't even opened the books; there's my first public sermon on Christmas Day. *The Winter's Tale; Paradise Lost; Wuthering Heights.* I stop going to school, each day driving away on my bike, into the country − somewhere, anywhere alone, to sit, drinking in the empty December silence . . . Sleet-white horses on red fields; lichen, like splashed blood orange on an old stump; a tractor jingling like an old typewriter as it scrawls back and forth. Then I fall asleep.

Late one afternoon, I go to Jim's. I let myself in − I've long had a key − and creep upstairs. In the gloom of the tiny bedroom, there is a mound in the bed as large as my Mom . . . I ease my way downstairs. Sitting on the sofa by the grate − the fire is out − I begin one of my English books. Almost two hours later:

'Edwee!'

'I've just arrived,' looking up from the moors,

'Thought I'd read a bit.' Then, testing: 'I didn't want to disturb your study.'

'Ahh − Thank you,' he lies.

One night soon after − it's raining like hell − Lambey comes round: Christ! I haven't seen him for weeks. He stands there, beaming. His motor scooter, an old, noisy, Lambretta, on the pavement behind him, hisses and fumes as the rain settles on the hot exhaust. He doesn't wear a helmet and his wavy red hair is plastered to his forehead. Opening the door, I couldn't be more shocked than if it was Father Christmas.

'Oh-'

'Do come in,' he provides.

'Mom, this is Mr Lambe, my English teacher . . . I'll put the kettle on,' I

[31]

add, retreating into the kitchen, hoping she won't turn off the television. She goes upstairs to get him a dry towel from the airing cupboard. I don't know what to say. 'Some sugar?'

He does the school play at Christmas. This year I never even went to the auditions. He always wears coloured socks: lilac, fushcia, sweetcorn-yellow with his elegant, Spanish-black trousers. All the other teachers come in cars. Sometimes in his quiet class you turn around and find this shape hovering over you, the Dracula-dark academic gown spread, wing-like, above your head. It was fun being frightened by him. One day he told us he wrote poems too. And we hear he eats ants coated in chocolate.

He is charming and soon all of us are laughing. Mom tells him about her singing, but he's not satisfied:

'Give us a song.'

'I couldn't . . .' she falters.

'What about' − he breaks into 'O come' like the archangel Gabriel himself. And Mom soars, her fleeting soprano steady as a fountain in the middle of the living room through several carols. Suddenly I feel very proud of Mom. And him. A wise man. He could have been my friend.

He sits in the wicker basket-chair, one leg cocked over the side, listening to me in my bedroom - the faint strains of the ten-o-clock news coming up from below − with a terrific smile on his face. A red sock glints.

'I don't know what to say,' I say.

'I know you don't'.

And he leaves it at that, though I go on about what I call 'my calling,' until he stops me − 'I'm not interested. I just want you to come back to school.' There are conditions: All work must be in on time and no, 'No,' he repeats, 'more absences.' Of Jim I say nothing.

With a flap of the kick start, swaying, the silver scooter shudders into life. He vanishes, mercurial, in a cloud of exhaust, the wind fanning his scarlet hair. It's stopped raining. The fact that he told me the head may want me to see a school psychologist once a week, doesn't bother me. I shall say nothing to Jim though. I still want to drive.

And I do everyday. He's opened an account for us both in Birmingham, at the Christian Literature Crusade Bookshop. Lives of missionaries, like Hudson Taylor, pass through my hands and several Bibles. One, of snakeskin-thin parchment, rustles when I blow the leaves; it is bound in black leather with gold, hand-printed titles, and makes a nice slap when I drop it. There is a massive, costly concordance that must weigh ten pounds. Within six months it fetches enough to buy myself an ice axe. When Jim isn't with me, I buy some other books. Driving there in the lunch hour with my bag of apples everyday, I run my first red lights.

On Christmas Day, 1962, in a small, rural Methodist church, at Brewood

[32]

near Wolverhampton, the congregation wait: for me to give the sermon. I am striding through the snow with my dog, to Jim and Elsie's, for cold turkey, since I'm going the long way round, and it's well after nightfall when I get there.

I have my books with me. Over the next five days, while they are out visiting Mission members, I am reading my third by Bertrand Russell, which I've bought on Jim's account. It has a soft, yellow dust jacket: '*Why I am not a Christian.*'

'Sixty feet please.'
'Sisal or hemp?'
Jim pays for the sisal, the cheaper, and we leave the ironmonger's in Fort William, with me cradling my first climbing rope, wrapped in brown paper. April, 1963.

Oh grow up! I think: he's just asked me if I'm trying to kill him. He withdraws himself painfully from the cavern of dead bracken he fell into through the surfsoftsnow below the surface. That's the fourth time. If it happens again: Watch where you're treading! I'll tell him.

'Not long now,' I say. I hope; he's been in a bad mood all morning. I got out of the van fast; made tea, porridge and packed before — like red pencil slashed across the sky — dawn . . . He hated getting up. Above us, black and blue, the Ben, like the backside of the moon. We've got half a pound of cheese, a block of dates, sixty feet of rope and we're going to climb the Tower Ridge — like it or not. When I can find it. It's the most difficult climb in Britain — (probably in the world). 'It's the longest climb in Britain — Look!' Showing him the passage in the book I'd found, browsing in the mountaineering section of the local library, somehow ordained this icy discipleship in his mind. 'I want to come with you.' The book had pictures of men in funny trousers like jodhpurs.

Jim has on his priest-black mac, and a pair of brand-new wellies; I'm in my shorts, you know, the ones I show a leg from on Great Wall, four years later. The brown, hippo-hoof-huge boots Mom bought for me, munch the crust — crunch-crunch-crunch: 'Must you go so fast?' he shouts.

'A hut, a hut,' rucksackhunchbacked, I ape Richard from a bleak hillock, hoping to raise a whinny of laughter at least. But my play is lost on this pachydermatous Moses, following in my oversized footsteps.

'A house Jim' — he snorts, 'I swear, a house.' Inglis — (Is that Scottish for English I wonder, pushing) — Clarke, has left the door open . . . We enter cautiously.

Inside, Jim bucks up. He takes stock. Oats, there are lots of oats: Quaker Oats, Scot's Porridge Oats, several boxes, along with tubs, jars and ubiquitous brown paper bags whose oats look a little wild; in a blackened saucepan there's a grey, gluey fluid which might once have been oats too. 'And they're free,' but he's not there.

'There's no water,' he says coming in through the door.

'I'll get some.'

Skedaddling down, away behind the hut, I sling the rubber bucket in the burn — tied to our rope — cannoning about the marble banks. Standing on a saddle of snow above the rushing current, it's like riding a horse, the bit the bucket.

I leave the rope outside. 'Fire!' — he's started a fire. Puffing like the devil, down on his hands and knees in front of the stove, spooning coal down its roaring throat. And what a meal he doles out: cheese and potatoes and potatoes followed by oodles of porridge with hot, sticky dates for dessert. Then whisky-brown tea, for he had no milk. He proposes — looking around I see the single bunks — that we stay the night. The first pinpricks of stars in the window. I sleep on the top one.

A late start. 'I forgot': the rope is like an Eskimo macramé. In my dripping hair shirt I move agedly up the gully that runs out near the top of the Douglas Boulder. I take my first steps, kicking happily, until I realise Jim's not there. He's pawing at the snow in his wellingtons.

'Edwin' —

'Coming,' I bound down, exultant he's agreed to use my real name, and tie him in, cinching the rope around his waist. His chest puffs:

'There' — tighter, and he winces; 'That's better.' We chassé slowly to the top of the gully.

I peer over and sink back. Looking down he's much smaller, but I know how heavy he is. I feel like I'm sitting on the tip of an iceberg. Watch his every move. He toddles stiffly from step to step, jerking me when his foot goes through:

'Watch where you're treading!'

Above and left: 'That's a crack,' (or is it a chimney?)

I try to recall the diagrams in the library book.

Spindrift smokes at my heels as I lurch up to introduce myself:

'I'm not sure what to do.'

'You're doing well . . .' his voice trails off. I feel as awkward as I did at the last school dance I went to, just before I met Malcolm. There was that big Polish girl, Danuta . . . she was a year older than me. Really big. She called it a polka. But I saw Cook holding his sides and doubling up . . . I put my left foot in, my left foot out, in-out, in-out — but I'm shaking too much to move, caught between a rock and a soft spot ten feet and forty years beneath me. So I really get into it, I mean, really, I get in it: embraced by my Gaelic dura mater, I wriggle for fifteen feet until I can stand up in a pulpit of spikes. After tying myself up in knots that I invent on the rocks, I heave up the rope.

Sprawling over the top, slapping out at holds, his fat arms are as useless as fins up here.

'I've ripped my mac,' he gasps. Suddenly I feel sorry for him:

'Well done Jim.'

Behind us, the ridge is a white wave of quiet Niagaras. We hold each other. I tie him in; and step out. No, not like Blondel, more like a char looking for money on her hands and knees.

'No laddy. I think y'ud betta awa doon, afor yu lose the licht.' It is mid-afternoon; the two, claw-footed Scots I noticed, astronomically-tiny on the snow, only an hour ago, move quickly past us, munching the last of the dates, at the foot of a small, ice-turretted tower. They look like knights; I wish they would let me go with them.

I lower Jim back down the chimney. Fibres of sisal cling like hairs where the hot rope rubs the rock. One of his wellies drops off, prancing down the gully, to stop, several hundred feet down, sticking out of a drift like a stove pipe. How do I get down? By inventing rapelling, limboing backwards off the ridge with the rope wrapped around as many appendages as I can find. My thigh turns blue. Then, after extruding myself twice, back up the chimney to free the rope, the third time I waltz it, throw the rope down and return, breathlessly, to Jim, slumped in the sun on the warm snow.

Ten, twenty-five − thirty times, I play out the rope while he hobbles down, holding his foot in the air like a gigantic land crab.

'This is going to take all day.'

'I'm tired. I'm not built for this.' While I pull on his wellie − the foot is white − I realise we don't have long left.

'Tell you what, lie down.'

'Lie down?'

'Lie down. No, on your back.' Doggedly he obeys.

The snow slopes below in one, more or less unbroken flow, all the way to the foot of Observatory Ridge. There are some rocks like crumbs of coal and a few larger ones like Bedouin tents.

Four minutes later we're there − it must be a mile − going so fast with me as his husky that at one point, whipping by like a top while I'm floundering around in a drift, the rope rattlesnakes about me, unbunging me backwards after him. We end up in the same hole, laughing like Ollie and Stan never did in the films, together, at how funny we are, tangled − not strangled − in each other's arms.

Remember how we soured through that long, long day toiling up the stealthily steepening snow, towards the cirque I was really worried we could never get over?

'Of course we can.'

'But how do you know?'

'Have faith.'

[35]

He grows surly, silent, slower, and I think I hear him swear. I start stamping out messages, when we reach the shadow cast by the north-facing cliffs, vertically, in the snow every hundred steps, for him to read: 'DOG . . . SI . . . EVOL' — we're nearly there — 'MIJ' they read to me now, looking back. The ground gives way, he's practically swimming in his wellies and I can't hold on much longer. I'm clawing like a fishmonger in the bottom of a steel-lined drawer at five to six on a Saturday night, for something not ice. I pull him out and, slapping him on the back, untie, throwing the half-cut cord, hissing, down the long, icy slope.

'We don't need that any more.'

Tomorrow is Easter Day.

We walk down the long, heathered slopes into Glen Nevis in two hours. In the dark the tarmac smacks my feet. A couple in a Jag who've been watching us with wound-down windows for the past half hour, ask us where we've been. They give us a lift round the mountain. When they see the mattress in the back of the van, they look at each other.

Six weeks later I'm back. I climb it alone, bearing the ice axe on my back. The ridge is bone-dry. In the clear blue sky the ice axe gleams like Venus. I leap Tower Gap. Jim is taking the long way round, the broad path Whillans drove his bike up once.

From the neglected observatory on the summit plateau, alone, I watch a climber, like a green caterpillar, inching its way up a pure white peak or pap, across the valley. Suddenly it falls, sparkling, spurting a long, silver streak of light that at this distance seems seminal; glissading I guess. I meet Jim on the way down, one of the crowd, his sunny face stands out a mile away with the almost academic black macintosh Elsie has carefully repaired. He doesn't seem to mind not going all the way and follows me down.

That night I wake in the back of the van, pulled off the road in Glen Coe. I've been dreaming of Linda at school, and that party after the last play I was in, when we went up to her parents' attic, and, while the floorboards pounded underfoot with the Beatles, and the rest of the cast were jumping up and down, we began tearing off one another's clothes — but now, in my dream we haven't stopped at my underpants and — until I find Jim's heavy hand clamped on my throbbing wrist. I let him have it. Right in the ribs.

And this is the last trip we shall take, even though it is the only time I see him cry, when, a day later, his step mother slams the door in his face: 'Why! Why have you come back!' I glimpse a haggard, white-haired figure at an upstairs window, looking down as Jim turns back to me. All the way back to England he hardly speaks. There are Christmas cards for a couple of years, even after the letter I send. I hear he went to the States.

[36]

I leave the photo on the table in the study and go down stairs. The children light up — especially at the climbing pictures. After dinner there's still a bit of warmth in the grate, enough to pull us to it when the guests have gone. Lía stirs the ashes and a couple of flames play lizards. Green and blue they soon vanish up the chimney. On my way to bed I find her in the study.

'Is this what's his name?'

'Yes, Jim Proud . . .,' adding, 'I've never really told you about him, have I?'

In the bedroom it is damp, gloomy and cold. But under the covers we're warmoistasapie. Lying on my side, with my back to her, her arm slung over my shoulder and round my chest, I fall asleep. Suddenly he is behind me. I can't move: pinned in his arm, I slam my elbow in his ribs, struggling to rise as he rears, huge over me, to smash his fist in my mouth. 'Aaaaah', falling, my mouth drowning in tongues and gnashed teeth.

'It's all right' — I'm awake — 'Edwin, it's all right,' she tells me, stroking my hair, stroking my hair.

I fell

in 1964: 'She loves you yeh, yeh' . . .
Yes, forty feet.
In Shropshire, from the tip
of the Pontesbury Needle.
Unable to make it as an angel.

I was eighteen.
It had never been climbed.
My girlfriend was on top
 — you can scramble up the back —
waiting for me to rise
to that pedestal in the skies

I'd sat her on.
I remember . . .

Forearms bloating
– her fingers scraping my wrist
the scribble of nails –
twisting in the air above the trees
'O God –'

Black sky. Applause of jackdaws,
going, going –

When something – out of my mind –
'I don't want to!'
spewed me onto my knees
beneath the floating sycamores . . .

I must – braying for breath –
have sounded like an ass: 'hnnnnh' – 'hnnnnh' –
Little did I guess the sentence passed
was Life: To thank, this

world.

Climbing back onto my feet,
apprenticed to a broken wrist
my body, this growth
– though I didn't know it at the time –
with a mind of its own,
had begun to believe in something . . .
At least this first big bang.

'I'll be back.'

A Dawn Walk

THE MAIN WALL GLEAMS, brilliant as the university.

'Over here,' he says, and we start in the trees and mud, for it has been raining for a long time. The limestone is black, and as steeply curved as a motorcyclists's helmet. I feel Victorian, an explorer, in my shined mountaineering boots with a rope in my hand like a dead snake. It's my first time with someone.

'Oliver': he had introduced himself one night after dinner, at Burwalls, the only "Men Only" hall, where we're both living as first-year undergraduates. At dinner we have to wear our academic gowns. At first, we had all talked quietly, moving the silverware like chess players, considering . . . Three weeks later, once prayers have been delivered, we're like jackdaws, stabbing at our food with the vigour of young men who know what the future holds: ship-shape, Bristol-fashion, mid-sixties.

It had sounded like "Beryl," or "Opal," there was something so definitive, geological, about the way he said it. And he is a real specimen to my defensive, working-class mind, just emerged like a miner after a pit collapse — from Wolverhampton — there at Bristol, Cabot's city then, not St. Paul's.

'Philosophy,' I tell him, which, I think, alarms him since he never refers to it again. It matches, perhaps, the fact that he is rich and had gone to Marlborough College. 'Where Hunt went.' So I feel safe, looking up to him, perched behind a small tree, looking down at me, while I hop on one leg like a young stork, attempting to dry off my boots.

My wrist has been out of plaster for about a month. The nerves have only regrown to the base of the thumb. Since I can't feel with three of my fingers, I have to keep an eye on my left hand, picking and clawing for what he calls out are 'sidepulls' and 'incuts.' It feels like a glove puppet.

'Pull!' I yell. He obeys and I feel a surge of terror as my feet pedal for the ledge my arms had clutched like a rugby player away from the rest of me.

'That was a mantelshelf.' he beams.

There is a shallow "chimney" ahead of us. Gracefully, hardly tipsy, as if they are the stairs at home he could climb blindfold, hands and feet just brushing holds he disappears.

'I've got to take my boots off ' I scream. Fish-footed I dab the scummy rock, softly kicked from behind by my boots as they swing from my waist. I

[39]

try holding them, first in one hand, then the other, as if I'm carrying both our handbags. Aping the way he went, when I finally part the bushes, muddy-faced, big clunkers dangling around my neck, I must look African and an embarrassment to him, reclined, taking in the rope, with a slight, injured smile on his face, sahib of Breakfast Ledge.

The ground is a long way down. I don't want to look up.

Get me out of here, I say to myself, retying my laces, wishing I'd never started again. My mind keeps going back to that unroped fall from the Pontesbury Needle (in Shropshire, Houseman country), that I'd taken in front of my girlfriend, that summer, before coming to Bristol. Clutching the summit like a figurehead, the blood in my wrists turning to rust, head-over-heels — 'Oh God' — the trees leaping at my head. Salmon-like, the mind returns to the falls . . .

This is easy.

'This is good,' I say, following his trail between the trees to Lunchtime Ledge. Looking up — my heart sinks. We can't go on. That's rock. I watch him from the trees.

Why am I here?

'Slack!' he orders. It got dark so quickly. Now I can't even see him.

'Watch me!' The shadow sprouts.

'It's loose!' the tentacle retracts. The cliff stands like a wave. Suddenly he slithers into blackness, Mine-dark, pitons tinkle; I can hear hammering. Then a great yell.

I will be killed. I peer through the trees: stars.

'If you allow me to live God,' grovelling for the rock I breathe, 'I'll never climb again.' I look down: street lamps glow; a car's brake lights flare, ruby in the river — for a second — red eye of a serpent winding towards the graceful Clifton Suspension Bridge, the most popular suicide spot in Britain. Which we can't even seen from where we are.

I feel a vague tug and start out, hoping you know I'm coming.

Why

— in the sheer face of things —
do I?

It's shaky . . .
tracing faults and intrusions
treading
huge, empty air-fields,
hoping nothing lands on your head.
Loose flakes that creak volumes.
Hanging in long, bomb-bay chimneys
and overhung off widths,
with no protection or tears.

Taking years to reach
an inn of seconds
out of the weather,
where fingers scrape
together the pennies of holds.

And grasping the clammering
ghost of falling,
clasping the madonnas of balance
— hammering the dry teat of fear —

did I find nothing but

— Swifts
like laughter round the cliffs;
a breath of wind . . .
Ants, epsilon-tiny
on the blank rock —

Then, last year, rain
like electroshock for two days
snow like a coma.

When the helicopters stopped,
at a loss for words
something stirred in the pit of my stomach:
'Help, help . . . HELP!'

[41]

Great Wall

'YOU'VE JUST GOT TO CLIMB IT NOW.' That was all the man said: Boysen slipping quietly off to climb. Seal-cold in my shorts I was feeling a little blue. Below us Llyn Du'r Arddu flashed black glass. On the line of the mountain the toy-tiny train crept, its gasps of steam signalling like heartbeats.

'Come on Lily Legs.' Crew didn't like to be kept waiting; it was him holding the rope.

Above me the wall beamed gleamy with rain, bald as a whale. Easter Sunday 1967. I gulped to see there was a line; my pub outboast still stoodered. This wasn't funny.

A paraphernalia of cameras, wormy ropes, comments, draggles of steel krabs, oh, and a talisman rurp I'd hidden in the pocket of my shorts; he said I wouldn't need any pegs. The camera shot me in black and white, glossing over my burning cheeks. My knees were news in wild Wales. Boysen was slinking up his route on velvet feet.

On blunt finger-tips to a jingle of krabs, I footjigged the first wall to the small overhang.

'That's as far as Banner got,' floated up. I can rest up there thought I, peering, manteling.

I could not and, mouse nervous, I not-rested for an hour, Crew spearing me from below.

'I didn't have a runner there.' But I did, after an hour, and then I rose again. Ten feet. There was a quartz break and I took one too and looked around.

I could just make out Llanberis smudged between hills; woman and child would be up now asking where I was. Below me a delighted Pete was blowing advice to a numbed Boysen. Above me was a peg; with an open eye. If I could poke my finger in, he certainly wouldn't be able to see. If I had a ten-foot arm.

I lift up to the left,

'Clements fell off that way,' bless you sir — a five-foot arm — my fingers start to finger the slippery dimples, toes walking backwards. A ten-foot arm.

Then he tells me he moved right, 'then a quick layback and then up to the peg.' I note the connective; he didn't say a quick layback up *to* the peg, so what happens when I get to that 'and'? Climbers arriving below would ask how long I'd been there. I felt established as a kind of gargoyle. Stuck.

AfivefootarmsuspensionbridgingyourlifeinyourhandathreefootarmIdon'thave

[42]

tofalloffSolesstickonicenice. Made it, snug as a nut, my *doigt* in the peg. While I'm not-resting at the peg he tells me he used it. I'm getting to like him.

Now you're big enough to fly, jugs come lovely, hands full of rock up I go like a slow balloon, pink knees bumping up after me. Two rusty pegs peep:

'That's as far as Brown got.'

Uncle Joe beams at me from his advert and Pete sounds a long way away.

Now once upon a ledge in the middle of Great Wall I sat on a jammed half arse and dangled. A tidal wave of rock swelled out all around. Above me a twenty-foot groove groped to a slim bulge; above this straggled a ragged crack. Where this began was a tiny sling, waving to me. Suddenly hungry I took off my sock and lowered it on the slack to the deck where someone put a block of my dates in which I pulled up to suck. For a while I'd turned cold. While someone else held the rope Pete ran on the spot for warmth. Climbers below moved off home silent as fish.

I was delighted now to bridge, push, flow, no runners since the ledge, warmer. The little sling was trying to reach me. Boysen perched, smoking, watching.

The bulge slid into my arms, frigid with cold. It was staring me in the face. Thirty feet above a runner, only noholds here. Sixty feet is long enough to see where you're going. The noholds in front of my eyes float up, slowly. First you see them, then you don't.

PAs on wheels I move quickly, fingers whimpering. The little sling stops to tickle my chin and I put a krab on it and hum. One thin nut on eyelash tape. Then I put my foot in the noose.

Down I glide, invisible, in the lift, and slip among the staring crowd on the street. He's still up there. He must be holding on to something. Then he moves jerkily. Suddenly no one is talking, upturned white faces eating the sight alive. You blink and stop breathing. He stands in the sling. 'This is like cracking a safe,' he yells. We look at each other. He's all right. I'm all right. Pete shouts something up.

Now the crack grins for two sweet nuts. Elephants bounce past trumpeting. I would like to put my fingers in its mouth, free as air, but I'm saving that for a sunny day. Then the crack shuts up and it shut me up until he said there was a peg behind a hidden flake to the right. After that parabola there's just a human sucker move with a ledge after, just lying there waiting for you to stand on it. Pancake-hearted I plopped a fist in five feet above, just as my feet skedaddled. I'm not usually lucky.

It was too late for him to follow now, and I sat chilling, the silly rurp still in my pocket, while he abseiled down to unstick my runners.

'Well done Scream,' he said. Five years ago. He was still in love with that wall. Lovely boy Crew, arrow climber. Wall without end.

[43]

Sugarloaf

A slap in the face

        – the wind

                                wave

thrashes past stampeding the trees,
scrubbing me

like a doorstep.
February: the cracks gape.
Not a lizard in sight.
White skies spit birds
blown about above.
The river, vinegar
running on the spot,
Frost on the tops.

When we got there
we were pink as salmon,
the missing stairs
beneath us once again.
Lichen bloodblots
the polished, dry rocks.

They're always asking why . . .

In the trees,
the sphinx granite

breathes

White Elephant, White Whale

IT IS A HARD THING to write about — nothing. There is not much you can say, except that you did not do it. You set out in an obviously homemade (or was it spun?) corkscrew of a boat, convinced that you could navigate your way, half blind with eagerness to the lack of a capable crew. Nothing was navigated, no great route was followed. The great wall was not a yardstick of your calibre: a general cock-up. A white elephant — not quite in the real world.

Yet not quite nothing. Not lost that agony of the South Buttress. Standing laughing while the white hail shook us cold, and windy hands tore at our ropes before failure. The water rushing from your granite side that we presumed to spear with inching steel. Not blood, but clear thought crawling up to you. Hammered by the sun, our metal faulted to a bronze replica of activity. And didn't make it; rather were broken by it. Too much passion, no sleep overnight. Who rolled the boots away? Leave the next morning, back to the earth. Phoney. A sort of Judas, or a climbing impotence. Going so far, petting the flanks five hundred feet up, but no full orgasm of splendid days and nights. A masturbating failure.

The moral of the story is: White Elephants are barren as mules are impotent. Although eccentrically attractive, their beauty is only skin deep. They are a worrying mistake bequeathing white hair or white feathers.

It was more than this before the beast of burden was lunked across an ocean and a continent. It was a vision — a very high adventure. Somewhere the white whale was sighted, but was lost. But the ruin of mediocrity which he gave will remain. Nor will I be satisfied until I come again, American, and share your secret, and live that ten-day life too full to last.

And what was it that was not quite nothing? Thirty hours in the Lost Arrow Chimney, too British in shorts; a tourist with puffed and bloody knees. A shouting friend — Schneider, irritated at my slowness, teaching me. Loyd Price crashing through the air. Before the ground he stops, but only just. Thrown from the heel of North America, unhurt; but only just. We don't return. A year or so too small. Madsen, two thousand feet tall and I hear his voice like some captain on a tossing ship who commands by doing what is required, superlatively.

And Robbins. I grew old with him and saw how young I was. Not a graceful climber, he seemed to walk where I would struggle; where he struggled I would follow with his tight help. His foot above his head in some flared horror he would rest and talk. He'd have me relaxed − for a while. Until my turn came.

And my first day in the Valley. The Apron, a great wave that bore us to its crest in twelve hours. A beginning that was its own end; that, in my subsequent failure on El Capitan, was a preparation for nothing.

And now I am six thousand miles away. Working, waiting to return. A little older and a lot wiser. Ready to leave the shore with a willing hand and equal captain. Out at sea identifying the obsession, but not at sea. Riding a wave. To be carried away? White whales are unpredictable. Will he come again? Will my aim be calm enough for long enough?

The Ghost (on Makalu)

1977.
On his white tower
sat the miser of icicles,
the millionaire of pebbles,
who gave up everything to climb.
A kind of saint
Bernard, sleet-shagged,
that's heard something . . .

Plodding, lost in the drift
towards the end
went round in circles,
reaching no final point
to look down and say, outloud:

'I made it!'
The Ganges' veins,
the glacier's dangerous tongue,
hung in the balancing cloud.

Deep, soft — ice axe lifted like a samurai —
he stopped.

Looking back . . . Far
below the wind, drumming
on the yolk-yellow tent,
for a moment allowed
many small steps to be seen coming
to this cold shoulder in the cloud.

That he could take back,
down, past
base camp,
winding the trail like a bandage
through the rhododendrons,
to the airport, to England, his son, to —

To prove
himself
part
— human,
afraid of not being followed
up there.

I turned around.

Out of the Midday Sun
The Lost Arrow Chimney

'THE BRIMMING SELF-CONFIDENCE shown in your letters and elsewhere borders on audacity and engenders in me irritation . . .' Robbins' words were a warning which nagged me as we slunk through the last of the scrub's defences to face the object of our desire in the broken dark.

The aspect shut us up for a while, sorting gear while obedient eyes crawled 1,800 ft up to Lost Arrow Spire, its tip thrust from the great limb of the Lost Arrow Chimney into the upper air.

The affair had been carried off in one long day on the first free ascent by Chuck Pratt in 1966, but we were to spend a night out with her, my first, not having the push and acquired subtlety of the valley man, which opens the secrets of the least willing.

The first long drain-pipe crack, at about Very Severe, flattered our virility; obviously a snare; the lift of a casual eyebrow. Illusions of attainment at ease were abandoned to extreme climbing in the hammering sun up a shallow crack system on poor pinch grips, and made me long for the cool falls of shadow above our heads where the chimneys began to close. The third pitch took us over a large "gritstone" overhang to the "Horseman's Ledge", before the "Safety Valve", a squeeze chimney which once it allowed admission would not admit of return. It had taken us some four hours to reach this point, a bad beginning and omen for the harder pitches above where my inefficient hauling and pedagogical belaying were to lose us hours. It was the most strenuous pitch that I had ever done due to a technique born of panic: I am not a strong swimmer. Schneider, the young American with whom I had teamed up for the climb, led through on what looked an innocuous pitch. All that was innocuous was my sense of scale after the confines of the intestinal hole.

A frog leaping downhill with easy indifference to the world of exposure lapping below us. Tiny, mocking my gigantic effort in the skin-tearing jam-crack where for the first time I seriously doubted my ability to free-climb the whole route; if it got any harder . . . Below, on a lower pitch, I had stopped my hammer from driving a peg into a tiny frog, occupying the gloom of a convenient crack. The strangeness of the climb, myself a stranger here with a stranger, made me respect a life that in its insecurity of lodgement seemed my own.

Schneider seemed inspired by the difficulties of the crack that I had led, in

[48]

spite of his prusik up it, to lead through on a fifteen-foot wide chimney, and in the cold twilight find only the second adequate ledge of our fourteen-hour day. Seconding revived me to lead through and, after a rapid pendulum, to bivouac as high as possible; I was relieved at a long easy-angled chimney stuck with overhanging chockstones.

The chimney gathers the winds to it at night and without a half-sack my duvet was insufficient to bring sleep for long. Long absurd sounds of empty cans clattering down the day below amused us before sleep came.

The next day was only four pitches in length to the groin of the Lost Arrow Spire with the trunk of the chimney, where we were to meet Josephine my wife, with friends who were to leave prusik lines from here, the Notch, as is usual to avoid the final artificial wall. These pitches took me all day to lead.

The third was very hard. Too hard for me at the time, but I had to do it or be faced with a next day of rappels, and days of shame. On the first fifteen feet of the pitch I had used some aid; tired, cold, and scared. Halfway up the pitch I was aware of a further seventy feet of air up which, against my gravity and fear, I had to move. Up the lips of this repudiating gargoyle I had to squeeze myself with cross pressure between knees and heels and downward-pointing palms. My puffed and bloody knees, ripe from the night, softly exploded in crimson berries on my dirty trouserless legs. If you are thrown overboard with your wrists and ankles tied, still you try to swim. I went inside the blackness of the mouth and waited. Nothing would happen; I had to make it so. I risked the flare again with fifty clear feet of air below; a nasty house to fall off. Back I go; look around. At the top to the chimney a nest of stones. I caved up the back and succeeded in threading these together. Less worried now I descended and climbed up the spouting flare from the outside, protected from above. A dead mouse unwrapped itself in my slings as I climbed, lifted by the able wind that held my hair on end as well. No matter, not even that spectre mirrored me; I was succeeding. A few feet higher I had to remove my chest harness, and retie at my waist, as the chimney was too narrow to permit me, corset and all.

That day and that climb ended one pitch above, the alley of my inexperience ringing with my shouting American friend, shouting at my slowness, teaching me. But the prusik lines promised an end, and for a while I forgot myself, and just screamed back, as virtuous as a god.

On Mt. Diablo (California)

Hawks carving the sky.

A sandstonehenge,
near Livermore
weapons' centre.

Dusty loaves of curves
between manzanita and live oak,
the eaves of former homes
swifts are replastering.

A figure: turned back,
from this distance
a hunch, rubbed by the sun,
among the yellowing leftovers,
the cyclopean buttresses
and rain-worn sheep bones
of more than four billion years, dreaming . . .

Then Michelangelo starts
turning stones into people.

My eye climbs
from its cave,

into the Twentieth Century.

The Incubus Hills

Thursday, 23 July, 1970: the end

HE WAS FURIOUS. His eyes marbled in a big rage like some Beethoven in heat, as he pounded at the pitons I had almost welded into the perfect fault. The crack diagonalled the wrong way, overhung like drunk and forced him to use his wrong arm. But all the time he was really laughing. We were nearly there.

The sense of awe was still bossing me as I stood on a cat-thin ledge and the wind hunting around me under the arches and pillars of rust sandstone. It was as though the whole wall were slowly toppling over into the crystal shattering sea. I remembered the time I saw on a television newsreel a helicopter lowering the spire onto a rebuilt church steeple. The helicopter suddenly stalled, buckled and dropped the mere two hundred feet to the ground, killing the pilot and his mate. I was twelve at the time.

A minute would pass while his left arm dripped hammer blows. Now we were limpets on the S.S. Great Britain, stuck to the prow of Brunel's great boat in white charge at the world's seas. The boat had recently come home to Bristol, which was where he and I began to climb in 1964.

It became evident to me that one of my strongest reasons for asking him to come on this climb was his inexperience. He seemed to guarantee failure without danger to my fantasy. But he didn't play it that way and I still find it hard to believe that he was that hard, was that mad.

At last. I welcomed him like a long-awaited guest to my belay. He was a long time coming but left no pins I saw as I took a long last look before stepping off onto the last pitch. I saw green and nodding cotton grasses, the green grass waving only a hundred feet away at the summit place. At last.

Thursday, 16 July: the beginning

From leaving Jack Rendel's farm, swaying like camels under our masters, up the incubus hills, it took us two days to set foot on the untrodden beach of St. John's Head. We had logistical piles. And after our minstrel from Afreet Street, Tony Greenbank (Greensleeves), left us, we hung our hammocks for the darkless night, then donned monk-cowled black anoraks for a walk along the beach. Like two unfrocked priests leaving by the back door of St. Peter's, we felt we were being watched as we upped and downed over bus-big boulders to grab a look at the West Wall. That was to take us to the North Face. Up there.

Friday, 17 July

I have a dream that one day I shall wake from a bivouac feeling like a child. Not this day. Oliver gets out first to brew tea-bag tea with tit-sweet condensed milk, making me feel like I've never been gone. But I have to and on the first pitch from the stonehenged beach in grizzling rain the cold gnaws my fingers to their bones and I nag him for slowness, and as well blame him for a haul caught so tight that the wind blows an organ note on the steel perlon bringing tears to a quasi-Quasimodo's eyes. The thought of a week on this wall is intolerable and at the end of the first pitch, begging but he doesn't hear me. I give him the opportunity to call it off, to give me a sanction. But he just blasts me for playing Grand Master chess with nuts, gets there, and I creep off on the second pitch. Which isn't too bad and brings me to Hog Ledge, vast and almost empty of the fowl that foul. And a roof over our heads. While the tomato soup warms I sloth around the edge of the roof smashing brittle plates at the lip, and fix a pitch, really lonely once I'm out of his sight. Get back, last light, a dim darkness, lips kissing hot soup in instant pleasure. At night the wind fills my scarlet hammock like a vast kite and my mind rides out.

Saturday, 18 July

Oliver is out first and brews tea like wine. The gull chick whose parent had fled on our arrival died in the motherless night. Heading north we cannot stop and to keep the heart warm I knit at the rate of twenty-five feet per hour for four hours, through a craze of traverses to land on a lawn, greeted by a hand of fat butterflying puffins, nodding like dons in the afternoon sun. Fifty feet higher we sleep on lush grass, the House of Lords that night. Herring fillets, dried bananas and a reading from James Baldwin's *Tell Me How Long the Train's Been Gone* and we doze in ermine.

Sunday, 19 July

Above us the wall won't go away. Until one lowers the eyes. Tongue rattling nineteen to the dozen when we see what's looking down at us. On the sea below hangs the shadow of an axe. I saw it last year but with the wuthering we've had since we began, this is the first time it's come out to watch us crawl.

Two easy pitches on grassy slabs then I'm off up rock so perfect we call it Tuolumne Wall after a California meadow that we know. While we are in such chorus Greensleeves appears on Lookout Point and we blow kisses across half a mile. Last Thursday, on the beach, as he turned to go he said to me, 'Good luck, Marra' (a coal miner's term for his pit mate), 'see you at the top in a week.' It sounded like a prison sentence in my ears and my enthusiastic 'Sure man' worried me. Later this day I climbed the Vile Crack. The Vile Crack is one hundred feet long and the width of a full-weight boxing glove. Boots skinheading, you have to fight it with slow uppercuts. One could have done without the roller skates on the boots, though boxing gloves would have helped.

Then a leftwards traverse on a ledge of window-sill thickness where my never-bending finger enables me to place a protection peg for Oliver. Then, using a box spanner for a bolt holder as the proper one broke when we were trying it out on the beach, I place belay bolts and rappel back to the Commons where vile gulls greet me with spits of hot yellow vomit. Not until the next day do I discover the value of a handful of dirt down their throats as an anti-emetic.

During the night it rains and my hammock weeps. A year previous to this I had been at this same bivouac with four rare lads: Jack the Sprat, Leo the Lionheart and Ben (without Bill). The route (the West Face) was no plum; more of a crab apple and such taste is unusual, though crab grapes were a popular choice during the three days we spent doing the route. The experience gave me a perception of what could be, tomorrow. During the night, rain and worry got into the hammock; tomorrow was almost today. Perhaps today will be different.

Monday, 20 July
It isn't. I wake up in a carriage of the last train to Belsen. Oliver has a cup of wine for me that tastes like tea and the train leaves without me. Then I prusik on a not-quite-empty stomach. Jumars would be easier, somebody says. One is not amused and goes on, knocking sleep from elbows and knees. Then he comes, so you photograph and try to forget. Above us sway weird flakes and horns of rock, a kind of right-left Unconquerable. While I'm arming up it I keep saying 'The Wipe-Out Flake' to myself, but like me it does no more than rattle when I put a fist deep inside, making it clear its throat. One of the things that bewildered me about the route was the stability of apparently insane flakes. Perhaps real instability lies in silence and uniformity, in keeping it all quiet. At the top of the flake I blow again. I almost go crazy at this gull which just keeps shitting at me. Not content with a four-foot deadly puke, rotating like a flywheel it must thrust its feather-fringed arse at the pole of my face and let fly. Then it whips around and pukes, the whole action taking less than three seconds. Christ I went crazy. I mean I was scared. The rock was dust in my hands and my protection below me was, well, below. I don't remember how I got away. The vomit, dyed into my stockings (which I was, of course, wearing over my

face) never will, and the memory is now precious. So we go on to fresh insights and foolishness.

Higher, just before an elbow of overhanging rock, I find myself praying like a miser and I seek charity with a four-inch bong. Pleading, this fourth day ends forty feet higher on Hanging Garden Ledge where we are able to boil water which we spice with antiseptic to lave our cut-tattered hands.

It was good to be there that night. At sunfall we saw the puffins, tipsying and hurrying, innumerable as bees around the summit of our world. Black bodied, white-chested with orange, nut-cracking beaks, nibblers of each other. We even talked of finishing, I did.

Tuesday, 21 July

This day was bloody awful. Branding-iron winds burnt the cheeks, and mad mists hid the tearing sea as I stumbled out on an easy ledge traverse past frozen birds with their gull-cold looks. In the middle of the ever-narrowing north wall I crept around the decrepit roof while Oliver trembled. Jammed nuts for aid and the wind was banging me about. The wind was gale force that day; we felt it, later we learnt it. It butchered us and I shall never forget Oliver's face, cold-purpled like raw meat, his mouth a kind of wound as he tried to complain. I found it hard to moan that day as the sight of Oliver suffering did something to me. Three pitches and already we were wondering where to sleep to escape the arctic lick. On I go up the three Giant Steps, each eight feet high. Then I have to crawl left, forty feet on my stomach, inside a two-foot cleft. This was comic relief indeed as my bundle of iron travelling horizontally across Oliver's line of vision was all that could be seen. But once a gargoyle peered down, mouth full of fear. I knew what I had seen and I did not want to sleep there. Surreal for real. I was under the thumb that night and I had a bad time. Worrying that the cleft itself might close, that tomorrow would never come, and that when it did I would not be able to face it. We slept in the gutter and I ate a tin of salmon, my last food and the tin slept by my head. Sure we had water for tea, but the wind blew away the flame and someone turned out the light. Self-pity fanned to seething anger. I tried to use Oliver as some kind of shield from the wind but it didn't seem to make much difference. Hell, we weren't married.

Wednesday, 22 July

Corpse-prostrate, we shared his food. Dark in here, out there the day beamed and we beamed too. If he resented sharing his food he didn't show it. The wind had dropped, the night was over. I felt it had to be the summit today. Nailing up this brittle crack in the wall, only way to go, I placed a bolt in case the insane flake above me would not be trod on. Above me to the right the fifty-foot roof of the north west arête prowered; altogether elsewhere. Not that way but this and I had no choice but to edge up to what, in my mock mockery of the night before, I had called the Guillotine. A fifteen-foot blade of red dark sandstone, tapering like a knife from five feet to six inches at the end I had to stand on.

The thin crack I am knifing in dies, so I ask for it and climb out of the trench of my aid slings and start running. Oliver is getting smaller; freezing me with a stare that is not nice and I can no longer hear what he is saying as his voice shrinks to mind size. My ropes run under the flake, butter to knives if it breaks. Fall forever, or run forever?

I keep running, the bolt kit is in my hand and I'm smashing at the door crying to be let in when the key breaks in the lock and hands are around my throat and everything goes black very quickly.

I have no choice, have I? There is a limit. That's it, we go down. I shout across to Greensleeves that I cannot go on because . . . he cannot hear me. Oliver finds it difficult to refuse; at least he can hear. But his anger shows he does not realize the vitality of bolts, I mean how vital bolts are. I mean would have been. Anyway.

Then I hear this voice. Some kind of male witch in hot gloat.

'At last. So this is what you're really like.'

I feel like I've been caught masturbating in church.

'This is what you are.'

And it hurts me a lot and I wonder whether my climbing is some kind of suicide; whether I am about to kill myself. Can a man know that he is mad? Perhaps I have gone, and I scream 'Who's that? Stop it.' And I scream it again and Oliver has come back. He's looking at me like that.

I do not know. I did not know then. How I went on but I went on. The black bag around my head burst and I died to get at the crack too far above my head and my fist locked solid. Then I'm away in this fist-thick crack, forgiveness making me sweat.

'Those skyhooks are flashing,' Oliver royaled up.

In fact they winked twice, but I'm married and he isn't and it's easy to confuse a flash with a wink. Perhaps fear is the possibilty of ecstasy. Oh we warbled. Then I reached, and prayed, and hooked and pleaded on fingertips, scratching to reach Thank God Ledge, invisible from below, where, being numbered among the angels I just Don Giovanni'd my head off for a full five minutes. Boy I was beating my chest.

I hauled our home and Oliver came up for air like he's being born, saying he doesn't know how. We were eatless that night but content, and while the sun hung about on the edge, curious, I walked out in its last light and found a thin thread of a crack in the sheerness. Impregnability perfected by a single perfect flaw.

Thursday, 23 July
We drink scalding hot orange at dawn, sweet like a thin syrup with the last

of our sugar in it, while gently we talk hopefully of food and success. I dreamt of her in the night. That hadn't happened for years. Swaying up the final leaning wall I feel the privilege of the lookout in the crow's nest on a whaling ship when he sights the whale first. Oliver scarecrow, below, out to my left on the bivouac ledge: peering, waiting.

Do you think you'll ever come here again?' He doesn't hear me. Tomorrow, next year.

'Will you ever come back?' But he doesn't hear.

The Way Down?

Two climbers, a rubble of muscles
and rucksacks, between a rock
and a dark place.

Holes   chop   ankles.
Legs . . . tentacleslithering
ahead.

Feet, shifty — overworked nurses
who may let the wheelchair
go

— Suddenly
in the doorway

of a kitchen
of bay laurels,
the wind simmering,
the utensils of the stars,

gleaming all about us

Mirror Mirror

WE REACHED OSLO in two days, nudging in under the shrouds of cloud spreading a thin fine rain upon toast-faced Norwegians and pale faces alike. It was the first rain for a month. Burning up to Romsdal on the bike, I found my cagoule was promiscuous in the rain, but Lindy, at the back of me, kept dry and fed me on chocolate and made me hum with her big hugs. I couldn't lean on her as I could my cold companion of other years who pulled on my neck: my rain-slimed haul bag, my meticulous Humpty Dumpty. She was continually delighted at new waterfalls; her oohs flew to my ears and near the end of the journey, my goggles crying with rain, I raised a soggy arm at the alp of cloud shearing up a white mile. 'That's the wall,' I roared. She gripped her hand on my arm, and yelled about the coming bend.

Where am I? I'm cold. Thin mists shift, touching me. Where is she? She must have got out of the bag. I shake my head out, struggling to look. There is another near me, raw-red in the white air. Hugh! A dream. I'm not on the Romsdalhorn. That was a week ago. Lindy isn't here. This is the wall.

So. Three nights. Almost 1000ft. Our second ledge, Lucky's. Seven pitches and a paper-dry cag. Hugh's still in bag, sleeping the sleep of the just, sound as a foetus, on his first wall. During the past three years I had, in three summers and a spring, snailed the mile-long approach scree twenty-three times and twenty times I came back. Not this time. "The Northern European Wall"; "The Mourning Wall"; "The Rurt Wall", (Realised Ultimate Reality Troll); "The Lord of the Walls", "The Drummond Route", (if we said nothing they'd call it this); "The Royal Wall", naw, what has Robbins ever done for you? You'll never level with him.

On our first cralk up to the wall — the scree is so steep that it's like trying to ski uphill — we had climbed the first slabs, 200ft or so, gritty, nasty, wobbling to extreme. There had been the snow pitch, cricket size, and the jokes about forgetting the ice axes, using skyhooks and étriers as we had no crampons and the ice was marble. Then the 'schrund and my little leap; it was all fun. After three trips we'd brimmed the hauls and I'd climbed the third, a squirrelly free up a great crooked slab, funnelling to an upside-down squeeze chimney that made me squeak. Then we went down, Lindy, who'd come up to watch, and I, slowly, like two old people, while Hugh flew off to the river where he swam among the salmon; the fishermen had all gone home. We just promised ourselves a swim when it was all over.

Returning, two days later, Hugh went first and the hauls went after, quite a while after. His first haul; his first artyfishyl; first hamouac; first air jumar (barring one from a tree in Mexico). Hugh was, slowly, going up the wall. So it was noon when I set out on the fourth pitch.

And it was seven in the evening when Hugh's jumars gritted their teeth to follow. What passed in those seven hours is unforgettable: my mouth, sock-hot; my larynx strangling for spit; a fine shivering as of a thin wind trembling through me. It began with a layback of twenty feet, wonderful but for the iron stone around my neck — it was a struggle, favourite uncle, was it not? Then the footholds faded away and I muttered on nuts under this thin roof until the only way up was up.

There was a crack, not a crack crack, but a line, a cra, the start of a crack say. At any rate the bolts were in the haul bag and this was the third pitch of the N.A. Wall as far as I was concerned. My rurps curled up when I banged their heads and refused to sit still. After five fingernail knifeblades I got out my hook and sat on that, about as secure as the last angel to make it onto that pin head. Then I struck dirt. Now dirt is okay if you can get dug in. I began and ended with a knifeblade which dangled sillily from my waist, and I was glad that it was not me that was holding the rope, for after four hours and forty feet I might have been caught napping. But Hugh wasn't and as it was I only went fifteen feet for the hook stuck and though it trembled it snapped not, O Dolt.

So then I had to free that bit, but after that it eased some. Nuts hammered in the dirt and at long last a ding dong bong. Hotheaded I'd reached a ledge, feeling a bit sorry for myself. "No Ledges" we called it and it all hung out. There we had a pantomime in hammocks by headtorch which was really not in the least bit funny. Hugh, as chattery as a parrot, floated above me in his one-point. He even said he was comfortable and had the cheek to take a shit. By a battery *son-et-lumière* I watched his anus like an angry eye; no voyeur but it might look my way. However, he missed me, my arms full of ropes like some deeply confused spider.

'Ed! Come on, it's light.' Oh, God, awake already.

'Look at the sun,'

'Uuh uh.' Why don't you go back to sleep?

There and then I decided that if he was unable to lead the next pitch, then that was it. I'd led every pitch so far (didn't you want to?) and it was unthinkable that I'd lead all of them. Not bloody likely. I'd make that clear. I tortoised out. What are you smiling at? Rather him than me. I've had about bloody five minutes bloody sleep. 'Right, coming.'

It was strange to be there, sitting up in the hammock, feet stirring in the air over the side, opening the haul, fingers weaseling in the cold stuff bags, tramp-thankful for food in the hand. Eating quietly we heard the whipcrack of breaking ice in the gloomy cwm below and I'd yell 'hello' with a dervish fervour (wake up, Drummond, grow up, you can't go back). The echoes yodelled and I'd say to Hugh, 'He's there.'

'Who?' he'd ask.

'That bloke,' I'd tell him. 'Listen.' And I'd do it again and we'd both cackle like kids with a home-made phone.

By 7 a.m. I was ready to belay him. I wasn't laughing now. One more pitch and there would be no retreat. I moled into the cold rope bag, my arms up to my elbows, fingers fiddling for the iron sling. I had a krab, empty, ready on the belay to receive it. My fingers curled in the sling; I moved my arm gracefully, slowly, (I was cold) to clip it into the krab before passing it up to him. If I drop the iron sling we'll have to go back down. From the end of my arm my little family of fingers waved at me. And it went, there, no, once, twice, there, oh, down, out, there, and under and into the heart of the icefield, clinking like lost money.

I couldn't believe it. Hugh was silent. I kept saying I was sorry. I didn't mean it. Not this time (How do you know?). I couldn't believe it. Hugh said nothing.

'I've done it now.'

Instantly, 'How long will it take you to get back up?'

He's got you.

I got back by noon, gasping. I'd come down to earth. A 600ft abseil, my figure-of-eight sizzling my spits at it, and then a free jumar all the way back. I was furious. 'Right, belay on.'

His pitch was perfect after a bit. Dirty at first, then a cool, clean fist-lock crack. Iron out in the air like a bunch of weapons, he groped at the sky like something falling. All around a sea-sheer swell of wall, untouchable. Him the one sign of life.

Then the rain came. A dot in the eye. I heave for my cagoule, one eye on Hugh, an invisible drizzle blackening the rock. New noises fizz in. Twitters of water and Hugh is yelling for his cagoule, but I point out the time and that he's leaking already. Well, for a couple of hours I kept pushing boiled sweets in my mouth and Hugh kept on moaning and kept on. After 150ft he had to stop and pin himself to the wall.

Early evening. There he hung, wringing himself like fresh washing. Thank God he had no cagoule, or we would both have been up there for the night, him perched above, if not on, my head like a great wet heron. The waterfalls would weep all night.

'Why wait for Godot?' I yelled up. He said, 'Eh?' so I said, 'Come on down, let's piss off.'

We stripped the ropes off the hauls, tied the lot together and down we went, happy as nuns in a car. A slalom down the scree and back before dark.

[59]

Back in the camp hut we listened with Lindy, gladly, to the rain hissing outside while we kissed at a snug mug of tea and drooled on the food to come. That night I slept like a child.

Eight days later, well pickled, we humped up the boulder-fields in epileptic sunshowers, snagged at by cold-cutting winds. The days were getting shorter.

The bergschrund had rotted back and we had to go down inside the mouth. Our ropes were 20ft up the slabs, strung taut to a peg. I manteled up on this mica jug, massaging off the dust, feeling sick with this white pit under me, thirty feet deep, rocks in its dark, lurking.

When I had the end of the rope I dangled a bong on and looped it to him. Three times I threw and three times I missed; each time the bong tolled dolefully. 'Hey, our funeral knell,' I yelled, but he wasn't impressed.

Two and half jumehours later Hugh brooded on the haul eggs, sucking the sacred sweet, as I botched up the freeasy and awkwaid of the next pitch. When I warbled down about the ledge I'd found, he said he'd kiss me, but on arrival I didn't hold him to the threat. In fact, the first thing that he said was that the next pitch looked a bit steep for him and ordered me to do it. But since it was dark I could wait until tomorrow. Under the tube-tent, scarfed in cigar smoke, we sleep like refugees.

Pitch 7 took me all the next day. It is 156ft long; our ropes were 150ft long, at a stretch. That last six feet to the belay cracks saw me lying flat on my face on the ledge, hammering like front-crawling. Hugh climbed up from his end, pulling the haul bags (one at a time, and there were three, each weighing over fifty pounds) onto his shoulder and then weightlifting them up so that I could get them through the pulley. Hugh studied Law at university.

So. Three nights. Almost 1000ft, Lucky's Ledge is no longer important. A stab of butter, a jab of honey; the pumpernickel crumbling among your fingers, a steamy censer of tea, packing your bags, hurrying as a jostle of cumulus smudges out the sun and the stove starts to fizz the drizzle.

As I remember we made three pitches that day in a rain as insidious as gas. For two or three seconds, suddenly the valley would come like an answer, and we would stumble into conversation, then numb up, sullen with wet clothes and cold, clubbed feet. In the downpouring darkness I jumed up to Hugh, squatting on blocks, owl aloof. While he belayed me I hand-traversed down to a ledge on his left, where I backheeled and rubbled away for over half an hour, making the bed. We couldn't find pin placements for the tube tent, so we hung our bivi bags from the rope and crept into their red, wet dark.

Sneaking out the next day at noon like shell-less tortoises, I realised as we both emptied a gallon of fresh water from our bags, that it might have been better to have had the opening at the bottom rather than the top of the bag. A point that had escaped me as I tried out the bag on the floor in front of the fire at home. Sneer not. Wasn't the first Whillans Box a plastic mac and a pram? The Drummond Cot would have its night in time. Well, we strung the tube tent as an awning, lit the stove, and wrung our pulpy feet out, sitting in the cloud, machine-gunned by water drops from the great roofs that crashed out over 200ft wide, a thousand feet above our heads. We wriggled a little in the tent, slowly gulping lumpy salami, a bit stunned, stuttering with cold.

At about four we took the hood off our heads and saw the valley for the first time in twenty hours: the curve of the railway line, the thin black line of the road, pastures of grass, the glitter of the river, the big stacks of corn like yellow firs. The red tractor a slow blood drop. Then we heard yells, words, my name, and saw a spot of orange jump at the toe of the scree. It was Lindy calling, calling, and I called for my favourite team: 'LindyLindy LindyLindy,' and the wall called with me. Hugh even asked if I was going out that night.

Morning. The fifth day. Cornflower blue skies, fiord-cold in the shade, and above us brooded a huge wing of white granite, its edge a thin black slab about as long and steep as the spire of Salisbury Cathedral. I had seen this from the scree. We go that way.

Two skyhooks raise me off the rubble — wobble ten feet without protection — a necessary enema after the thirty-hour sit-in. Then I'm staring at a poor flare where I belt a nut. Little chains of sweat trickle down my back. I'm struggling to free-climb and Hugh's not even looking. Jerkily I straggle to a ledge, not a word of wonder escaping his lips as I braille for holds and shake onto this ledge with a flurry of boots. With time against us I was doing all the leading. Hugh sat still on his stone throne while I squirmed about, greasing my palms with myself. Still, a cat may look, and he was the one rock, the one unshakeable, all the way there and back.

Abseiling down in the dying day the bergschrund breaking its wave beneath my feet 1500ft below in the cold ammonia air, the tube tent was a rush of bright flesh, raw on the ledge, and Hugh, his back bent, peering, was a black bird feeding. After a soup supper, watched by the smouldery eye of Hugh's cigar, I blew my harmonica, and brought tears of laughter to our eyes. We were doing okay. Hugh even said he liked to hear me play.

Two days later we were barely 300ft higher, and what I could see was not pretty. It looked as though, during the night, someone had pumped Hugh's foot up. His skin transparent as tracing paper, the foot was a mallet of flesh, the toes tiny buds; thalidomide. I didn't want to say too much. Perhaps the strain of his jumaring had done it, or the rotting wet when we were at Lucky's taking the waters. It was early yet; we had a long way to go. He said he just needed to rest it.

[61]

The ledge was lovely and I was glad to linger there. We spread ourselves around, Hugh blowing gently on his foot while I had a bath. A snip of cotton for a flannel, lint for a towel, and a nip of antiseptic to give my spit a bit of bite. With behindsight I don't recommend the antiseptic neat, my dears. Let me tell you it wasn't a red face I had. The funny thing was it didn't hurt at the time I dabbed it, lovingly, my back turned while I blinked over the drop; but the day after. Well, as they say, there hangs a tale.

A week later, his feet out like two heady cheeses in the dim pink light of the tent, Hugh has the mirror. He's checking on the stranger — the first time in twelve days, squeezing his pimples, humming some Neil Young song. For four days we've been in and out of this womb tube, harassed each time we go outside by the web of stuff bags breeding at the hole end. They are our other stomachs. We feel in them for our pots, our pottage, and our porter (although the porter is water since we've finished the orange). Cosmetics ended, we turn to draughts, drawing a board on the white insulating pad and inventing a set of signs for pieces and moves. So we pass an hour; doze, shift, fidget, sleep, talk, yawn, fart, groan or cackle, plan, doze, and watch the light dissolve like a dye in the darkness. Snuggled together we are pre-eminently grateful that there is another here at the end of the day. We don't talk about failing and I hardly think about it now — we've been here so long it's a way of life. The pendulum's done now and the only sign I'm waiting for is a weather one. The valley in my mind is out of sight.

In raggy mists we moved quickly, leaving our hauls on the bivouac ledge. Hugh, some deflated astronaut, swam slowly up on jumars as though someone had taken the gravity away. Breezes whiffed up my cuffs and my icy cagoule etherised the back of my neck. After those two pitches I frog-legged left, my numb hands bungling on the flat holds, to reach a little ledge from where I would go down to pendulum. After each pitch I was getting a bit desperate with the cold and I'd can-can to keep warm. Hugh, only forty feet away, was a white ghastly shadow.

Below us, Norway was at war. A volcanic pit of bursting water; the cwm boomed, a vat of slashed air. Stones howled around us and avalanching crashes trembled the wall. And me. Nothing could be seen in the gassing mist. No pendulum today.

Going back to our home, Hugh passed out into the cloud first, using the haul lines as a back rope to the bivouac ledge, which would otherwise have been impossible to return to because of the overhanging wall. When I got down he'd a brew ready which lit a fire, briefly, inside me. My thanks that it wasn't snowing just about made it.

During the night it snowed.

In the morning it was still falling, so we rolled over; better sleep on it. In the fitful sleep of that day I had my dream! The editor of *Mountain* had arrived at the foot of the scree and, with a foghorn or some kind of voice, had managed to wake me, telling me that he had come all the way from England to let me know what a great job I was doing for British rock-climbing (he never mentioned Hugh), and also how we were contributing to better Anglo-Norwegian political relations.

By the time I awoke he was gone but Hugh hadn't; he was just vanishing down the hole at the other end. My watch told 4a.m. the night had gone. I oozed out of my pit to find lard-pale Hugh with the blue black foot, sitting stinking in a skinful of sun. For half an hour we wallowed, exposing ourselves to the warm air. New creatures we were, able, if not to fly, at least to jumar, up there. And up there, today, I had to swing for it.

I try, flying, at thirty feet below Hugh, then fifty, then eighty, then at over a hundred. I'm a bit too low so I jume up to about ninety-five 'Ed Leadlegs,' I tell him but only the wind hears me. I'm getting a bit tired; Hugh has given up asking me how I'm doing and is just hanging, staring, his pipe alight — the wind brings a tang of it to me. No doubt he's thinking of his girl in Mexico.

The white wall is so steep here that I can barely keep hold of it when I crab myself right for the big swing. But my first swings wing me out into space away from the wall and I have to pirouette to miss smashing my back. This is ridiculous. Like a spider at puberty I toil but spin not. It's after 2p.m. Lindy will be here soon.

When I've fingernailed back as far right as I can (and this time I manage about four feet more) I'm nearly eighty feet away from the groove that I'm trying to reach.

I'm off, the white rushing past; out, out from the wall, way past the groove, out — I tread air, the valley at my feet — Hugh moons down, he's yelling something — can't hear a word — rushing, coming back, crashing in, wall falling on top of me, I kick, jab, bounce my boot, bounce out, floating, an easy trapeze. Then the unknown groove is running into my open arms and I strike at a flake and stick. Fingers leeching its crack.

I hang a nut in (my jumars attaching me to the rope are pulling me up), then I get an et and stand in it. The nut stays put. Jumars down. Now put a knife under that block. The press of the block keeps it in as I weigh in on it. Out flips the nut. Whoops. I know I'm going to get there. I can't see Hugh but I know he's there. A tiny nut like a coin in a slot. Watch me. The knifeblade tinkles out. Thank you. The nut gleams a gold tooth at me. There you go. To climb is to know the universe is All Right. Then I clink a good pin in at a stretch. Can't get the nut now (it's still there). And then I'm in the groove, appalled at the sheer, clean walls around and below me, baying for breath, my heart chopping in my chest.

We have lost 100ft, but gained a narrow track of cracks that will, I believe, lead to the "Arch Roof", the huge, square-cut overhang that from the valley looks like an old press photo of the Loch Ness Monster. I saw a crack in 1970 through binoculars going out through the top of the head. 'Loch Ness Monster sighted on Troll Wall.' I'd out-yeti Whillans yet. Just before dark Hugh lands and goes on ahead to order dinner; we're eating out at the Traveller's Tube tonight, a farewell meal. The pendulum being done, our time was going and so must we.

But it snowed for two days.

On the thirteenth day the sun rubbed shoulders with us again, and Hugh jumared up at a snail sprint. He found that the yellow perlon he was on had rubbed through to half its core, so he tied that out with an overhand before I came up at a slow rush. Halfway up I worked loose a huge detached flake which had hung 100ft above our tent; it took me five minutes so we had had no need to worry. We watch it bounce, bomb-bursting down to the cwm, and the walls applaud.

The crack above the pendulum's end was a nice smile for standard angles except where a ladder of loose flakes is propped. Bloody visions slump at the belay below me. Silence. Care. The hauls zoom out well clear.

The next two pitches, up a bulging, near-blind groove, were ecstasy. I had to free climb. The hooks were only for luck, and I was quick in the blue fields. Above, suddenly, two swifts flashed past, thuds of white. 'That's us,' I yelled to myself. Lindy may not have been here, but there she was. I could hear her, naming my name, and I flew slowly up. Four fine patches of ledgeless pleasure that day. In the dark Hugh jumared up to the Arch, me guiding his feet with my head torch.

But that night the sky shone no stars. Packs of black cloud massed. Not enough food to eat. A sweet or two. No cigar. And too late to fish for hammocks. All night, four hours, I squirmed in my seat sling. I speculated on recommending to the makers that they rename it the Iron Maiden, but it was too suitable an epitaph to laugh about. My hip is still numb from damaged nerves.

Came the morning I was thrashed. The sun did not exist. The roof over my head was a weight on my mind. Suddenly, over Vengetind the weather mountain, clouds boiled, whipping, exploding, avalanching. Over Lillejfel, a low shoulder on the other side of the valley cauldron, a dinosaur mass of white cloud was creeping toward us. We could hardly run away; we were so cold and hungry we could hardly move.

I was scared as I moved out under the Arch, a clown without props, all these things were real, there were no nets here, only dear patient Hugh blowing on his fingers.

No man walks on air was all my thought as I melted out of sight, upside

[64]

down for forty feet, my haul line dissolving in the mist. I couldn't feel that I was connected to anything solid. Fly-sized, I mimed away under three giant inverted stepped lips. Not a single foothold, not a toehold in a hundred feet. Just over the final lip, in a single strand of crack, I pinned myself to a wall of water and started to land the hauls.

They must have seen me coming. I couldn't believe it. Raindrops ripped into me, making me wince. The cold rose an octave, catapulting hail into my face. The wind thrummed a hundred longbow cords. I could hardly see through my Chinese eyes. Only while I hauled could I stop shaking. My fingers, cut deeply at the tips, were almost helpless. People at upstairs windows watching a road accident in the street below. My feet were dying. My silent white hands.

Hugh came up for air, grinning. He'd had no idea down there. Up here he had the thing itself. Murdering, washing out more than ears. I led off, hardly knowing where, except that we couldn't stay there. I could only just open my karabiners with two hands. Sleet had settled thickly on the bunches of tie-offs. Both of us were really worried. Hugh cried up after an hour that he was getting frostbite. What could I say? I had to find a place for the night.

If you ever go there and have it the way we did, you'll know why we called it "The Altar". I remember the rush in the drowning dark to hang the tent, the moss churning to slush beneath our feet. Back to back, our backs to the wall, we slumped on three feet of ledge for three days. We had nothing to drink for the first two of those days; our haul bags were jammed below us and we were diseased with fatigue. Lice trickles of wet getting everywhere.

I remember Hugh drinking the brown water that had collected in his boots, instantly vomiting it out, and me silently mouthing the gluey water from my helmet. You didn't miss much, Hugh. He shared his food with me, some cheese and dates and a bag of sweets; rare fruits. After a day he had to piss and used quadrupled poly bags which I politely declined to use; I had no need. A day later my proud bladder was bursting. But sitting, propped in a wet bed of underwear, I was impotent. For over two hours I strained and grunted in scholastic passion. Hugh said it was trench penis. A sort of success went to my head, however, or rather onto and into my sleeping bag. After that I felt like some great baby, trapped in his wet cot, the air sickly with urine, and sleep would not come.

To get more room, both of us, we later confessed when there were witnesses present, developed strategies of delay while we shuffled the status quo. 'Could you sit forward a minute?' Or, 'Would you hold this for me?' At times I'd get Hugh to tuck my insulating pads around me to bluff off the cold stone. It was deeply satisfying to have someone do that. Grizzly, bristly Hugh: what a mother.

We wondered if this could continue for more than a week. But we didn't wonder what would happen if it did. We never talked about not finishing. (We were just over 1000ft below the summit.) It was no longer a new route to us. It was not possible to consider anything else as real. There were no echoes from the valley. There was no valley. There was no one to call your name. No wall now; unhappy little solipsists, all we had was each other.

We began to get ratty, like children locked in a bedroom. An elbow scuffled against a back once or twice as we humped back to stop the slow slide off the ledge. A ton of silence rested on us like a public monument, for hours on end. I felt that this was all sterile. I ate food, wore out my clothes, used up my warmth, but earned nothing, made nothing. The art was chrysalising into artifice. A grubby routine. Trying not to die. Millions have the disease and know it not. My sleep a continual dream of hammering: banging in pins, clipping in, moving up, then back down, banging, banging, taking them out. A bit like having fleas. Searching for an ultimate belay. Unable to stop: the Holy Nail. My Dad, my Dad, why hast thou forsaken me? At times I was pretty far gone.

But it wasn't all self-pity. We talked about the plight of the Trolls and could clearly see a long bony hairy arm poking under the tent, handing us a steaming pan of hot troll tea, and although nothing appeared in our anaesthetic dark, the idea lit a brief candle.

Three days later we were released.

Lindy yelled us out. A giant marigold sun beamed at us. Everywhere up here — and we could see hundreds of miles — was white, perfect, appalling. Across the river I could clearly make out scores of tourists, a distant litter of colour in one of the camping fields opposite the wall. Cars flashed their headlamps and horns bugled as we struggled into view and flagged them with our tent.

Then, quickly, the charging roar of an avalanche. I flattened to the wall. And then I spotted it, a helicopter, gunning in, a stone's throw from the wall, a military green with yellow emblems. A gun poked from the window. 'Hugh, they're going to shoot us,' then, tearing his head up he saw it: an arm waving. We waved arms, head, legs; danced, jigged, yelled, while they circled in and away like something from another world. Later we learned that it was Norwegian television. But we fluttered no blushes on the wall. The spell of our selves was broken.

Five hours later, after a long lovely 130ft of aid, intricate and out in space, I was on the final summit walls, the last roofs wiped with light, 700ft above me.

All that night, while a white moon sailed over our shoulders, we perched in our haul bags and cut off the blood to our already damaged feet, too exhausted to know. Sharing our last cigar while the nerves in our feet were suffocating to death, we shone in our hunger and smiled a while.

As soon as I put my weight on my foot in the new dawn I knew I'd had it. Hugh's foot was an unspeakable image, and I had to tell him when his heel was grounded inside his boot. He could hardly have his laces tied at all and I was terrified that one of his boots might drop off.

All that day the feeling was of having my boots filled with boiling water that would trickle in between my toes and flood my soles. Then a sensation of shards of glass being wriggled into the balls of my feet. And upon each of my feet a dentist was at work, pulling my nails and slowly filing my toes. Then nothing but a rat-tatting heart when I stopped climbing. I would tremble like water in a faint breeze. I knew it was hypothermia. We had had no food for three days. Maybe it was two.

All the last day we called, a little hysterically I think, for someone on the summit. They were coming to meet us. Sitting fifteen feet below the top, with Hugh whimpering up on jumars I heard whispers . . . 'Keep quiet . . . wait until he comes over the top.'

There was no one there. Only, thank God, the sun. It seemed right in a way to meet only each other there. At the summit cairn Hugh sucked on his pipe while my tongue nippled at a crushed sweet that he had found in his pocket. We dozed warm as new cakes, in a high white world, above impenetrable clouds which had shut out the valley all day. We were terribly glad to be there. After midnight we collapsed into a coma of sleep, half a mile down in the boulder-field.

We met them the next morning, quite near the road; it must have been about half-past eight. They were coming up to meet us. Lindy flew up the hill to hug me forever. I was Odysseus, with a small o, I was Ed, come back for the first time. Hugh grinned in his pain when I told the Norwegian journalists that his real name was Peer Gynt, and that he was an artist like Van Gogh, but that he had given a foot for the wall, instead of an ear to his girl.

On our last hobble, he had, before we met the others, found himself dreaming of the walks he used to have with his Dad, as a child, into the park to feed the ducks, and of the delights of playing marbles (we were both pocketing stones and rare bits from the summit on down). When we arrived in Andalsnes with our friends, I saw the apples burning on the boughs, glowy drops of gold and red (the green gargoyle buds, the little knuckle apples had lit while we were gone); and the postbox in its red skirt shouted to me as we turned the corner into town. Bodil washed Hugh's feet, sent for her doctor, and everyone in our house was alive and well. Only the Troll Wall give me black looks, over the hill and far away at last. Black iceberg under sky − not eye -blue skies.

Back in England my feet were as irrefutable as war wounds. I was on my back for a month, and I had the cuttings from the Norwegian press, as precious as visas. But nowhere to get to.

[67]

PART 2

Terrorist Minerals

Starting Up

'It's me! I'm back! I'm ...'

Gone
Never makes the bed.

I pull back the covers
... where we fermented

the wee, small hours.
After nearly a year

without rain, in bed
there's a red dawn ...

And I feel like a climber
finding strawberries under the snow.

Then a face.
Warm,

yours.

Easter Island

I'D ALWAYS WANTED TO GO THERE. I had a picture. Incredible, a tusk-white rock, tropical, like Treasure Island: childhood . . .

Hamish loosened his grip — immediately my loins felt the cool draught. He leaned back. I didn't say anything. Besides it was stopping and we'd soon be there. Leaving Sheffield, the gravelly rain had turned to big blots of snow going through Chatsworth, then to a fuzz, here and there a wet, white feather. By the time the Honda purred to a standstill, the air was warm, the sun was shining and the snow lay in tatters on the fields, its wave passed.

The world remade. Shakespeare's though, not Christ's even though it was Easter Sunday morning. Magpies flashing through the trees; blackbirds noisy as parrots; a gold finch simmering for rose hips; dippers weaving in and out of the small waterfalls the Dove made slipping over the stepped river bed. An English jungle. Not a soul about. I felt like Thor Heyerdahl. Ilam, it sounded Samoan.

Jesus Christ! Scarey, lonely. It looked more like Thor's blood-spattered anvil, up-ended centuries ago in the forest. Something was dripping. A white patch of snow drooped over the summit like a flag.

Well. We can have a look. Hamish followed. He'd been pretty quiet. Three years now we'd known each other. Tall, pale, chivalrous; though he'd never been in any of my dreams, an anchor in the waves I tended to make. Now he had to decide what to do. University? Work for his father? From the street outside his house, I could see half a bedroom wall being taken up by the Mt. Everest he was painting. I would miss him.

The face leaned over us. I felt like a painter in a shipyard.

'Where's the ladder?' But neither of us laughed. I looked up: Proctor country . . . I'd climbed a bit with Tom. Gentle, mild-mannered as a shire. Once he'd told me of a wild birds' egg collection he'd made as a boy. Every bird you could think of, hundreds and hundreds, from the lapis of a robin, the ivory nut of a wren, down to a peewit's muddy nugget. He had the crown jewels of Derbyshire in his bedroom, all correctly named and labelled, with the discipline of a mathematician, the patience of a painter. And to watch him climb! Taxonomic down to the fingertip, it was as if he was standing on eggs: so deft, and unbelievable his strength, you felt he could crush holds, yet he floated up. When he put his glasses on he looked like Clark Kent. And, though I never told him so, by his side, I felt like Lois.

[72]

I was clinging to the edge about fifteen feet above Hame's head, trying to get my foot up, onto a tufty hold in a little dish.

It was like trying to shave while driving.

'Watch me —' He licked his lips. I'd found a scalloped edge, about as thick as the handle on a British Railway's tea mug. I had to go. I started pulling out — if it broke I'd be thrown back onto the station. Pitons clanging I started moving

'We're off!' I yelled.

The Dove was steaming. The sun was directly above now, hammering down. The rock was as dry as a freshly ironed white collar, and, for a while, I just stood, at the bow of myself again, swaying gently.

'How are you doing?'

'Hamish, I think —'

I felt like an angler with three rods. To my left, a ripple of incuts led to a gash, a crack — but no footholds. Not having Tom's thumbs up for power moves, my feet would be like wheels. Nevertheless, I made a few perfunctory twitches with my left hand:

'Too steep.'

Too deep. Ahead of me, the arête rolled up like a wave. And I wasn't a strong swimmer. Though I've crawled like a snail where some, stronger climbers have got butterflies and drifted back down. So I went more to the right. A bit of knees-up Mother Brown to get me over the bulge — I pulled my horns in, slithering rapidly back.

A family was having a picnic across the river. I was being watched . . . I looked away. Defensive, pinched for holds, with my hands in the air above my head, like I was being held up. Eyes searched me. Climbing is strange. We want to get away — from different things — but once beyond the lawn, the cat, mail in the morning, her face across the table, we can't go too far, because they wouldn't be there. I turned around. And waved, because they were there, interested, happy, like ponies in the sun, having a rest. They'd probably earned it.

So. Back to work. The problem is — like darning: Appliqué yourself Drummond. The rock is a fabric. There are holes in it. But I need repairing — I put in a pin. There, that won't rip. And I start weaving — will's the loom — shuttling back and forth, fine lines of feeling, hemming an atoll from the waves, tucking the loose ends in, fingers bobbing up and down, a bit of sewing machine leg — Then, strange as ripples, after making a splash, coming back — the sinking feeling disappears and I strike out of fear and elation, one wave that carries me up onto Whillans' shoulders, Brown's head and, with a quick pull on the Crew's halo, I'm poised, on the crest, diving for a jug, dark eye of a needle deep in the rock. It accepts my hand like a letter box slot. Snarling a bit I rush out to whoops and barks from Hamish.

[73]

A group of climbers had arrived and were passing around a pair of binoculars. I was battering out old wooden wedges from the summit crack, hanging on a fist jam like a drunken sailor. The ropes billowed out below on the white sail of the rock. This was to be our last climb . . . Hamish would go on to study Philosophy, headstrong on Logical Positivism, getting higher at Aberystwyth. And, after three years teaching, I was leaving school too. By the time he graduated, and began shipping second-hand cranes to Norway, I'd had my Gaugin-like pretensions stripped away by a beautiful and abused native of the States, the same age as him, whom I was to meet in Yosemite. But that's another story.

The wind was just right. Not a cloud in the sky. I could see the green waving in the distance. We were almost there.

Night-Fall

His face crashed awake:
'DON'T LEAVE ME!'

Gripped — tugged — jiggled
juggled — flakes — fingers
fumbled — footholds stumbled
— but only the ghost slipped
back in the pit
of his stomach . . .

In ten seconds
he's more than a hundred feet tall,
his head on the pillow
next to yours, snores.

A beanstalk of dreams
he's climbing
down
towards
dawn.

Ah, the golden eggs, broken.
On a plate.

End's Land

I HAVE NO NAME. Not guilty. How long will I be here? The wind burns my back. Not innocent. I hunch my knees to my chest, trying to stay dry beneath the overhang. Where did I come from? The rain spits in my face.

Bony, ankle-clutching heather with tiny, silent bells, coughed dust all over me when I fell on my face. They were reminding me of her ear-rings. The sun looked down. It was not what I had expected after driving so far all night. Stopping once at a neon cave of lorry drivers, I saw a woman old enough to be their mother, half-asleep at the cash desk.

Almost there. I stood by the cairn-man, my arm on his shoulder, gazing at the sea. I'd made it. Blue milk lapping a headland, creaming the beach, a thousand feet down at my feet. Between finger and thumb I picked up a ship and put it . . . there. It could have been painted on a postage stamp.

Underfoot bursts a magnolia — gull! On the edge where I'd dragged myself on my stomach, after leaving my satchel in the bushes, it hovered above me, sitting in the sky, waiting for me to drop off perhaps.

Gaze in. Far below on the wave-scalped platform, maggot-wriggly things were busy. Cries reached me, like the squeals of piglets being skinned and suddenly hundreds were heading up, flowering around, snapping and snickering from bashed bonnets of seaweed and snowy down, getting on one another's backs, treading on their own eggs in the general struggle to get a better look at this ape in search of a jungle, on the north-west coast of Notland.

The cliff leaned, a headstone for the sea, set by a giant, who dumped an island on the horizon, scattering offshore rocks in his haste and forgetting to write the name.

A wave — mopping its brow on the platform — got a round of applause from the white things, throwing their hats in the air. They returned to their seats at length, screeching. The sea remained calm.

I fell asleep in the swaying grass at the cliff-top, the sun setting the forest-green ocean on fire as I rolled over on my side . . .

It felt like the tree I used to sit up at night. When old ladies passed beneath, I'd owl softly. Sometimes one would stop and look up, even, once, calling and making noises, as if I was a cat and she had milk. Opening and closing my eyes in the dark, high wind, my hand gripping the slim wrist of the last

[75]

inches of the tree, the stars were my sparklers. Sometimes we had contests, the lads and I, to see who could tie the ribbon highest. As if the tree were a tall girl who let us admire her. Red ribbon running in my fingers as I tip-toed the pencil-thin twigs — slipping back branches smack-cracking — the pavement leapt.

I hung upside-down looking at a bergschrund of waves: waiting to start falling again. Throwing a hand up I heaved myself into the glutinous cavity I had almost slithered out of, sleep-climbing-down the spongy, red cliff.

Next morning I found a baby gull had died, inches from my head, during the night. My cheeks were wet. Had it rained? Five more minutes.

A day later I opened my eyes. And looked down. The sea was making the bed, tucking white sheets in beneath me. I could move my fingers. But I didn't smell good.

Next night I slept better. An old Chinese recipe I remembered for "Thousand Bird's Nest Soup" — though I only had the dry ingredients since it hadn't rained — kept me philosophical, if not warm: I could be in a worse mess. I might not have stopped. And the great pyramid of eggs I'd scraped together came to my shoulder. So I could have a cooked breakfast if I liked, poached by the sun; or if I felt over-hung, raw. And after the rain stopped I could have eggs and orange-juice-coloured sunlight, assuming that my boots — suspended from a spike of rock — held water too. And there were always eggs *à la* night, with or without a slice of moon melon.

Five days. The pyramid lost its point. The birds began to return. I crawled along the ledge for an hour. My back didn't hurt as much and the swelling in my chest was less. Six feet in an hour.

I washed my clothes. The sun didn't drop in to do the drying. I thought about wearing my birthday suit.

A ship! When I woke up the sea was empty. I took my second ugh. You could last forty days I thought. Locusts and honey. Moss and old eggs?

Voices! I prop myself on my elbow and wave. A yellow and two orange figures, on the neck of the land that juts out past my place. They must be looking for me. They aren't waving. I'm probably hard to make out. But they can still hear me calling surely, even that far off. I haven't spoken to a soul for weeks then, now I mean.

'Aaaaaaaak! Kirrrrrr! Phssssssss,' is all that comes, croaks, puffs and hisses, helplessly childish, that I can't even write. If only I had a rock! When they're below I'll roll some eggs over.

They are spending the night on the promontory, the two orange ones blobbed together in one bag, the yellow alone. The orange ones hold each other a lot. One goes. Now the yellow and orange dance back and forth uncoiling long lines. They are lowering bags and themselves down a long gully to the sea, seething at the foot of the cliff.

[76]

Two days they've been down there. The first morning a boat came by, its red bows smacking the waves, the other orange one jumping up and down among small black cages. One of the covered hammocks under the eaves of sandstone spewed a sleeper. Standing on a boulder the size of a cottage, he called to her: that voice from the sea was no man's. The boat turned away.

All that day and the next night, waves like white elephants charged the cliffs. When they woke this morning they found one of their ropes trailing into the sea, its end rising and falling and tugging as if something was trying to get away.

Around noon, foam simmering in the sun, one waded out to un-noose the rope from the boulders, gurgling and gasping at the ebb.

Now, late afternoon, at the lip of the huge bottom overhang, neck straining like a lizard's — bulbous-eyed seeing the gulls looking at him like that, one has fossilised.

He pulls a plumbeous bag up after him, as if, at the same time as climbing it, they're finding the true level of this highbrowed cliff.

The other appears from beneath the overhang, flashing into view — blue-anoraked, long red stockings — like a marlin jumping. They've stopped. I scream (I think), but they're unable to hear me over the hammering, as they hang themselves for the night. It starts to rain.

I can't believe it: they're leaving. And burying something in the grey mirror breaking below. A body? Or a bag? The sea gulps, shivers, flings it back. The cormorants stand like spectators under black umbrellas. They pull down the ropes. But leave a pink tie, several hundred feet up, to remind them.

At the top of the gully, where the other orange one has been watching for several days, they glance back. One of them, Ed I think, waves to me. He knows I'm here. Goodbye Ed, In and Om. At least I've learnt their names. Ed and In — the two orange ones — keep touching faces.

Three weeks. My ledge is much longer than I first realised. By bridging the gap at one end — swinging on a horn all woolly with moss — I find myself in the workaday world of the gulls, lined up on their doorstep of a ledge like so many 6am milk bottles, endlessly repeated on level after level of this grandiose sandstone highrise. By the time I reach the last pint on the shelf, it's no wider that a shirt cuff.

But even if I could climb higher, there's no guarantee it will give me a way out. The sun rises, the sun falls. The gulls multiply; big gulls, little gulls; big girls, little girls; eagles, seagulls. Just birds . . .

September. Fine weather has returned. I'm exercising again, in preparation for Ed and Co. I can help them by climbing down a bit. I can do three pull-ups on the ledge beneath my roof. And I've reached ten sit-ups.

At the head end of my ledge is the tunnel of slimy rock down which I first slumped. It's about forty feet long. Some days I see blue flowers, waving like boaters from the rim. If I can restore my strength I might be able to slip into this orifice and wriggle back, grunting and puffing in the soft crack, until I collapse on the bed of lush grass at the end.

I could take a running jump.

Another day. Two seals roll by, nudging one another with coal-black noses on their backs in the spittle.

All night the lighthouse fences the sea, double-crossing the waves — which always come back.

A ship passes in the night. A house built on water? Or rock? I'll know next time. Time . . . I'm twenty-eight, twenty-eight shells, the calendar of my brief life at Cape Wrath, between the golden egg of the sun and the moon's stone one. My breath smells of cod liver oil. My hair is a glossy, hard cap that the rain bounces off.

'Illo! Illo!' There are two of them: they're looking. 'Illo!' My mouth has shrunk, and I can't make the same sounds seem since my teeth began to fall out.

They are creeping nearer.

Most nights now it rains, though I hardly feel the cold. I've so many feathers sticking to me that I don't even get wet. My feet, from squatting here so long, are flat, black and damp. Their thick, curved yellow nails are quite useful for cleaning myself.

They are spending their nights in a large bag. After they've hung it — like a blue beer barrel bound with gold hoops — I hear them singing. They are so close I can read "Cloud Nine" on the side; and "Karrimor." While one of them climbs, the other lies on his back in the tent, keeping dry; he does occasionally stick his head out to see if the other's still there. At night I hear their cat. Or is it a harmonica? I used to have a cat.

My eggs are bad. Each, for the past week, has had a red sac inside. I wonder why they changed the colour. And the birds have stopped laying. Last night, the moon hurtled past like a broken saucer.

The gulls like me! At night they fit around me, breasting into me to keep me warm. They offer me fish tails.

Less than fifty feet away!

Somewhere under the roof that's been preventing them from seeing me, I can hear them arguing. One, Ed I think, wants to go back. Om's not sure.

It has been raining for two days. A trillion water clocks are dripping down the rock, ticking into the sea, the one blue tear seen hanging in the blackness of space, for all we know the universe's only regret. Tapping me on the shoulder from the lip of my overhang, remind me I must drink, I nipple the drips.

The gleety passage I had hoped to try, has turned into a slick slit that I'd have to be a snake to stick in. Venereal-green, the risk of slipping is too great.

They aren't giving up! Om spends all day climbing the bulge above their tent. He wipes egg off his fingers every few seconds. He has been fitting tiny question-mark-shaped hooks on, or in, whatever puckers and niggles and nubbins the rock concedes. He brushes a raindrop from his sharp nose. Then like a watchmaker fits a tiny hook. Looks at it, hangs, steps up, in — blinks — out and down. Thinks. Looks. Shakes. Studies. Pulls — Then: gripping a peg in his mouth — you've got to hand it to him — he climbs up muttering onto the hook. Wipes his black-framed glasses and — Seconds later — there's a tinkle — I see the sea take the hook and Om coming back, jumping up and down in mid-air, a Cassin sardined between his teeth. 'Well caught!' cries Ed.

Who spends today getting up twenty feet. From where I am he's on hands and knees, fingers like chicken's feet in the watery gruel coating the slab. A white blob drops, steaming, on his arm. That's it! he thinks, I've had enough.

Just ten feet away from me, their meal is sizzling — I catch a whiff of garlic and onions, with parmesan cheese over pasta. My eyes water. I have my birds.

Going . . . On their way down, Om stops and lifts a kittiwake from its nest. Ed, huddled on a foothold below, intones: 'Beautiful, isn't it?' Om says, 'She's perfect.'

On the wave-lathed platform they are packing their bags. Piles of cereal and snowy peaks of powdered milk — wiped away by the first wave, boiled fruit sweets plopping like paint bubbles. They slop several pots of jam around to be spread. Last thing they do is to empty a large bag of white sugar out, sweetening the sea.

Gone. The gulls have a party. After, they feed me bits of salami, bread, raisins and snippets of cheese that they peck from the plastic packets. As if I was one of them.

If I can only hold on until spring. I'm sure one of mine will be back. Next time he'll reach me. The look on his face when he pulls onto my ledge and finds me asleep on my eyrie of shit, hatching plans if not eggs. Or could it be her? Could a woman come here? I wouldn't sprout wings or squawk. She might talk to me; or even listen to my odd voice. She'll share the cord they tore me from — tied to our waists as we fall — dragging each other down to earth.

[79]

Deer to Me

Crack of a twig . . .

I glance back into
two, huge eyes.
A wet, black nose
twitching oak leaves,

while the milk of my cereal
drips onto my trousers.
Long velvet ears
like ballet slippers.
Plum, pursed lips.

Flitting through the trees
like Diana's understudies
from those satyrs,

whose antlers are prised out
by men with certain doubts.
Barishnikov-buttocked, camera-shy.

Gone. Dear,
I have to say,
she is the other woman.
Naked, fey,
her stare back at the cars
is Asian, erotic
the way she trots off
with her white arse bobbing.

Although the green diet
doesn't draw me to her pine kitchen
– and I'm not tempted in her bed
of leaves, her small feet
are so hard and sharp –
I bet her breath is sweet as grass.

And I would like to stroke
her trembling face,
and rest her head
on my tangled chest — your forest bed —
for an hour or two.

Quick private wild
animal, I could never capture or train
— who reminds me of you —

come again.

Frankenstein and Linda

Linda: it is the Spanish word for beautiful, though she spoke perfect French
and came from Yorkshire. On that warm, September day when she sat down
facing me, in the staff room, and began talking eagerly — we'd both been at
Bristol it transpired — our eyes darting back and forth like chipmunks
checking nuts, while my apple turned brown and Whitman remained open
at the same page for the rest of the lunch hour, I knew that soon I would, at
last, be leaving my wife . . .

Only a thin, ragged crack, maybe ten feet tall, hardly worth dying for
you'd say, yet it gave me more insight — for all its viciousness — into the
nature of climbing than Joe Brown's smile, Don Whillans' scowl, or Royal
Robbins' stare. Peeping into the soft-lit Sheffield street, (the child, Haworth
asleep upstairs), on that gusty Sunday night in 1969, like a bug-eyed frog in
its last seconds watching knife blades and tied-off lost arrows being smashed
into the shallow crack in the granite that is its home, I was petrified. The two
figures approached. Holding hands, they halted outside the house. She looked
up — face a sudden honey under the street lamp — and, while I writhed,
punching my eyes, gasping and slamming my head onto the sofa, they
kissed.
If only I could have made a strength move, ripped the curtains open and
gone for it — them — right then; smashed my fist in his face, dragged her in

by the hair up the stone front steps and then chased the Yankee bastard up the street in true South American fashion, snatched the kid and slammed the door behind me for ever. Why, I could have become a general, a politician, even have rubbed toes with Messner on Everest, instead of a ghost writer, pouring over his diaries and first poems, in order to find someone seventeen years after he disappeared.

Ah, but then I would never have met Linda. At our best we were perfect. There is a photograph of us that Hugh took, on the day before he and I began living together on the Troll Wall. He jumped out in front of the Honda as Linda and I left to be alone for the day. We look like Justin Hoffman and Dayne Fonda, the bike gleaming, our teeth gleaming. In fact my mother used to have it up in the front room, between two toby jugs. Which was where it remained until Christmas, 1974, when I came back from the States with Grace . . .

We moved in together — set up shop — a little cottage close to school, with two single beds that we roped as one with an old 9 mm. And held hands in the staff room. She wrote and told her parents: her father commanding the international division of Lloyd's in Radford, her mother — an ex-WAAF — the local branch of the Women's Institute; who wrote her out of the will. My letters in general, my parents probably regarded as they did the weather maps on television, neither understanding their over-elaborated analyses of change, nor believing their sunny forecasts.

'It's Haworth I worry about,' said Mom, several times during the two fast years that followed before Linda and I left for the States. At school, both of us were warned at length, by the headmaster and mistress, of the damaging effect 'It could have on your teaching career,' we chorused, laughing, naughty at home that night after the interviews, saluting one another with a nice cup of tea.

' "You'll never get another teaching job" he said, which, after a day like today,' I said, pouring myself a second, 'sounds awfully attractive.' Then I went upstairs to write. After a year and a half of teaching all day and trying to write at home in the evenings, feeling more like an octopus in an aquarium facing the kids than the captain of a second class destroyer, his argument against seemed, really, more one in favour of our administrative adultery. More and more it was those intractable walls in Norway and California, ones I would never dream of trying to remove, that attracted me.

'He is married,' Miss Freeman, the senior mistress said to Linda, who, though she wasn't, had taught the milkman a thing or two while still a schoolgirl, she'd told me, in Hardon, Yikes, on those days her parents left early to go to Radford together. Which, in my hate of the art marriage, really whet

[82]

my appetite, since, not just a good looker, Linda knew love was a four letter word like the verb to cook — at which she was also superb.

At home in the cottage she made lemon curd; my favourite, cheese cake, and baked bread. She took with wide eyes lashings of my pre-Copernican poetry, and, after I'd been climbing out on Stanage, washed my back — we had a tub in the kitchen — handing me hot, sweet, tea. She cultivated raspberries from the dandelioned wilderness at the bottom of the garden, and made pies that could have tempted the devil to behave. And on those days she went to town after school, she'd buy food from Marks and Spencers. She was not cheap. Waiting for three weeks at the foot of the Troll Wall, calling up their names to those statues after the storms, until they moved; defying her powerful parents and risking her new teaching career, to go to America with a married man; looking after my son while I was in Wales doing you know what; supporting me in Mexico when I got hepatitis and stayed in bed for two months, reading over a hundred books that she'd get from the British library — Oh no, you can't say she was immaterial. When I began to get up at dawn, sitting alone on the beach, trying to write: the way an albatross skims the waves, like Hemmingway's pen on his best days I thought back then, with — seeing crabs whirl like catherine wheels, spurting sand if I came too close — words that kept their distance, poising like an eyebrow-slow porpoise, lifting out of the still, blue sea one day — like an apostrophe of a world at my feet that, while climbing, had looked flat, why, though she was lonely she had left me alone.

An expensive education. Yet she paid; through the nose. It was just a pity she didn't — even though she had done Snake Dike while it lightninged, under heavy duress, and jumared the first pitch of the Nose in a downpour, as well as having got up something on Stanage once just after we met. But — in spite of having spent three days at Cape Wrath, in a ruined cottage on the moors within earshot of heavy gunfire from the Royal Navy using the headland for their annual target practice, until Tom Proctor and I finally scuttled back from the nine-hundred-foot face we'd been in suspense on in our hammocks — lowering our sights before Her Majesty's lowered theirs — and cooked us fresh lobster before we crept away home — still, she wasn't a climber.

We walk the three miles from Camp Four to the foot of El Capitan, on a cool October morning in 1973, holding hands. The North faces of Half Dome, Sentinel and Middle, are dark. El Cap is a lilac mile, flat and calm and lifeless, unless you know where to look for the tell-tale tears and blood-drops of the hammocks. Both of my haul bags are at the base of the first pitch, along with my equipment: nuts — the only Friends I had in those days — from pumpkinseed-sized wedges, to hexagons and Moacs that clacked like a bag of brazils; all on wire. Although I plan to use no pins, just in case, I take some lost arrows, angles, bongs, a rurp and a knife blade — a fair selection of the usual cutlery for any fat or thin granite cracks that, cooking in the sun, I cannot swallow or swift, but must just peck away at like a chicken. So I do have a hammer, which, when I was packing back at camp, I kept discreetly hidden — as if it was a gun or something; since the recent first, hammerless ascent of the Nose, word is out that pins are not *in*, and nuts are normal.

'Sounds a bit crazy to me,' she said, 'I'm glad you're taking a hammer.' Well, with Christmas getting closer, I needed something to crack my nuts with. At night I sleep with it under my pillow. I have five ropes, two for leading and rappelling since a solo climber, like an only child, needs extra security; an 11mm for each haul bag, and a lighter, 7mm line, with which I'll pull up my bundle of pins and nuts whenever I need it, leaving it hanging by a fifi hook from the last point of protection — that's my theory. Oh, I have a book, *VICTORY*, by Conrad; which may sound heavy, but is a lot lighter than a TV.

Climbing, at its best, is like crawling, the current strong, toes lightly pushing, hands brushing the holds; a feeling of floating that, on great pendulums like the King Swing I'll be facing later this week — jumping on the toe of the fifty foot Boot Flake with my own tiny ones — brings back with a rush those first, gay, placental days when we held the world on a string and gurgled for joy. So it — the first pitch — goes, beautifully, fluidly, Linda playing out the ropes with casual, croupier strokes.

'I wish you were coming,' I call down near the end of the pitch, my fingers cinched in pockets made by my percussing predecessors.

'Not this time,' — turning — blushing — away to check a slight tangle in the lines. 'This is yours.'

Snap. Snap: the teeth of the jumars clamp the bright red rope like a tourniquet. A long, last, hug.

After raising the two, huge, hauls, I sit there for a while, my arms round the old bags like some kind of single parent with two dumb kids to bring up alone. A bleak prospect on four gallons of water, two pounds of cereal with added powdered milk, four boxes of dates, four packets of cheese, twenty tea bags and one can of sliced cling peaches, for ten days. I do have five packets of hard-boiled fruit balls, which at thirty per pack, makes for ten, fifteen-sweet days, or fifteen not-so-sweet-ones, i f I g o s l o w. I aim at doing at least three pitches per day. For each pitch I allow two for leading, one for the rappel and clean, none for the jumar and one for each haul. That's five balls for each pitch. Still, to solo the Nose you need a lot of those.

Popping a red one, cherry, I think, I plop a per — 'There!' — fect nut in and layback up, nuzzling sugar, my tongue-tip rolling the sweet round my mouth like a seal a ball, while I inspect the austere, silver-grey summit a week away. Looking up to the Great Roof — looking down at me, I realise I can't move — it's like trying to tug a train out of the station: What the — I lower my eyes: I'm out of slack . . . Backing down I bite the dusty rope, chewing and sliding the prusik along, regurgitating enough slack to get me to a resting place.

There to begin again this un-free climbing, paying for every inch I make. Just when I have my hands full, legs gently epileptic, eyes rolling, the haul bags start tugging at my waist, reminding me I'm going nowhere without them. Call slack all I will, until the day that apes move up to slaves, creatures who solo big walls are going to find themselves, from time to time, caught with their heads between their legs, looking where they came from, hoping the harness is on tight. Octopushing and pulling, I spend the rest of this first day getting drier and higher, marinading my white tee-shirt to a delicate, kippery hue, as I try to persuade the two big drags to let me go. The problem is that if I give myself too much slack I may end up where I began. And if I give myself too little, I may up-end; or — unable to move — shift neither hand from neither hold as the sweat drips down my nose, as I drip down the Nose. And, learning this process by the skin of my teeth, not going too far before I grip the lead ropes — like a bit — and slide the Pemberthy knot as far as I can, gaining a foot of slack each time, I realise — as the hardware sling crashes across, jangling like a slammed cash register — that I'm probably going to run out of sweets.

She comes back before dark. I'm near the end of the cryptic traverse onto Sickle Ledge, shoplifting my weight on to bashees and hammered nuts that look like toffees plugged in kids' lips, with miserable dribbles of slings, that, as I clip in — heavier if I hold my breath? — quiver. Am I the last camel?

'Linnnn-Da!' — throwing her name out like a bouquet.

'A-i-r-r-r — ed' — tiny bubbles of language drift up as I haul myself, dripping, onto the ledge. I rig my lines across. There's an orange pip of moon, by whose light I ease each haul out, from the belay at the top of the third, until it hangs, motionless, below the bolts in the middle of Sickle. Night fishing: three, a good bag. Then, moving the prusik knot and the jumars — like a set of hand-held dentures — along the grey lines, I reclimb the pitch twice, clipping from point to point with increasing fluidity, like in a barn dance, not gripping so tightly as you get to know many partners' hands. Moving along Sickle for the third and last time that night, I'm removing 'biners and popping protection as easily as Dad rolling a fag while he's driving.

It's hard to believe what I did here four years ago. On this very ledge, in the dark, with that arrogant young American, Petersen.

. . . . It was 1968. I was twenty-three years old and had been a father since

I was twenty-one. It was "The British North America Wall Expedition", the brain-child I'd dreamed up in England as a penurious student, to get me to Yosemite, and, who knows? as I learnt to say in California, maybe an audacious ascent of the NA. The real child, Haworth, got left out in the process, abandoned to grandparents, since the actual ones weren't feeling too grand, and, after a year and a half, were ready to be surrogate students. The attempt on the North America Wall never materialised. You could say my fellow Brit and I had a ball, but the problem was that neither of us was willing to accept it as his:

It's your lead.'
'No, really . . .'
'Please, be my guest,' each of us hoping, I suppose, that the other would, magically, sprout − if not wings − then at least one more, so that we could give it an honourable try. Well, after we'd yo-yo'd around on the first pitch of the Nose, which as you'll know is a good quarter of a mile from the start of the NA, brow-beaten as much by me as by the sun, my partner agreed he wasn't 'up to this sort of thing,' and that 'we'd better call the whole thing off.' Back in Camp Four, he signed almost a hundred identical postcards that I'd composed, attributing the ex- of this 'pedition to his inexperience in leading difficult aid-climbing. Of course I didn't mention that my only difficult aid-climbing had been from a tree branch in Bangor, using five inch nails driven in upside down, to simulate the roof pitch on the Black Cave, in a harness homemade from a car seat belt . . . 'Mooooo,' a cow commented, as the branch bent lower and lower, depositing me on the damp grass it had been studiously chewing. He signed and we sent them, back to England, like wedding invitations, cancelled on the big day, thereby adding, to the arrogant figure I had been cutting for several years, a long tail of lies. And we hadn't even spent a night together. Near the end of that hot summer, after Simon left Yosemite, having had a constructive middle-of-the-road season, while I either browned off in the sun with my wife, or exploded vicariously at routes such as Lost Arrow Chimney and the North Face of Sentinel, with Americans whom I was hoping to persuade to lead me up at least one big wall, I met a young, confident American. And we decided to do the Nose . . .

Now, four years later, alone on Sickle at night, I am recalling the steps I took: the devious, creeping things I did. And hid. I threw my boots off. The blue suede ones that the king had given me. In the dark − flinging them out so that they wouldn't kick the wall and warn Petersen. When they hit the ground, 550 feet down, the stones gave a little cough. Next morning I pretended I'd no idea where they were:
'They must be here,' I insisted, emptying the haul bag for the second time.

And you wondered why I have these chains round my ankles?

After we had trudged back to Camp Four, Royal's only comment as I offered back his old boots, was a cold, slow, stare. We never climbed together again. Four years later, lying on my back, looking at the constellation of Pleiades, I'm keeping my boots on. When it's over, I'll tell Linda what really happened.

During the night furry fingers rustle in the hauls, scuttling across my sleeping bag when I lash out. So one hungry mouse misses the chance of a micetime to make friends with a simian called man. I was so wild mind you in those days, that even St. Francis, let alone Linda, would have had a hard time being my pet. Later, the clang of tin cans banging down the walls above my prone face, wakes me:

'Filthy swine! Someone's trying to sleep down here!' Silence. Then, rising, with the sleeping bag around my ankles, to an unexpected American stage, I pitch: 'It's like living in the Bronx!' at the darkness. Nothing. So − to the heavens − 'You should be ashamed of yourselves!' Close by a frog hickets. Like a true slum landlord, whoever it is up there is keeping quiet.

Now this occurs just before the ecological movement of the seventies really gets off the ground in the United States, so far as climbers are concerned. Only when they took up Galen Rowell's democratic suggestion, that issues on big walls should be passed into brown paper bags, was − with a show of hands − the motion carried . . . Now, Spring, Summer, Fall, the lean trees at the base of the monolith are empty-handed no longer: bags of excreta hang from their branches, roasting in the relentless sunshine, and something the consistency of coffee may drip onto your head − brushing past − after a shower. Is this progress?

Sleep ruined, I flop around in my polypropylene pyjama suit, too hot by a long chalk to drop off again. I even consider − since I'm sweating so much − chalking up. This is the first time I've carried chalk. It's only just appeared in the Valley, but while I'm climbing I don't even think about it: the sleek, mango-yellow sac − the size of a bull's testicle − swings behind me, unnoticed, all week, until, suddenly, it starts snowing . . .

But I'm not there yet. Here, beneath the magnifying glass of the sun − Linda nowhere in sight − I start moving house. Blotting my cereal dish dry with my tongue, I scrape together my bits and pieces, clothes, sleeping bag, headtorch, food, toothbrush. Packing them into the separate stuff sacs racked on karabiners, hanging from the belay bolts behind me, I generally butler about in best British fashion, picking up errant sweet papers, brushing my hair, to present a neat and business-like appearance to this great white elephant that has lifted me out of my rut in England.

Sickle Ledge lumbers right at this point, an easy stairway of uneasy blocks

[87]

and earthy cracks. Stripped to my underpants for the next two, short pitches, the sun glaring, I feel dazed, vaguely colonial, as if I'd been made gardner at the Taj Mahal. It is impossible to haul here so I have to manhandle the bags like drunken uncles up the tottery steps, belayed by jumars from the lines I've strung.

To anyone in the meadow with a glass eye that morning, I must have looked like a nude ascending and descending a staircase, or a sort of ant, shouldering two royal-blue eggs to safety, after some catastrophe in the nest. Wino-red in the sun, I start drinking much too early, guzzling the hot, plasticky fluid as if I don't know what I'm doing.

Bright as a ladybird at the end of my finger as I wave, Linda sits in the sun. Now I feel like a man digging the back garden, his wife watching at the kitchen window. Planting a jam, I inspect the tiny black ears that have just appeared from the granite. Tying the bolts together, backed up by two nuts, I lower for my first El Cap pendulum; nervous, almost thirty, unemployed. Will I get it?

Dashing like a stockbroker's jockey snatching ticker-tapes of price crashes, the wall fluctuates, rising and falling with my bids. Accepted — after the third time of asking — to distant applause from the little lady in the front row, I quickly work my way up the eighth pitch, rubbing shoulders with the hard-nosed granite. Hurrying, I let the last haul go into the groove without a back rope. Crossing for the last time, I see in the cold light of the evening sky a large, spreading, silvery patch, below the bag: a waterbottle, like an overblown egg — burst. I end up that night, wedged between big flakes in Dolt Hole, like a piece of chicken in a sleeping dog's mouth, with one of the haul bags jammed somewhere below. Strangely familiar accents, like stale cigarette smoke, drift up in the night from Sickle Ledge.

'Bastard!' Bunkered in Dolt Hole, the sight of that grave English face hammering his way up the chunky crack below, makes me feel depressed, angry, English. They might have waited until I was above the Great Roof.

'Hello Ed. How are you doing?' Peering down from my perch in the hole:

'Cold.' I keep it brief, annoyed to be caught napping. Dolt Hole is in a corner, back in the shadow from the early sun, and, if you're a dreamer, you can drink in bed until you realise — as the sun shatters the black window — the house is on fire.

'Can you get that bag for me?' A real gentleman, he obliges, while I bang about like a navvy, without breakfast, a hot drink, or a shit. Underfoot, the loose flakes growl. Gravel pitters down the cracks. He looks anxiously up.

Bridging past Dolt, I see Linda, eight hundred feet down, between my legs, probably puzzled to see me so low this late in the morning. Calling, waving

— it couldn't be anyone else — at the bright spot on the scree, I see the English exchanging grins, wives in England no doubt. More important things to think about now, I scuttle back to work, fists flashing, boots thudding into the off-width.

My desk today is blank, stretching endlessly away, not a letter in sight, not a speck of dust, washed and polished day and night for a hundred thousand aeons by the minute ministrations of raindrops and feathery snow, brushed and buffed by warm westerlies and biting easterlies. Its only signs of life are twelve old bolts — one or two of them hanging out — that I must use if I am to rise at all in this ruthless world. They look like triggers. Cautiously clipping from one to another, always spreading my weight between two, which requires deft étrier pliés, in case, overloaded, one snaps — right between my eyes — I feel like I'm shaking hands with a firing squad. At the top I feel at home, once I've strung the last four bolts together with two big Cassin screw gates. Like Napoleon on Elba.

'Funny things, pendulums, going up to go down to go up,' I observe, running over the skulls of my fellow countrymen, crunched down in Dolt Hole as I gain momentum for the long, hurdling jump over the wall of the corner — airborne — all the way to the Stove Leg crack. First time. I can't believe it. Leaning out on the perfect edge like a Botticelli angel, pink cheeks a-puffing, I should be in a film . . . Drummingbird or something.

One of the English, Ken? Mike? is going to release my last haul, saving me another trip down. It springs into view on the rope like a punchbag and I slug it up like Don Cockell, in training for the big one, Britain's answer to the monstrous Marciano, whom I used to see on the British Pathé Newsreel, at our local cinema with my Mom, after school, eating sweets, and holding hands in the dark.

It's now about four o'clock; Linda should be back soon. Brooding over my tiny family I take stock. The food hardly matters: one bite of cheese and I lose my appetite; the Monteray Jack in the plastic packets looks more like soap, and the dates that I put in the top of the hand-haul during the day are like a viscid brown tar I can hardly get down. Water is life up here and I've less than three gallons. If I'm a good husband I can probably make it to the Great Roof. That's a big if, since, once I get started on those hot, lip-sticky mouths, I find it hard to stop. So, if I'm going to back off it might as well be now. There is a rappel line. Isn't there?

'There isn't?' voice — out of sight — in Dolt Hole.

'I can't see one,' says the lead climber, holding the topo of the route as if it's a ticket, issued by a little-known travel agent, and here they are, standing on the longest, emptiest, airfield in the world . . . The English are coming.

One of them has stuck his head out of the corner. It looks like a huge baby being born rather late in the day — out of the rock.

'Down man,' I Yank, translating at the same time into me udder tongue: 'A little bit lower down,' punctiliously dripping EnglishEnglish into his open mouth, as if I was feeding a baby bird with an eye-dropper. As soon as he takes off, I'm off, in best Duke of Edinburgh fashion, pulling my three fingers out of the sweaty slit — knowing I'm being watched. I complete a whole rope length up the dramatic, easy crack, placing stoppers and hexs with broad, sweeping gestures along the way; here, tut-tutting nuts into place; there stamping and champing like a flamenco dancer as I jam the last forty feet without a stop. When I finish the pitch and start bowing and bending at the waist to lift the haul line into the pulley, I must look a bit like Barbirolli after a prom, acknowledging, acknowledging. I throw a smile in the up-turned face, 'Thank you, thank you.'

Are they arguing? Huddled over the belay, wind flicking the ropes, swaying, wrestling with the haul and one another as they tie in again, the happy couple seem to be having some trouble. The same one continues to lead.

He's being very heavy-handed with the crack, jamming in so far that for a second I get this Dali stamp of a man with no arms, crawling on his belly towards me, my severed, Siamese twin. He's making me feel nervous.

'It eases up soon,' I yell — he still hasn't put anything in, heading, apparently, for the fixed bong, gleaming like the evening star ten feet above his head.

'Bloodyopeso.' His hands slur at the crack — three feet — his friend's face shoots up — two — I don't want to look — one — backwards — the crack spits him — crucified in mid air — plunging past the buried head of the second — stop, stop — at the ground, a thousand feet down. What do I do? A dark stain, spreading like oil now that the sun has set, leaks from the corner of his mouth. His glasses are gone. I can't hear:

'Are — you —' — I take another breath —

'I'm all right,' he calls up faintly. His friend has an arm around his shoulder.

'I can easily rap down.' What will I do? Is it spleen? I think of the worst; kissing him, his blood on my hands, the First Aid course I was always going to take. Is he crying? Head down, shoulders shaking . . . Evening seeps in like treacle, tying my hands up with organising my own forced bivouac. I do nothing. Moving about below, tying themselves in as best they can, they look like a short, twisted tree, briefly growing limbs in the slate twilight, before slumping thickly together.

Night spreads. Squatting as comfortably as a wild goose on a clutch of golf balls, because the haul I happened to choose, in the dark, to be strung up horizontally, is the one with the water bottles, I watch the autumnal streams of vehicles, arriving and leaving. The gold-brushing head-lights through the pines on the far side, the quick, red pulse on this, speeding past our astronomical house in the woods.

Some would be going round that old circle, from San Francisco to Yosemite, each weekend in the fast lane, climbing, hiking, skiing, bicycling, a bit of peace and quiet. Past the quiescent nuclear weapons complex at Livermore, the battleship-grey canning factories outside Merced — whose products travel all over the world too, becoming in time, a Nepalese tea cup, Somalian ear-rings, a football in a Rio slum, even an oil filter on someone's perennial VW Bug in Baja — they would drive: middle of the road, proud, generous, one-eyed, deserters of their pasts, Liberty's lemmings, those other English, the Americans.

One or two would be making their once in a lifetime visit to Yosemite. From all over the nation, Alabama, Rhode Island, Alaska, crammed in the family Plymouth with the kids, to live on Cokes and Coors, with hot dogs barbecued on the Park Service grills provided at each numbered camping spot. From where they would walk to Mirror Lake, and read the notices about that process by which what was deep and reflective, becomes shallower each year. But the highlight would be that eye-popping orgy in the meadow at the base of El Cap, when they sat in the tour bus and joined together the coloured dots of the likes of us going up the wall.

Maybe I can go on tomorrow after all. I call down and ask them.

'We'll decide in the morning.' The moon, like a black big toe with a thick yellow nail, sinks below Middle Cathedral.

Sometime during the night, bursting to do one — I haven't since Sickle — writhing out of my Hellies and harness, after fashioning a rather spare bra from my étriers — I do, trying, as it were, to give nothing away to my sleepy compatriots. Modulating, aiming, prettifying such a happy, barbaric process, is like playing trumpet and chewing gum at the same time; things can get a bit messy. I hope I haven't put my foot in it. Night seeps away . . .

They are filling my empty one-gallon bottle. Before going down.

'No that's plenty,' I tell them, afraid to reveal the depth of my need, austere little wallflower.

'Good luck,' both of us chime. We laugh. He looks happier. I feel like I've missed the dance again. I wish I was going with you, I don't say, though I do.

Another day. 'What a drag this is' I tell the haul bags, 'It's like reading the Bible in one go, I'm not even halfway. We should complain.' They don't say a word all day.

That night I sleep well, stretched out on El Cap ledge, that king-sized slab of golden granite that a pharoah could have slept untroubled on for four thousand years. Until the first caravan of climbers arrived back in 1958: Warren Harding holding his nose as he raises a glass of chablis to its stiff lips. Relaxing, I take my boots off for the first time in four days. A warm, doggy smell rises from the matted woollen socks. And that's how it was, climbing the rest of the Stove Legs, then angling off diagonally right for three pitches to El Cap Tower: as easy as writing to the point and as easily forgotten.

Could I? Piano, piano, as the Italians say . . . I think of Martin Luther King, singing gospel songs in the dark, standing by a candle-lit piano in Montgomery, while the Klu Klutz Klan (New American Dictionary) were gathered outside with their rifles: 'I have a dream . . . ' I am staring across at the North American Wall. From here anything looks possible.

For this is a ledge that, like Helen's bed, makes it all worthwhile. The years of struggle, the long, selfish war, the betrayal, not seeing my son the past four months. The sort of place where Zeus could have a week off from Hera . . . Up on the shelf, weary of lightning strokes, he could assume other forms like mice, or men; maybe even climbers. A place where, puffing on my Hamlet cigar, Begin and Arafat could begin again; Nixon and Dean; Adam and Eve. Really high, I drop off to sleep.

It is late October, and the blue sky has a scatter of cloud like bits of oyster shell. Standing in the alcove behind the hundred-foot Texas Flake (what day of the week is it?) I feel I'm too late, a kind of 1939-in-Vienna-chill in the air, as if there's someone I'm supposed to meet to help me get away. Slipping into the deep black chimney, I look up. Not looking forward to this. A wide, smooth, totally unprotected pitch, formed because the flake is not flush with the wall: like climbing on a floating whale. Because I've heard that the belay bolts were fixed, not into El Cap itself, but the tip of the flake by the Dionysian Harding — rather like anchoring a liner to someone's deck chair — I've put the bolt kit in the top of the hand haul. I've also got this stupid fear I'll lever the flake off if I push out at all: lightly as a postcard dropping through the air, to explode on the screes fifteen hundred feet down. 'Dear Mr and Mrs Drummond, I am sorry to have to inform you.' Face climbing as much as I can, only bridging as a last resort — eyes shut, unexpectedly, holds and the odd, lichen-encrusted crystal appear. Stroking the lucky ovals and crisp incut curves I feel the joy of boyhood birdnesting.

Perched on the tail of the flake, I warble thanks to climbing's Columbus, for having the savvy not to put all his eggs in one basket: on the wall facing me is a line of bolts, gleaming like unopened bottles of Dos Equis along the long polished counter of a dusty cantina in the Senora Desert. And Linda, in the corner of my eye, watching from the scree.

'Orange juice, *por favor*. On the rocks. Oh and a tequila for the lady over there. *Gracias.*'

Ever since the English retreated, I've been talking out-loud . . . I don't feel mad, though I must admit with my food-sprouting beard, furry trousers — a pot-pourri of liquorice, onion and all sorts of smells when I lower them — and my pelt of hair, like a mechanic's rag hanging, I'm getting there.

I follow the bolts leftwards in a rising line, my ropes, green, red and blue, twisting, wistarial, through twenty or more 'biners, making it difficult to move without tugging. Solemnly, Boot Flake appears, with the grave step of a Pinochet. The cloud has gone. The sky is unambiguously American; 1973, aggressively sunny. And with the hot air rising from the valley floor, I'm like a fly caught in the drier with a Texas housewife having a beehive hair-do.

The bolts run out. Now I have to place the rurp. It's like trying to get into Caesar's with a dime, dressed in ursine underwear. I'm either going to be thrown out on my ear, or ignored as the janitor. Sweating, I stand tall, level with the shoulder of the last bolt, offering: thin lips spit it back. A different angle: just a tip . . . I don't even bother to pick it up. This is getting serious. I whip out the knife blade and, keeping my hand on it as I press it hard enough for the tip to stick — a couple of quick blows — it's done. Point taken, I slide by, popping a nut in the open mouth of the crack above, 'keep the change.' I settle down to make myself comfortable before the show.

Mick Burke had told me that when he did the Nose, making the first non-American ascent with Rob Wood in 1968, just before I arrived, the first pins he placed in Boot Flake, (angles I think), fell out due to the expansion of the flake by later, higher placements. That's why I'm going to free-climb it. Again the image of a huge piece of rock, flying from the parent body because it wasn't attached, shattering the afternoon.

Standing in the first nut, I re-rack the hardware sling and try to relax. It feels like nylon, the sweaty, thigh-thick edge of the flake crack I must appear to be trying to pry open, tentatively slapping, pinching and laying. A change of tactics. I proceed like a fencer, jabbing quick slick jams while I tango with my shadow, my two front feet rapidly growing — eight — nine — ten — more, until, hanging upside-down, my head in a cloud of snow-white chalk, I realise I'm going to need a ladder. I finish the pitch on nuts for aid. Which is like getting soybean burger after ordering a steak. I drink long and deep, Linda at my feet asleep in the sun. She didn't even see me fall.

The top of the Boot is the width of a window sill. I could sleep here, but it would have to be on my side, fastened to the four massive coach bolts in the wall behind. There are two hours of light left I'd guess; maybe I can do the pendulums. This is the King Swing. Trying to get the three haul bags to balance on the ledge I feel like a window cleaner with unruly flower pots, while the lady of the house leaves by the front door . . .

A flicker of red in the dark green wood. She'll catch a ride into the village, shop at the store, then settle down in the Awahanee lounge for tea. There

[93]

she'll read for an hour, chat amiably with visitors who might ask her the way to the restroom, or what she'd recommend for dinner: who, thrilled to discover her a true blue Englishwoman, would then find her eager to embroil herself in their life story: who the husband works for, how good he is at his job. They might even go for a dessert together. Then she'd wander back to Camp Four, looking out for a chipmunk or squirrel to write home about. Sitting at the camping table with the borrowed Coleman stove warming up some soup, she was a lonely figure, to whom the climbers, grooming moves on the famed boulders like Big and Little Columbus, or preparing the tackle for the next day's climb, rarely spoke. After dinner she'd go to the lounge at the Lodge. There to write her postcards and gladly point out the way to, as she'd say, the Ladies. So it should come as no surprise when I tell you how I – suddenly – hated her, stuck up – as I was – in the Stove Legs on the fourth, exhausting day I wasn't going to say anything about.

'A fat lot of help you are,' I had yelled silently, hanging from the eleven hex in the widest part of the crack, at her petite figure, savouring Flaubert in a cool drawing room of shadow at the edge of the forest below. I remembered, not long ago, in response to some perfectly minor criticism of mine, she had admitted she was:

'Like my name: mean and unimportant.' And I pointed out,

'If that had been my name I would have changed it!' Her cheeks burned, mine shone and I strode ahead like the petty officer going for the captain after discovering there's a woman on board.

Losing sight of her among the trees, I get back to work. Sinking, my weight taken by the ropes running over the clean-cut boot top, I feel detached, cool as an old coroner. After a while they all look the same, bodies, cliffs. Taking note of a fixed pin forty feet away to the left, I stand, gingerly, on the toe. It is highly polished: obviously a man who cares deeply about his appearance. And the other one? Here experience shows. As any old sawbones knows, there are many in this world who got their leg pulled a bit too hard by the powers that be, as well as those like me who don't have one to stand on.

From the ground, if you happen to look up at this moment that I catapult past the toe of the boot, it looks – having got my finger in the fixed pin – as if I've just been kicked into touch. With the third try I've poked my finger through its eye, only to find I can't get a krab in when – pulling my finger out as I have to – I'm snatched back by the eager kicker. Hmmm. Clipping a long sling to my waist, I hold it in my left hand with a karabiner and start running again, scuffing the toe of the boot with my own as I pump past. It is like trying to feed a giraffe.

Smearing on a bloodshot crystal, sidesaddle in the setting sun, I clip both ropes in. Lowering down, I realise the autopsy is over.

[94]

It's obvious. To the left the rock sticks its powerful chest out, glowing redskin granite. To overcome it and the natural resistance of gravity, swinging up and around, into the out-of-sight corner on this, the second leg of the pendulum, I must transmogrify. Since this term is not included in Blackshaw's dictionary, let me draw a picture. Of this stick figure, two thousand feet high, clinging to the heel of his master's boot, who, letting go, bursts through the twilight — slings swinging arms flapping hair on end like Frankenstein rushing to the bathroom — its whole being being booted round the bend and onto the belay at the end of this, the eighteenth pitch. A new man.

I ferry the haul bags in the dark. It is, to my surprise, relaxing. The night-blue tide returned, I gently bob back along the lines.

Rapelling back down with the first and heaviest haul bag hanging from my harness, I realise as I jumar up towards the fixed pin, what a stupid and dangerous thing I've done . . . I don't know how the belay is holding, it's just nuts — not in upside down as they need to be to stand an upward pull like this: all because I left the ropes clipped in as I jumared diagonally back to the top of the boot. Expecting at any second to be hurtling earthwards with a fifty pound weight attached to my waist — the ropes slicing across the top of the flake — I feel like a human guinea-pig about to be dropped. Say it's a useless experiment — everyone knows they can't — still, believe me it wasn't funny at all, suspended by a thread from the fixed pin, krabs chattering, swaying, sweating, yanking in the slack, making last second deals with my invisible support systems. Like the final apple left on the tree.

I look out. No one in the meadow yet. A white sky. Except that where the sun usually is, there's a ghostly full moon . . . No, it's the sun, like an egg, a bald pate lost in the clouds forming over Glacier Point. I look up: Now I've done it. There's only one way down: Up. I can't if I want to. The King-Swing is gniws-gnik; I mean it doesn't make sense backwards. Climb, rap, jume, haul — so far I do seem to be getting the hang, winching up the bags I leave in suspense by fifis from the belay below as counterweights, as efficiently as a crane operator plucking containers out of the hold. Though they do look tired, torn in several places. Will they last, or will one of them catch on a jagged pin as I drag it up, regurgitating its contents into the happy valley behind my back? To arrive at the belay like a sea-floor-cloth and not the stubborn marlin-red and blue creature that's been following me for days.

Cli - ra - ju - hau - so - far - I was going to say that it's like practising musical scales. But this is hardly practising. This is it. There is no more public stage than this titanic auditorium, these one night stands on Dolt Tower or El Cap ledge, aloof pantomimes whose only audience is those

[95]

flowers in the meadow who throw no bouquets at the end of your tremendous, silent soliloquies. Only your heart applauds wildly the laggardly madrigals you make up the blunt prows and shields of this bastion of eternity, and probably no more than a haul bag spinning in the wind will ever thump you on the back, when you climb El Cap alone. As for music . . . True, you have been known to whistle when all's well, jingling your tools like a cap-o-bells as you skip up a tricky crack, or hum a hymn while you're fixing dinner on a ledge with plenty of light − but, let there be the merest rumble on the drums beyond Half Dome, a cymbal flash of lightning, or the wind rise, booming bassoon behind some hollow flake, or flaring the slack from the trailing haul line like a vast, trembling clef as you pound on the jams, and you don't want to hear. Why, the tinkling pan-pipes of icicles outside the bivvy tent, would bring you to your knees, beating your head in despair.

There − just coming out of the wood − she is. Like a little old lady making her way every day to the foot of some implacable stone idol. She probably has no idea I'm watching. Each day she's smaller, her dark-blue sweater harder to find in the early morning pools of shadow that lie at the foot; her faint cry just another bird's. Mornings now it's the swifts swishing past that wake me, blurred brown boomerangs around El Cap like bees around their hive, looping, spiralling, diving a mile in the wink of an eye, making love at a hundred miles an hour. If I could tie onto one of those!

Actually I'd like to be caught by a storm. Just as long as I find a ledge to spread my pans on to catch some water. That would save me. Is there one? I feel silly not having brought a topo, like going to the theatre but, deliberately not taking the ticket because you've paid. Didn't I?

I'm looking at the Grey Bands. Though they sound like a Russian punk rock group, actually it's the name of the only punky rock on the entire route; the imperious, aquiline profile scarred by a deep intrusion. From the valley floor it looks like a line of dirty sheets hung out to dry.

The first pitch of the day starts with easy free. There are so many holds to choose from that I feel I'm a juggler having a particularly good day, picking up speed, frisking the rock like an old cop who knows all the tricks, brushing delicate cavities and suspicious bulges, enforcing my right of passage through the chaotic minerals with a few rapid blows from the hammer on the heads of rusty pins. Higher up I dismiss a hold, bouncing past the slumped hauls, volleying out baseball-white, to shatter, eight seconds later − (using $S = UT + \frac{1}{2}FT^2$, the initial velocity zero, F the acceleration due to gravity, and S the distance − about two thousand feet) − on the dense skull of our terrestrial umpire. More precisely, I was getting cocky, so it should come as no surprise to learn that I ended up flat on my face a little higher, unable to reach the belay bolts no more than six feet above my head because

[96]

I'd used too much rope at the belay below. And of course this just happened to be the longest pitch on the Nose; bar one that — though I don't know it at the time — I'm getting to . . .

I extract some loops from the thick web of my bivouac and finish the pitch. The sky is darkening. At the end of the next, long, pitch it starts spitting rain. I can make out a ledge, thirty feet away, horizontally left. It looks good. But the rock is wet. I get out my headtorch. Spacewalking on the faint gleams at the brink of a huge black hole I feel extraterrestrial. A long way from home. By the dim view of my headtorch on the silent film of water running down the rock, I look like Errol Flynn's stuntman.

Once I've hung the bivi bag and spread my pots, then shuddered inside the stiff folds of the Drumlin, I begin to feel better. I named it that back in Sheffield. After Linda helped me to make it on her machine, we put our names together.

Headtorch beaming, the air pillow in the small of my back, drinking to my stomach's content — hearing the wind sniffing around, flinging the first salvoes of rain against my bullet-proof nylon capsule as the storm builds — I know I shall sleep well. Melding dates and a fleshy slab of white cheese in my mouth, I have a real appetite for the first time in days. The flavour is exquisite, almost mystical, as if — taking Mass — I really tasted something . . . Although the water remains water it doesn't remain long. Thankful I had the determination to gather some overnight — otherwise I'd only have one gallon left for at least three day's climbing — I down a third of a jug in ten minutes. Tomorrow I shall begin the Conrad; drinking, resting, thinking, maybe even singing in the rain. In fact, climbing now continuously for six days, tomorrow should be some kind of Sunday.

I'm sitting in a ball of fire. The storm never came. My pans — ducking back through the porthole to make sure — are barely damp. The wall glares.

Dressing fast, just as a flea excited by higher temperatures will abandon even the most saintly old dog if it slumbers too close to the fire, so I start throwing out certain expectations of what I wanted — for what's happened. I must look after myself. Packing my bags, chained to a great blind rock, it is the heat that is Promethean not me. My fingers are fiery, the ends tender, red grapes of wrath after a week of nothing but climbing eighteen hours a day, picking and pounding at rock with the assiduousness of migrant workers sharing a tin hut with no water and ten others, off the beaten track in Stanislaus County any long, hot, Californian summer. At night I rub Nivea in.

At the end of the low-angled pitch, I use the two haul bags like hostages, crouching in their pathetic shadows to get out of the mad light. Imagination working overtime, I drive the spike of my hammer straight into the fish, leaping from the bleached sea on the label of a can of John West that a climber bequeathed to the ledge, in the hopes someone may have made a mistake at the canning factory and put in pineapple or mandarin oranges. Wiping expectorate of salmon from my eye, I would have settled for tomatoes.

Almost level with the summit of Middle Cathedral, I take my first drink of the day. Hot water. I swill it round my mouth, squirting it between my unbrushed teeth. My breath smells brown, like the inside of the old wooden desk I used to have at Junior School. Then I swallow it with the delectation of a venerable cactus as if it was *spumante* of a spring sprinkle; not sputum.

I feel faint. Everything leans to the right as if swayed by the cobra-hooded roof rearing overhead. My shadow is a brass rubbing in the midday sun. The air is swimming with gossamer, millions of filmy lines rising from the valley floor as if some great nest was being dissipated upwards, its fine long hairs carried to all four corners by the casual winds.

Jumaring back up after cleaning the pitch and freeing the hauls is like raising a flag of lead in Hell. Halfway up I have to stop and rest, turning slowly in the hot air as if I'm being preserved.

The Great Roof — like a geyser of rock — soars, its clean, Corinthian curve introducing the rest of the Nose with the aplomb of a sombrero tossed in the air by the bull before a hushed crowd. A breath of air whispers past, blowing coolly down my neck. A tattered sling under the roof, flicks.

Grasping a big horn of rock behind the belay I wobble up, half mantelling, spurred by the grip I have, to crank out ten feet before I realise what I'm doing. But it's too late, we're off, me clinging, him swinging his majestic cranium from side to side as if trying to dislodge me. Knowing I'm being taken for a ride, I bury my fingers in deeper, clipping my rope to old arrow heads buried to the hilt in the stony face. Where his blood has mineralised over them, they look — in the light of the setting sun — like violets.

The rock is bone-dry and warm. Rearing, inexorably he forces me out — feet flicking and dabbing at those impassive jowls. Hanging a sling in one of his many empty eyes, I bring my weight to bear. He doesn't flinch, but as I string together five or six, begins to relent, the stern brow bending until he kneels in silence at my feet. Dangling from thick, sweat-streaming nose-rings with my three haul bags, I hear something. Listen: 'win . . . win' Or was it the wind?

More like a sitting duck than Sitting Bull, I struggle forty feet more on nuts and chocks that I feed into the lean crack with trembling fingers. By headtorch I hang my bivi-bag level with a thin ledge. Inside the tent it glows like a persimmon. Emboldened by my good fortune in finding a doorstep at this time of night, I treat myself to a tea. English tea, strong, hot, and sweet. I feel happy. A crown of stars hangs over El Cap. If the cap fits.

A day on the rails, laying track to Camp 6; five stations passed in record time for me. No Flying Scotsman — though my name be Drummond — I'm the fireman on the slow train to Harlem that ends up on the rubbish heap, surrounded by sky-scrapers. For this immense, detached pillar of the rock-climbing establishment's most famous route is crammed on both sides with refuse. Fifteen years of cans and faeces, with a few dropped karabiners and slings for roughage. On hot nights it smells like a dirty old man sleeping in a doorway. And during the day, if you happen to be climbing up below after it's been raining, the cracks shiss on your hands.

Yet nothing of the sort could have been predicted from the morning of that fair eighth day. I woke rested, feeling as at-home on the edge in my sac, as a sea shell dependent between the breasts of one of our wild female ancestors, going into labour without midwife or doctor.

And I certainly am letting it all hang out, legs dangling over the side, rubbing my eyes at how much I've come up in the world; or as anyone taking a god's eye view can see: what a long way down it is. If you look closely, observe those little rituals that, over the years, have established my reputation — flossing and brushing my teeth, wiping the look off my face — for clean climbing. Using an Easi-Wipe, an astringent, scented, cotton pad, like a large, circular postage stamp, from your point of view it must look as if I'm doing my make up.

So? Is it important? You pee, he pees, she pees, and, between friends, we, though probably not They, do, too. Tea-pee arcs into space for a quarter mile, casting pearls before that old swine the earth, basking in the shadows, the river with his arm around her. For breakfast something fishy. Although it looks crumby, in fact it tastes, sort-of, Sezuan, the digestive-biscuit-powdered lotus of apple rings, fried for the last week with just a hint of hand cream, redolent of take-outs in Chinatown. I take stock of the hardware, rearranging it for the day's trade-offs, negotiating cracks I cannot afford to spend time trying to convince they should be free, with fast, direct, aid. Then I brush my hair. After yesterdustyday it's like shaking out a coconut doormat. I mean business. With a jingle, I stepped out.

The end. Spent. Not a drop of water left. The electricity's been turned off, and it smells as if the toilet's blocked. Since the chances of getting a plumber at this time are remote, I decide to leave home — this w.c. (wall colon) — hoping to find a cheap little bumpy as the only flats in this granite topsyturvydom are for the bats. Forty feet on, the stench is overwhelming. I feel like a bee, drawn to the deadly flowers, trapped in a fast-filling grave, confused and angry as night pours down, on and in me, filling my nostrils like soil, rubbing my face in it. Forced back to the isle below, Defoe-like, I hold my nose in a sea of smells and hot air rising from the valley floor.

For a while I just sit here, pretending this is the life: Remembering the warm toilet seat at home in the garden at the cottage. I loved to go down there after school and sit in the stone outhouse, right next to the pavement. The door faced South-West and being on a hill, overlooking Sheffield, we caught the sun until late in the day. It was funny hearing people walk past, holding my breath or whatever. A crown of dandelions gathered at the open door, the whites of their oblivious, gold eyes slowly dawning. Butterflies would occasionally blunder in. From the aged, wooden seat, I could see the cos lettuces Linda had planted for salads, their long green ears piercing the newly-dug soil. On damp nights I would find black slugs on the sunken brick path. Dangerous fingers to tread on, slimy, secretive, I used to move them out of her way so they wouldn't be crushed. And I liked to let them try and grasp the difference between us, rasping away with their crisp, kittenish mouths. I had them eating out of my hand, fascinated by the silvery, seminal trails they left and amused by Linda's squeam of delight. Does anyone live there now?

Tonight I feel like a slug, french fried. *Haute cuisine* indeed for local shoppers like the peregrine falcons; if they get peckish in the night. My hair is like chocolate shoe laces.

There's a thought. There might be a sliver left. I ease my throbbing fingers into the haul, extracting, one by one, the many, mostly empty, stuff sacs, as carefully as a surgeon. The one with my personal effects, hairbrush, book, spare batteries, matches, dry socks, balaclava, first-aid kit and a little bottle of antiseptic, has, inside the ball of silver paper − no chocolate. Antiseptic?

'I pronounce you,' getting up rather unsteadily, holding on to the ropes that snake down from my high point in the darkness, 'Sir Freddy Laker.' Not until I have sipped in religious miniscules for an hour, am I finished with toasting my host on the charter flight, three months previous: for the plastic, micro jeroboam of French cognac, my free, in-flight drink, anticipating by several years his elevation to the peerage. I had thrown it in at the last minute for the summit. It cuts my thirst like acetylene. I'm ready.

I wake. Still dark. Cold. The wind rattles the rigging above my head, blowing down the Nose for the first time since I've been climbing. Moving calmly to my high point, I tie in and begin hauling. Dark cracks accept my fists, clean, deep bites that urge me on as dawn bleeds through the pines twenty-six hundred feet down. After its eight-minute journey from the sun, today, the light is broken, crawling at the rim, no Excalibur flash on the Dawn Wall as usual. Its sombre tide turns overhangs buoy-blue and sheds a weak lime light on the meadow. Five pitches to go.

The sun breaks through, a great golden bell pealing colour everywhere. I feel cheered. Linda promised to be there at the end, somewhere just beyond the mounting wave of stone poised above me. I get a Gauguin-like picture of this fine white woman holding out her hands to take me home — now a tent in the valley. Maybe she'll bring some cheesecake. A pitch higher, a flock of honks from the car park among the woods tells me she's on her way. She'll drive the Tioga road to Tamarack Flat, park the hire car and walk in to meet me off. Three or four hours at the most then until the summit, that flat, bald spot the patient climber — after his nervous ordeal below — recovers. I've been there once before, three weeks previous, by the West Face. On the sweltering final day, at last making it — albeit by the back door — to the top of the Mount Everest of the rock-climbing world, was like having an amorphous white blob in a steam bath pointed out to me as Churchill. Today will be different.

The hauls are coming up like treasure, royal-blue amphoras from the shadowy depths, scuffed and ripped, but still intact. Artificial heart-lungs, external to my own, but just as vital, tying the tireless red and blue veins of nylon in with my own needs and greeds. I'm moving faster and better than ever; the honeymoon over, I feel like I'm climbing to my wedding.

When I set out on the final rope length, though the bulges look damp and visibility's poor, the slab's a doddle. And I can see the bolts. Why waste time getting a sweater?

Out of nowhere wind hits me in the face, smashing against the mountain. I hunker on the bolt. Cloud boiling around me — the meadow like spilt ink, people fleeing for their vehicles — Don't go! Humpty Dumpty for a second I consider getting back to the hauls and breaking out the bivy bag.

The next bolt is close. Fingers stutter at the sling. My elbows drip. Maybe it will blow away. Sensing my thought, the wind stops playing with my tee shirt. I wriggle it under my harness. A deep breath, turning, snatching the shirt, scratching rain down my face like a polar bear warming to its opportunity, the wind roars, flattening me against the rock as the first snow hurries in. The tiny, downy flakes soon give way to sops of sleet that gather on whatever lends itself: the bolts' black ears become arctic seals', the ropes ice. My eyelids feel heavy. The blizzard builds, swarming around the lip, twenty feet away. Stung, now I feel numb, too weak . . . I don't even have a balaclava on, flopping from bolt to bolt like a cockerel with its crest cut off, as the featherbrained wind knocks the stuffing out of the skies.

El Capitan's a silverscreen, an inferno of water, spurting, fire-like from every crack, fissure and chimney; a towering skyscraper with a solitary fireman at the top of the tallest ladder in the world, trying to get onto the roof.

It was at this point the boy fell. Not me you understand, but that lad, in the Spring, fresh out of high school in the Bay Area; up for the Easter break. Came to the valley to climb El Cap for the first time. Sixteen. Hadn't tied in to the end of the rope, a single 11mm from him to his partner, belayed at last over the summit bulges. He was using jumars, as he had for the preceeding two days. The youngest ever.

At this point, from the top bolt, you must traverse right for fifteen feet. Unexpectedly I find one, no two, bolts are missing . . . Only a shallow crack, like an open fly. On that unimpeachable blue day in April, it evidently came as a shock, finding the magisterial countenance with its trousers down as it were. 'How do you do this?' he may have yelled. But the other was too far away to feel more than the feather weight shift as the jumars gnashed thin air, although Beverly Johnson, twenty-two hundred feet down, about to pendulum into the Stove Legs, did have to move fast to get out of the way of a boy falling out of the sky at over a hundred miles an hour. Before climbing on.

I nut the gurgling crack with a tiny hex, tapping it with my hammer like it was a hazel. Once it holds I pound it until it's buried in the crack like a bullet. The exertion warms me, I'm almost there. I leapfrog right, dabbing a bat hook in a tiny drilled hole, and – at a stretch – reach the belay: three silver-dollar-size eye bolts, made in the U.S.A., good enough to hang on for ever if I have to. The wind has dropped. It can't be:

'Lin - da!' A faint call back:

'. . . kay?' No.

'YES . . . DO - YOU - HAVE - A ROPE?' No.

'I - JUST - WONDERED.' Silence . . . I don't believe it.

'STAY - BACK.' I don't want her to fall for me.

I've run out of rope. And facing me, hidden by the rock until now, is a twenty-foot slab of thin snow. No one told me about this. There's ten minutes of light left. I can't go back, even if I want to, my hands stupified starfish. Nine: and too little time. I scuffle the snow in the hopes there might be a ring, and maybe another – and another – like marriages, to get me back on my feet. But there are no more bolts. Eight.

Seven. I'm shuddering. Can't stay here. Freeze . . . Six. Unless I move. No rope. Five. Untie . . .

Think fast. What is thirty feet long, metal, found growing at the edge of a three thousand foot cliff in California in the middle of a storm? Four.

That fast I make a chain for myself, twenty karabiners linking forty nuts on wire. Three. I creep across the brow of the Nose, the incidental chain of life looped below me, slowly straightening out. Two.

Dashing the snow from the holds, imbalanced like Van Gogh among the desperate blues and greys of an inhuman face, I edge away from the corner I've painted myself into if I stop – one – now.

The Climb (for Haworth)

My sprat: sixteen.
We go to climb,

at Tremadog.
Wearing trim, polyprop fur
and new, blood-red boots
— I bought for him —

who'll follow me . . .
Whether he likes it or not
he turns off his Walkman
when I leave,

this time crawling
on my hands and knees
for two hours,
beneath cloud-dabbed granite.

Sinking — decisions,
do I
layback or stem?
He lets out the rope
— 'Carefully!' —
not giving me
too much again.

'Slack!'
If he was a fly
and could see me
— having turned the corner —
hugging the overhang
like a child nothing could pull from my arms,
he'd cry 'Well done Ed!'

A figurehead Dad,
I climb from the waves
that never move.

Now, near the bottom
draw of the crag, my lad
is rummaging through
hold after hold,
looking for footsteps,
trying to let go . . . Floating

out, below me,
so simple, dependent,
I'm tempted to take a little weight
– the red rope throbbing between us –

'Don't pull me!'

Vaulting-hung-hauled
yourself out,
tall as a marlin,
standing, shaking,
next to my shoulder,
for no one to photograph.

What was the problem you ask?

I laugh. Take a deep breath.
'Now it's your lead.'

Child, Woman, Man

I DIDN'T KNOW WHAT TO SAY when I saw my dad. He didn't telephone last night. They said he was going to before I had to go to bed.

('Hello. I'm sorry to be late calling but . . .'

'No'

'You're refusing to wake my son?')

Next morning I was playing on the bed with Lindy; she said he'd call any minute. I slept with her last night. When I used to stay with them in England, in the cottage, I had my own room. Her nightie felt nice. I saw her this morning. My dad wasn't there.

Suddenly he just rushed in and we grabbed each other.

'You've grown,' he told me. I felt silly, like in a school photograph. Then we wrestled.

'You're a lot stronger,' he laughed. He felt my muscles. Suddenly Lindy ran out.

'Son, this is Grace.'

Isn't she brown? She must have been in the sun a lot.

'And how do you like America?' She looks a bit Chinese to me.

'I'm going to Disneyland,' I told her. I haven't been yet, but Aunty is going to take me — my Dad's sister they said. I haven't got a sister. Then Grace and me played in the field next to the house in Pal something, where we're staying before we go to Yesummertee, where my dad lives. My dad played too. We flew my new helicopter. And dad chased me. Grace and me got spears of sticky grass and shot my dad. We chased butterflies then — cabbage-whites like in our garden, and lemon-yellows which I'd never seen before.

Dad and Grace are coming back for me tomorrow. We're going to the Valley. I thought we were going to Yesummertee. Aunty says I think it's just round the corner. If it is I can walk there I told her, because I can see the corner from the front of this house — where my dad just disappeared. I'll go in that van tomorrow, the Volkswagon my dad said he borrowed.

'We drove through the night,' he told me. I'd still got my pyjamas on this morning. I didn't know what to say.

'I'm seven now,' I said.

The van is red and green. It looks as if they threw paint at it. Grace says we could be mistaken for hippies, whatever that is. I'd heard my dad and Lindy arguing in the bedroom. My dad's new wife didn't come into the house. I went and sat in the van. I never heard them argue in England.

'We're going to climb Snake Dike.'
It must be an American snake.
'Is it poisonous?' He told me not to tell Aunty and Lindy. They think we're going up Half Dome. Well we are: 'In a way,' Dad said. It's a secret.

And my dad's getting married. 'What's married?' His words were too long. He used to be married to my Mom. I'll tell her when I go home.

I'm only seven. I'm the youngest boy in the world to climb Snake Dike. My dad said. Grace says she hasn't done it before. She's only been climbing a month. I've climbed before with my dad. She likes my dad I think. When I stop to read one of the notices along the trail they hold hands. I had a girlfriend to tea in England. She's seven too. Juliet.

'And Romeo?' Dad asked smiling. He must be in another class at my Junior school. 'Romeo who?' I said. They both laughed then.

'I'm the youngest to climb Snake Dike.'
'We haven't done it yet,' he said. We're doing it tomorrow. Tonight we're sleeping out. We're going to make a fire. Dad says there are bears.

I like her. Her tooth sticks out a bit. My teeth became frilly this year. Grandad got my loose tooth out for me. He put it under my pillow. Some money came. I know Gran put it there. I wonder what I'll have for Christmas?

I'm nearly up to her shoulder. She's older than me though. They're always kissing. Why? Her hair is long and black. I think she's a native. They don't wear any clothes. She's ever so brown. I'd like to see.

'Shall I take my clothes off?'
The fire was huge. She said the shadows were like bears dancing. I'm next to the fire.

'No, keep them on. You'll be warmer,' said my dad. He still had his on.

He and me made the fire. It frightens the bears. I haven't seen any. That's only a bush. They're kissing again. She's covered his face with her hair. That must be hot. The soup she made was nice.

I'm awake first. Big and gold, two of them. Then I look away at Half Dome.

'It's like a loaf of bread,' says Dad, 'proving'. I didn't know his eyes were open. It is. But we have square loaves at home. The stars have gone back in. I wish I could touch them.

'What does proving mean?' I ask him, but it's breakfast time and he doesn't hear.

He cuts up the apples and I mix in the oats. He used to make it for me and Mom in England. Then we have some bread the same colour as the Half thing. It was cold. The hot chocolate was nice. He never drank it before he says. She's like chocolate a bit. She calls him Honey sometimes. I think he's itchy — his whiskers tickle. I'd like to call him Itchy. I like honey.

'Bears like honey.' Does she feed bears?

'Why are they afraid of fire?' I ask her. She says they don't understand it. 'It would keep them warm too . . .'

They did have their clothes off. I saw her — then she put on her shirt. I've seen my dad before though. He's bigger. I'm like him. I felt funny when I saw her. Mom has broosts too. She was brown as Hovis. Perhaps she takes her clothes off more than Mom. Was he kissing them?

I was fed up. It made me say bloody. On and on. Then we had a drink.

'You're doing great.' said Dad. He always says that. 'Can I have a sweet?' I like it when he sings, even though he frightened the snake. I saw it first — he was just about to tread on it. Snakes are frightened of my dad. We watched it go into the bushes. He said it was a rattler. She had her mouth open but no sound was coming out. He used to catch grass snakes when he was a boy. He says they're nice to touch. Not slimy. She says he'd better not. Anyway, when they come to England, he's going to take me to find some. He knows all about grass snakes. But he was wrong about that one: it didn't rattle at all.

'Maybe the rattle was broken.' I didn't see why that was so funny.

My chest hurt. He said I was old enough to carry something too. I'm only seven.

The rock kept growing. It was bigger than our house. I was looking out for the Dikesnake. I bet that other was one.

'Do Dikesnakes rattle Dad?' I didn't know what he meant. I'm not afraid of it anyway.

He went first. Then he shouted. The rope slid up like a snake, then started biting my waist. The rock was as smooth as a ball. I couldn't find any of those holes he kept calling about.

'What's friction?' I bet he had glue in his pocket. He said cat-pad. He just made that up. I know him, he does that. But then I saw a lizard doing push ups, so maybe cats do come up here too. After the snakes? The lizard came like a finger, wagging out of a crack. I made them laugh when I farted. We were hanging from circles of metal stuck to the rock, all spluttering and pretending to cough. She said she does too. He laughed. I'd never known him laugh like that.

Going up the dike he got smaller and smaller. He was so far away.

'Pull!' Why wouldn't he pull!

[107]

'Pull Dad!' Sometimes I hated him. He was dropping me.

'Try,' he mewed. Too tired. He was making me cry again. Why couldn't he see how much harder it was than the tree at home? I'd show him. I pulled and suddenly he pulled and —

'Hand-foot, Hand — over there,' he pointed to a little bump like a drawer knob.

'Thanks Dad.' I held on to his foot while he tied me in. He was looking at me like when he used to read to me at night. Unwrapping a sweet too. He only helped me a bit though.

'How much farther?'

'How much farther father?' Grace says. I've never called him father, have I?

'Not far now.' I've heard that before.

While he's climbing it's nice holding on to her. She gives me kisses too. And more sweets. While we're waiting we snuggle. She's as warm as Mom.

At the top we saw some mountains. One was like a gothic cathedral he said. I could see some smoke coming out of it. He said it was cloud. The snow was great. My dad said,

'Energy is eternal delight.' Then he explained that eternal is like your left hand and right hand going apart for ever. And they would never meet again. That must hurt. His arms aren't that long. I threw snowballs and got my pumps sloshed in the bed of snow we found on the summit. My Mom says I am full of energy. I took a stone from the top to give to her. It was my Dad's idea. He hugged Grace and me; he could just get his arms round us both. I was so hungry. He said I should have saved some sweets. Why didn't he bring more?

It was stupid, like walking over sleeping elephants instead of being carried. I had to keep going up and down, down and up, up and down. He wouldn't carry me. He said he was tired. I know he's never tired. Sometimes Grace stayed behind while Dad and me walked ahead holding hands. He didn't carry me once; almost. Just the last bit near the river when I was asleep he said. Before it got too dark I wanted to give them something. I had a jewel I'd found on the top, when they weren't looking . . . My dad said it was piece of glass that had melted and then re-fused in a fire. It was like a small Half Dome. I could see all the way through, like one of those boiled fruit sweets when all the sugar's been sucked off, or an egg with no yolk inside. I wanted them to have it in their wedding rings. They'd said they wanted to cut a stone in half and have half each. But Dad said my jewel would break if they tried to halve it.

[108]

'Half-Dome, Half-Home,' he said. Lifting me up in the air, we all held hands. Then by the river. Then I fell asleep.

I thought I was dreaming. They had no clothes on. Just lying in the sun on top of their sleeping bag, holding hands. I slipped out of my elephant's foot as Dad called it, took off my clothes; and held her other hand. My dad was getting browner. Especially his legs. But his chest was still British.

'I thought I was in a strip club,' I said after a minute.

'What?!' They almost jumped out of their skins. But I really did. I told them about what I'd read on a newspaper billboard one day recently back home.

' "New facts about women: Raquel Welch exposed." And I didn't know where I was when I opened my eyes this morning.' We all laughed and jumped and thumped each other on the back: 'Three wise bares' Dad said.

But we had no breakfast. Dad said a bear came in the night. All the food was gone. He heard it in the pines, crashing away. Eyes like brake lights. I was glad I was asleep.

'Maybe a she bear who'd lost her cub,' said Grace. Dad said it could be. We didn't talk about it anymore.

I was angry on the way back. I didn't hold their hands; hardly. I'm only seven. It's not fair they had no sweets. He carried my bag a bit. Then we went to the store and my stomach hurt but it was all right.

Aunty and Lindy asked me when we got back what I'd been up to. I pointed at Half Dome, rising above the valley. Dad and Grace had said I could tell. It wasn't a secret.

'Quite the family!' I heard that, but I didn't tell them everything. And next time I'm taking my own sweets.

God

Crouching out of the wind
I get the message,
from the bottle: Written
on blue-lined paper,
recording ascents of this volcanic udder,
Las Tetas de Cabra:
The Boobs of the Goat.

Here's a man from Houston
who's reached the same, crumbling
conclusion, seventeen times.
Half of his students
in Outdoor Leadership say
— if they get down alive —

they'll never climb again.
Several find proof
in the distant view
— rows of tin shacks
behind the shining refinery,
the black river,
children on the tracks

— of a reason for everything.
A local, in Spanish,
left a postcard
showing Jesus, the unusual carpenter,
with two beams in place
— the lintel
of his crude, incredible house:

faint, brown words like dried blood.
I can't make out
if that wren
that touched down and took off again,

saw me or not.
Nor where that lizard like a wagging finger
— runnerbean-green — can be.
And as for the flies
that followed me
like an old nag — whining disciples —
what did they expect to find
on this lonely shelf in the sky?

Or I?
A book? Extraterrestrial scorch marks?
Myself?

Look: If horns and a long white beard
clatter into view
— with a snort — finding me
here in this draughty heaven,

I'll jump for the old goat.

A Grace Period

'The personality of a mountain is more than a strange
shape that makes it different from the others — just as a
strangely shaped face or strange actions do not make an
individual into a personality':
The Way of the White Clouds by Lama Angauka Gorunda.

AS A MURDERER RETURNS to the scene of his birth, so has my mind many times
to the Christmas-white woods just beyond the summit of El Capitan, where I
followed sleepily in Linda's bootsteps as she broke trail, her cheeks glowing,
to get us back to the road, the car, England. She would turn, making sure I
was still there, hadn't fallen asleep, snow-white among the deep drifts by the
side of the trail.

Soaked-sweating-shivering — clad in nothing but a tee shirt and sodden
climbing pants, after tying my strange cord to a sapling just past the rim, I
sprang at her, cramming sandwiches and kisses into my mouth while she
dressed me. 'My man,' she sighed, holding me at arm's length for all the sky
to see. The wind hissed at the lip, twenty feet behind. A mile . . . Thirteen
years. I still don't know why I did it.

Something spicy, pine or skunk, struck me from the dark forest. I stopped and took a piss. She waited patiently, looking the other way.

Six months and three volcanoes later, I left her. Ixtaccihuatl: 'The Sleeping Woman,' I kicked my way over and — with a blinding headache — up her icy breasts, wearing crampons for the first time: with Mexico spreading before me like the Middle Ages, I chipped "LINDA" in the frozen snow with the borrowed axe. Popocatépetl: where Cortez got sulphur for gunpowder and demolished the Aztec empire. Orizaba, the summit of Mexico: there I stumbled upon a way of breathing at altitude that made me feel like the one who invented beer. 'What about Aconcagua?' I asked John, the Olympic hurdler I'd buddied up with, when we stood on the top, sipping the thin air.

With severe retinal haemorrhaging that had begun to blur faces at twenty feet and went undiagnosed for a year, I kissed her goodbye, in Mexico City in March. We had not made love since last year. Recovering in bed for two months from ostensible hepatitis, with three weeks in Yosemite before she returned to California after teaching, I couldn't wait. In bed in the hot, mosquito-pricked nights, visions of dusky native women from my recent tropical Christmas, skin diving by the sea, had kept me wide-eyed. Skindiving . . .

Laughing, I gasped, 'ran all the way from El Cap.' She was holding a tray and looked embarrassed. Wasn't this her?

Last night at the dance in her short white dress, she said yes straightaway. She looked Indian: long, glossy black hair swaying under the strobes, blue, yellow and red beads bouncing at her dark neck. And such legs! Muscular, chestnut, fast — legs that could shake a government. And she didn't wear a bra. When I spoke, just standard King's, she looked at her friends as if she was Ms Simpson.

She had on a grubby maid's uniform. A tooth protruded.

'Excuse me being so dirty,' I said, 'I've just been climbing.' I restrained the jingling karabiners as we went to sit down.

'You're so polite. And hot,' she grinned, looking up at my sweating face.

We hardly touched lunch. That afternoon I climbed like a bird. And that night I wrote to her. Three days later, waiting alone in the house at night listening to music, I got my answer. 'At the weekend then.' I glanced at the clock: we had talked for over an hour. I played more Beethoven and went humming to bed.

Saturday afternoon. I floated up to Yosemite in the warm, March air, driving a twenty year old De Soto with three foot dorsal fins on either side of its light blue body. I'd bought it for a hundred dollars. Armchaired at the wheel, push-button gear change on the dash and electrically operated windows — the windshield televising the flowered foothills — I felt more like David Attenborough on the spice trail crossing Samarkand, than an English teacher from Sheffield. Near the entrance to the valley, from a hillside that would have made Monet murmur, I picked a huge bunch of flowers. 'Look!' I presented them to her as if I was the first traveller to bring fireworks to the West.

We went climbing; some long, slow, hot, easy, slab in the sun, her dark hand slipping inside my chalk bag. Then she had to go to work: 'I get off late.' After midnight; the leaves rustled at the foot of the tent. I dropped my book: 'Tea?' She tore off my jeans. Snow in the night, slow, cool, thick, white, like butterflies unable to sleep, drifted in the door, melting against our hot cheeks.

Linda was so beautiful on her return. The sea-green blouse she'd treated herself to after months of diligent teaching, her rose cheeks — Renoir as I opened the door of the room, where she was waiting for me at our friend's: I hesitated. Then let go.
'Why didn't you tell me —'
'It's too late.'
' — before?'
'I —'
'Why didn't you say something in Mexico?'
'tried, I . . .'
I won't gore you with the details. Let's say I met Grace.

Linda returned to England alone. Then the De Soto died. 'Transmission,' said the mechanic. I was sad, it had been so easy to handle and the most comfortable car I'd ever driven. I'd never done it in a car.
'Welcome to the American Family Car,' she'd said, flicking off the lights in a lay-by we'd pulled into, setting the handbrake with one smooth movement. As if she'd done this before.
'Second hand cars.' She sighed comfortably, as though a great uncle she'd never known had died of natural causes in his sleep. Had we driven it too hard? I wrote it off to experience. 'That's the way it goes,' she said to the mechanic at the garage in the valley, who agreed to take it off our hands. They knew one another: 'No problem.'

It was Summer, we were heading for Canada, The Bugaboos and the first free ascent of Pigeon Spire with my client, a craggy, whisky-haired teacher from the Bay Area, with a heart of silver and a Porsche. Patty was over fifty, a grandmother, part-Irish farming stock with a master's from Stanford . . . Quote, unquote. But I liked her, found her trust pushed me up when she could have called me down. Which was a problem for Grace. Wedged in the back of the tiny, fast, overheating car, whining along with Neil Young and Gordon Lightfoot and Patty, beneath rucksacks and gear, she looked as if she was being snuggled out of the States. Who, at nineteen, having run away from — or been thrown out of — home, hadn't gone to college and seemed to think that I was at any moment likely to elope with my mature climbing partner. About as likely as Prince Charles taking off with Golda Meir.

Grace and I gobbled Bing cherries whenever we could get them, stones and all, and slipped away in the dark, giggling like naughty kids, avoiding the evening's star-gazing class with my benefactress, to keep our own fires burning.

Washington State, the coast; down to our last ten dollars. Sleeping on the beach; hitchiking everywhere. Reservations: herds of Chevrolets in various stages of disembowelment; war parties of kids on 50 cc Hondas, screaming into the night. Forks, the logging capital of the world. A job, steaks, hotel. Elta's blackberry pie. Whispers of ptomaine.

Heartbreak Hotel we called it. Each night I came home the Indian on the metal bed in number 6 twisted to stare, my arrival signalled by the tick of my nailed logging boots on the linoleum. The rat in the corridor that sent Grace running back to our room. The time she woke from a nightmare of me back in bed with Linda, and locked herself in the bathroom, beating her head — or could it have been her fist? — against the tub. The tree outside our window with all those dusty, red plums that had never been picked. Counting my fingers each day.

'Poor old Nixon,' said one of the redwood-necked loggers, the morning after that tearful Watergate farewell that made even Kissinger blush. Behind those wooden stares there was a real soft spot: "Kiss my Axe Sierra Club" was the favoured sticker on the rear window of the pick-ups; just below the shotgun rack. A bell-jawed moose and a cougar with her cubs — all stuffed — looked down on the diners in the restaurant in town where Grace and I ate our last supper; before we moved on.

British Columbia: Squamish Chieftain, and Jim Sinclair, the *il capo* of Vancouver climbing. He got me a job in a steel mill when the rains came; where I drunk drove fork lift first. And he taught me to crane, so that, after a week or two, I could throw my weight around as quietly as the men who'd worked there half a lifetime. A former fugitive from the law — he said he'd been saved from a life of crime by climbing — he knew the ropes, who was who, how to get things done. Though he was the one who stopped yawning

[114]

when I squeaked up that groove he 'knew could never go' − like a mouse past a sleeping cat. And I mustn't forget it was he who told me the story and showed me the sculpture, of the man climbing out of the rock that an artist had done at the foot of the Chief, while the first ascent was going on. Grace worked in a toy store. We had a cat. Strange, wild, rich, days and nights. 1974; I was almost thirty and my Sixties had just begun. I wore beads, grew my hair − but drew the line at grass. Hippy? Happy? Sort of . . . Grace had her first petit-mal seizure, just before we went to England. It was her first time abroad.

'Do as I say!' The wind was screaming in my ear, fastened into the hillside. Grace was trying to lie − not plié − down, on the stretchy crux of the last pitch. In the dark. The lighthouse streaked the zawn every twelve seconds, lighting the way like a hand-grenade. The sea was going wild, black horses dashing at the white cliffs. She fell into place.

'Just feel!' Hoarse, hungry, angry I'd brought her.

'Hold the rope!' Führious I barked orders at the dark. She wasn't moving.

'Sorry.' She'd been crying.

'What d'you mean? You were great.' Wind slapping my face, I tied her in.

'You pulled me up.'

'Nonsense. Hold my hand. This way.' We groped over the hill, holding on to one another like Crusoe and Friday, leaving the island behind for ever. A bad dream.

I failed my bus driver's test in Sheffield. When I overtook another double decker, it only convinced the rosy-cheeked inspector gesticulating in the window behind the driving seat, that I'd better walk up − and down − the aisle. Getting such a job for a year, to save enough for us to get back to the States, would have been like going to sea, me in my navy-blue uniform, a Chichester of the rolling Sheffield roads, at the helm, not pacing the deck clipping passengers' tickets − or, as I knew from school days − ears. So when he said 'a conductor,' I said, 'thanks for the ride.'

Driven to joining the fire service, while Grace worked, first at the Children's Hospital, then taking the bar exams at a local pub, serving the straining hopefuls strong beer and long, dark looks − I coped. Theoretically, we were both in the business of cooling it. In practice, I hardly saw a new flame − a van in the night up on the moors above the station, burning like something from another planet, while − at the Crosspool Tavern was it? − Grace raised more than hopes.

One emergency call that sent me down the pole for a change, was to

Middlewood Mental Hospital: In our gladiatorial yellow helmets we stormed in . . . Hundreds standing by their single beds with shaved heads bowed; one young woman punching bread into her mouth, quacking 'Fuckfuckfuckfuck' — to find a posse of patients ahead of us, throwing the balls they'd made from their socks, up at the smoke detector they'd set off by their clandestine dawn drag.

At the fire station, "Sleepy Valley" — Rivelin — to which I'd been appointed, they soon got used to me. So, after a week of coming into the empty office I went to in free time to write, only to find I really was awake: 'How many poems have you written today then?' Terry trying to hide a smirk, Geoff looking serious, and me too tongue-tied to try to talk about what it was I was after — scribbling an image here, a noise there, thoughts that hit me like scents — they got the message. Clip, clop, clipclopclip — table tennis resumed and pretty soon my pencil started to fidget. Grace occasionally came to the station to meet me. Once she brought the men some banana bread, which we had with our tea.

'Is she Hawaian?' asked Terry.

'Philippine-American,' I said.

'She speaks English good' somebody else commented. I didn't bother to explain; they made her feel welcome. Terry showed her the engine. The calendar, a local garage's, of other exotic bodies than BMWs — well thumbed through to December — was rehung on its nail, after she left.

We were married on St Valentine's Day in 1976, in El Cap meadow, by Judge Mueller of the Mariposa Judicial District. Jeff Long was one of our witnesses. Out of the snow we found a patch of sere grass from last summer. It didn't rain. One of Grace's high school friends sang a Judy Collins song, and we released two sparrows that we'd brought up from Berkeley. We were going to free white doves, but, being informed that the resident Cooper's hawks in the Sierras would tear them apart, we opted for survivors.

After the ceremony, the sun made a brief appearance, glancing across the immense south-west face. Streaks, from melting summit snow, looked buttery in the morning light and would soon be gone. There was no one up there. At last, she was mine. Will and I made plans to do the Salathé after Easter. Jeff mentioned the vague possibility of the Himalayas. 'First I gotta get a job.'

I didn't leave the building for a week. I cleaned as if my life depended on it. Scrubbing the vacuum into the hallway carpets, washing the walls, even disinfecting the garbage chute, the foot-wide sheet metal bowel at the back of the house, down which most tenants dropped their bags of trash into a cavernous wheeled dustbin. It was all new, creative: collecting rents, washing windows, interviewing potential tenants. When I finally left the house — crossing Pacific Heights and dropping down to the ocean — walking over the Golden Gate I felt like Lindberg circling the Eiffel Tower. Life had really taken off.

Grace got a job with Wells Fargo and put me on her dental plan. I soon had American teeth, my craggy, caramel-carved molars and bicuspids rapidly shaping up under the attentions of my new dentist. He designed the world's first disassemblable yo-yo, skateboarded brilliantly and paid at least as much attention to the words that came out of my mouth as the teeth he was so successful at keeping in. Each day I climbed onto the large, flat roof of the building: The Twentieth Century reared around me: skyscrapers, churches, houses, docks; where lean, predatory cranes waited to scoop out the innards of the liners and tankers, at anchor in the bay. Chinatown, Hunter's Point, The Haight, The Castro; the streets of San Francisco, and, like the Dru, right in the heart of the city, the Transamerica Pyramid . . . I learnt to sweep sidewalks, buy tomaytoes, see trucks and write checks. I met people I'd only heard of: Neg — I mean Blacks, Chinese, Jap — anese. And then there was the old Russian couple, Mr and Mrs Pleshakov. It puzzled me they should appear to be so thin. Almost everyday I'd see him return with big, brown grocery bags in his arms . . .

After emptying the lightshaft that ran past their bathroom and ended at Mrs Miura's, in 201, a floor below them — for the third month in succession — of cigarette packets, newspapers, paper bags, used tissues, rags, hair curlers — once, a bicycle tyre — bus tickets, leaves; the daily dandruff of city life, I wised up. Nailing shut the Pleshakov's bathroom window, 'And, I hissed, a word at a time in between driving home the nails — 'If' — BANG! 'I' — BANG! 'Catch' — BANG! 'Him' — BANG! 'Do' — BANG! 'Ing' — BANG! 'It' — BANG! 'Again': hammer poised, I left it at that, slamming the door behind me. Shortly after he did a dummy run with a real bag of groceries: 'The bag stops here!' I said calmly at ten paces in the front lobby; but, after frisking it, I had to let it slide. Secretly I was enjoying my role as doctor in the house — unblocking sinks and bathtubs with a plumber's snake, getting that rush when I dredged up a pygmy scalp of hair from a plugged pipe, or a flush of pride as my first putrifying toilet gurgled, the clinical pleasures of swabbing scuzzy refrigerators and food-tumored stoves — so my occasional reversions to Mr Hyde, only added to the fun.

I ran a tight ship. When someone deposited a human turd in the elevator, I held my breath, and removed it. And when maybe the same someone, battered on our apartment door at five one Sunday morning, for the clothes I'd removed from his slowly-emptying apartment — he was skipping out on the rent — and, backed by his rather large friend made thinly-veiled death threats, I wrote out an agreement. Witnessed by a shivering Grace, while he

[117]

read it over before the goon signed too — that he would pay what he owed within a month — I phoned for the police. They witnessed the document as well, noted the return of his clothes and heated denials of those threats. 'Good day officers, gentlemen,' I said as I ushered all four of them off my clean front steps. Supermanager.

I went to the valley every third weekend. In May, with Will, I did the Salathé — the most beautiful route in the world they say. Cold, hard, work. Stepping onto the dusty summit lugging the haul bag, I felt the same excitement as going to the launderette on a Sunday morning.

'You missed it!' Grace cried as I stepped in the door, 'I caught a burglar — ' she paused: 'Almost.'

Evidently, that Sunday morning, while the Wongs were away, a cat burglar had climbed the fire escape to get into their apartment, which was directly above ours. Grace gave chase.

'Between the two of us we could have pinned him down.' With her in hot pursuit — after he'd climbed the tall-spiked gate alongside the building — he didn't get far. She was fast and still held the sixty yard dash at her junior high school. But he threatened her.

In the Summer Haworth came. First we went to see it. Mists dizzied the aluminium, copper and concrete summits — a new, interior range, thousands of feet above our heads — in the city! Mt. Bank of America; Embarcaderos 1 2 3 4, towers — of pain I learned later — and soaring above them all, Patagonian-bright, The Pyramid . . . We went fishing almost every day on local beaches, after I'd done my chores. He was growing fast, knew a lot about fish, how to cast, how to wait; how to let them off the hook. So I could sit there, keep an eye on things, and wonder about that metal-sheathed spire. At night the glass-iced summit winked to warn low aircraft.

We went deep-sea fishing one morning, walking over Pacific Heights to Fisherman's Wharf. Lance-long rods jostling, about fifty of us clambered on board. Armed only with pencil and paper, I felt like Sancho Panza's great great great great grandson by the side of my diminutive Quixote. He caught a shark. It was an eight pound nurse, with large, leopardy patches.

A big plastic bag of rock cod, striped bass and the shark — the grin of creation still on its face — slung over his shoulder, he looked like a little Father Christmas, doing the rounds of the shops on the ground floor of the building. Peter the Pizza, Elizabeth the Rice and Mel the Antique, as well as our cats and we three, supped well. We both cried at Departures. 'Good luck on the Pyramid,' he yelled to my horror.

There was a letter from Jeff:

'I've been invited to go to Makalu.'

[118]

'Wooah.'
'I don't know . . . Wouldn't you like to come?'

Jeff agreed to the Pyramid. I to Makalu, provided Grace came.

'Grace, it's okay.' She was in tears.
'I'm sorry, I'm sorry Ed.'
'It's okay, just hold the rope.' Bracing on the sloping window ledge, I lowered her back down, like a charm in her bright red turtle neck against the blank, grey concrete, watched by scores of early morning office workers in a near-by skyscraper. As she touched down they gave her a round of applause, deaf-muted by the glass. The first guard came out, rubbing his eyes. The rest is his-story, Jeff's that is. *Of Roosters and Lunatics* I think it's called, In *Ascent*. A tall tale? No, though it is a Long story . . .

Although it raised my hopes, our alpine-style attempt on the Pyramid, raised no money for the International Makalu Expedition. In fact . . . I studied the officers in the room. I noted the handcuffs dangling from their gun belts; bunches of keys. They were relaxed, almost jocular. They knew we would give them no trouble. Though I had lingered for a minute on the narrow window ledge, contemplating other possibilities, they had us both inside. We all sipped coffee from plastic beakers, courtesy of the management, who were at that moment studying the building to see whether damages charges were to be preferred. Jeff and I looked at one another over our coffee. He had had no problem in pulling out the baby angle I'd nested with two sky hooks in the rubber caulking — in order to reach the window ledge. But he was afraid they would see the torn caulk.

'No charge officer,' said the white-haired manager. You had to know where to look.

'To the Pyramid then:' I raised my plastic cup, but Jeff had already turned his back.

Then my Dad died.
    A month later, Grace:
'I'm not coming.'
'What do you mean?'
'To Makalu?'
'But —'
'I'm in school now,'
'But everything's arranged'
'I'm not coming godammit!'
Mr Calm, woman and children first.
'How will you manage?'
'I can get food stamps.'

[119]

'Well, I will be able to see Haworth in England, since we — I, do have to pick up that equipment.' And Mom was in again.

'There you go, two birds with one stone.'

The last thing Dad said to me when I left, in 1975, was, 'I'd love to come to America.' In our letters over the year between, it seemed as though we were becoming friends . . . One stone I would never lift.

I decided to do it. No woman on board; HMS Makalu: His Majestic Solitude enfolding me.

'No problem,' said Jeff, 'they'll take back the ticket.' He turned: 'See you in Denver.' After checking baggage he waved his boarding pass to us, then walked to the departure gate. Dianne and I agreed what time she would collect me. We hugged. Well, to be honest, she hugged while I, really, held on.

A week later she was in my arms. We were sleeping together out in the snow, in a roomy double sleeping bag, near Donner Lake. Icicles, inverted, unlit candles of the real world, fringed the hut where Lanny and Lynada were sleeping. The early morning sun was toasting the right side of my face. It brought out the silver-grey in Dianne's dark, chestnut hair. Last night:

'What about Grace?' Confused, warm, close. Grace, back in the house before we turned the corner at the top of the street.

'When we hugged after Jeff left' — I pulled my hand back, 'I thought.'

'Oh no,' she groaned, as if this had happened before. Were there others like me? I lay like a log, hand by my side, wide awake for a long, long time, while more and more stars crystallized.

A full moon rose over Denver as I drove down from Ford, where the expedition was gathering its wits, gurus, acolytes and token Englishman. I was going to meet the editor of *Mountain Gazette*. Jeff had said she was lovely. Anyway, they'd already published some of my poems.

We had dinner.

I flew to England. Ian had lined up a car in response to my urgent phone call. Wolverhampton; Sheffield; Glossop; Accrington — back to London. I had four days. Just a thought: 'How's Cathy?' He'd liked her too. 'They split up. She's got the baby.' 'Where is she?' I got her number: 'Just in case.'

'Just thought I'd give you call. I'll be in Bristol tonight.'

'I'd love to, just come round.' We talked and talked.

'Look, I must go to bed, I have to teach in the morning.' It was two o clock. She showed me my room.

I couldn't sleep. She could only say no. I pushed the door. 'Ed?' she was

wide awake. She pulled back the covers and moved over — a warm, milky
smell —

'Cathy.' I couldn't believe it.

'No!'

'But-'

'I thought you were cold.' She turned her back. I lay there with my heart
pounding, one arm stiffly over her powerful shoulders.

I drove fast the next morning to Wolverhampton. She was in B4, the
psychiatric unit at New Cross. I strode in:

'Oh my Edwin.'

'It's all right Mom.' Her lips hot on my neck. She smelt. Her tears on my
cheeks. There were several people in the room. The television sound had
been turned off. No one moved. A mist of hair, her huge skull, lunar under
the perennial fluorescent lighting. She told me that the ring they'd put in to
hold her uterus back, had fallen out.

'Bouncing down the stairs,' she said, flopping both hands in a hopeless
catch. I wondered if someone had picked it up.

'Did someone give it you back?'

'The bugger, he tried to strangle me!'

'I wasn't talking about Dad Mom.' But it was too late. Spluttering, cursing
the man she had been married to for thirty-seven years, my Dad, she quickly
became speechless, opening-closing her mouth like a fish on the rocks, while
her hand hit the plastic chair. My temper started to rise. Mad, my sister,
had warned me: 'We couldn't stop her at the funeral. She sang "Abide With
Me", — Dad's favourite hymn — four times in succession.' Then laughed
until the tears rolled down her cheeks as the coffin glided to the off-stage
furnace.

'I'm going.' I got up. She started crying again.

'Don't go eh?' imploring me with those deep, brown eyes. I felt myself
sinking — she was trying to get out of the chair, her face shaking as if she
was about to break the world weightlifting record for women: 'Don't go eh?'
She couldn't make it. I remained on my feet. She was holding her head, that
grail of disaster she'd borne through three suicides and the second world war
— bringing up my sister alone while Dad was in India: Her twin sister's
success and her own two failures; dredged back on stomach pumps and
electro shock . . . Her dress was up over her knees. The hairs were dark down
there. I could see it. Nobody was moving. That's it. I'll never see you again.
Makalu.

'Bye Mom.'

Haworth brought his friend Shawn. We drove to Glossop first. Peter, still there, still willing: 'This will keep you warm.' I tried it on the wooden floor of the old factory. He told me how he used to test his bags by spending the night in a local meat packing factory's deep freeze. He thought that would be about like Makalu. In Accrington, Mike gave us several haul bags. Ebullient, brimming with ideas; like a snooker cue his slap on the back helped me ricochet across the Pennines. Until I couldn't go on. 'Go and play,' I murmured, before falling, inexorably asleep at the wheel.

They were shaking me awake. They were plastered in mud.

'We found a horse,' he beamed. Two hours had flown by.

'You need a bath,' said his Mom. We played boats. It was the first time I'd given him one since I left. That night I slept in my new sleeping bag, in the same room where, in 1969 our nuclear family came violently of age. Alone, his mother slept upstairs in the bed she'd made.

'Go and see her Ed. She's better this week,' said Madelaine. She handed me my Dad's war medals. I hesitated.

'She's expecting you.' As a boy, my greatest treat had been to see them: The star of Algiers, cinnabar, silver and sand; and one from India that was damask and violet with a parakeet-green flash.

'Why did you get married?' I'd ask Mom when she was crying.

'I loved him.'

'Don't you love him now?' She never said she didn't.

The last visitors were leaving. I slipped quietly along the darkened corridors, passing no one. She was in the same chair. The television was off. There was no one else in the room. We looked at one another. I sat down.

We held hands. They were soft and warm. Someone had brushed her hair.

'Be careful.'

'Don't worry. I'll be all right.' I stood up.

'Get better Mom, for when I come back.'

'There's nothing wrong with me!' The old fire. I didn't argue.

The door was locked. Damn it! And I hadn't seen a nurse anywhere. I tried other doors, other ways. It was ridiculous. And she would be asleep by now. Then a door I hadn't tried: Staff Toilet. I turned, I'd have to find the night sister − then turned back. There was another door further in. Inside the cubicle, by standing on the enamel tank above the toilet at full stretch, I was almost level with, and about ten feet away from, a small high window which was open. Feet on one wall, hands and back flat against the other, I chimneyed out. The paint was a slick, limestone colour in the light cast by a street lamp through the high window. Had anyone come in, flicked on the light, dropped their pants and sat down, looked contemplatively up and

[122]

found my bundle of arms and legs suspended above them, they would probably have agreed I was on my way out.

I shrank headfirst through the window, slithering down to earth in a convenient bed of flowers. Eight hours later, after driving through the night to get to Heathrow, I took off, smelling of geraniums. Ian returned the car:

'Grace called.'

'Any message?' He smiled

'She loves you.'

A moist, warm weight as if I'd been buried up to my neck in summer sand, the air hyacinthine, familiar as the bathroom after she'd showered and left for work. I was trying to wake up. My eyes felt like stones. I kept them closed while I felt in my bag for the tiny hand mirror I always took on long routes. They were bloodshot, like two old cherries. I sat up. Government propaganda was going round in circles on the black state television screens. Gandhi was up for re-election. I wandered outside. Knots of small, brown men were standing around, wearing, what at first glance, looked like large white nappies. Flowers like drunken parrots swaying in the breeze. And hadn't there been forced sterilizations here? I couldn't see any women about. I wondered how my dad found the heat. I patted my back pocket; the medals were still there. Wasn't it here, in New Delhi, he saw the prostitutes?

It was our only talk about sex.

'As long as you don't do it too much.' Mom wasn't in.

'But will I have to wear glasses?'

He puzzled, caught it and made a smile.

'That's an old wives' tale.'

'Not a young husband's?' Then he was laughing and, lighting a cigarette, proceeded to tell me how he'd visited a brothel: 'Just once,' in New Delhi, during the war: 'Only to look.' I believed him. I think he said something about women in cages. 'Don't say anything to your mother.'

When I returned to the passenger lounge she was there. Long, long dark hair, almost to her waist. Not tall. Large, dark eyes. Really well built. I looked away. When she looked back I was gone: Watching her reflection in the glass front of the timetable display, with my back turned, she was looking at me.

'Edwin.' She had been issued the seat next to mine on the Air India flight to Katmandu. 'Linda.' From Massachusetts, and headed for Tibet, to spend time with refugees, she might 'Perhaps,' spend the monsoon season in a monastery. 'With lamas, living at seven thousand feet.' Alone . . . Two hours later I was carrying her bags across the dry grass into the airport lounge. Jeff and Dianne were waving me over. 'See you later.' She was staying at the same guest house. Dianne glanced after her.

[123]

'Did you see them?' Jeff asked. Dianne gave me a big hug: 'How are you?' 'Okay. What?' I asked Jeff: 'The Himalayas.' Her legs were a warm, coffee colour. She played flute too. She disappeared into the press of taxi drivers. 'Yes, beautiful.' But I thought that what I'd seen were just clouds.

It was like playing football all over again. Like after the match with Bushbury that clinched the league championship for the school team I captained; my right knee sliced by someone's stud, I had played on. Crowds of little kids milled around, touching us, gabbling, thrusting flowers. Women glancing from dim doorways and darting back with a laugh, men staring with a translucent passing interest as if we were no more or less than creatures, like camels, that often waddled that way, swaying beneath our colourful nylon humps, along the narrow, unpaved streets. The air smelt like dying flowers, from the flowers and the open sewers.

After changing I ran out into the courtyard where the team were to meet before dinner. I was feeling better. Jeff and Dianne, Fego Locney, Geoff Childs, Mike Lowe, Peter Quesada, Steve Mullen, Mark — , Jim Willis, Lanny and Lynada, and Margaret: all from the States; with Matia and Boris from Eastern Europe and you know who — you don't really, yet — from 58 Hilston Avenue, Penn, Wolverhampton, dreamland. So: the International Makalu Expedition. And there I was, in a way, representing the world. I felt like asking if anyone had brought a ball, imagining trailside games in the evenings, with me in goal for the Sherpas perhaps, against America. But Jeff had something to say to us all.

A rangy, gentle giant, who strode with a slight limp from unnecessary corrective surgery, Jeff was not so much a captain as, with his panoramic vision, sweeping the ice field above Advance Base where the climbers soldiered on, a director; looking for the best angles, the most aesthetic lines, for the big picture he had of the west face of Makalu. He led from behind, for although he climbed, it was not as well as he wrote. In *The Soloist's Diary*, he had laid claims to a vast and totally unexplored territory, almost extraterrestrial; a sort of climbers' Waiting for Godot. With long, sculpted sentences, he had mapped a haunted, vertiginous world, where recognizably human creatures climbed endless, monotone walls: Sisyphus — without that moment's rest. He had hated Makalu at first he told me — he had been on a previous exhibition to the south face — but: 'Then I fell in love with her, and ended up wanting to stay all winter, to write.' Jeff in his ice cave, bent over a stone tablet like Ahab in the belly of his whale. 'With an icicle instead of a pencil, right?' He didn't laugh; he was serious.

Dianne was beautiful, honest and fun. Though she stood a little in awe of Jeff, she was really no less able to cope with his writer's tendency to have the last word, than a young tree swayed by high winds.

[124]

Geoff Childs a Hemmingwayish Nam Vet — who'd pulled a gun on a major once, and had, I gathered, shot one or two — gutsy, fast and loose as a cataract — unnerved me. He entered into conversations like a paratrooper: feet first, through the cloudy, youthful speculation that he, a Maine man, would term — with a snort — 'Californian.' 'A real survivor,' Jeff called him. If we were forced to climb together, I — would what? Refuse? Insist he be searched?

I was just as defensive with Mike Lowe. He organised uncertainty as efficiently as MacDonalds hunger. Not at all to my taste, though he manufactured superb equipment — to the letter. The booster stage of the expedition, I wasn't all that surprised to learn he fizzled out at higher altitudes.

Steve Mullen, an impish figure from Colorado, brought out the policeman in me, just as I thought his friend, Peter Quesada would when I first met him, wearing a CAT operator's peaked cap. 'I want to make it perfectly clear,' I had announced in Denver at Mike Lowe's when we all met for the first time, 'I (for I had been appointed as "Rock Climbing Leader" by our leader) don't want any drugs to be taken on this expedition.' I was playing the Whillans' advocate in a way, trying on the straight jacket to see if anyone squirmed; trying to fit in. When I learnt Peter had done a thesis on Blake, was descended from Don Quixote and had a US Army general for father, I felt inept, fastidious, even lonelier.

Mark, whose last name I never learned, was quiet and kind. A newcomer to high mountains too, he saved Peter's life later, when there were those who would simply have added it to the costs.

Matia, a Czech, who'd been very high on the south face, was the carburettor of the expedition, through whom doubts were ignited into decisions. Boris, the other Eastern European, was the piston. What was the connection I wondered, given the record of Soviet bloc climbers in the cold spots of the world, between political control and the kind required in mountaineering?

Jim Willis, the doctor, taught Sherpas classic rock choruses he knew by heart: "A Doo Ron-Ron-Ron A Doo Ron-Ron," and "A Whop Bop A Loo Bop A Whop Bam Boom," quasi-Asian diphthongs that must have sounded almost homely to our tireless porters. Borne along by the tidal optimism of the sixties, he is one of those rare people who never quite come of age, never quite settle into the mould, but like a tree wrap the years around them unsparingly, preserving deep within their first, soft heartwood. Student protests, the Vietnam War, Acid and Grass, tremendous social changes after the Voting Rights Act of Johnson; Watts, the Panthers, Watergate, Pollution, had all left their mark on his rugged intelligence. He decided to become a doctor. And, he was to tell me later, he and his student wife — and

[125]

here I got the impression he'd married her partly in order to help her surmount certain financial difficulties of an official nature — were separating. Illegible as he might be when it came to the fine points of ice climbing, his nightly emergency first aid course and scrupulosity about our drinking water, his tragi-comic demeanour and passionate whackiness, combined with an ability to make one feel safe with pharmaceutical amounts of gentleness and anger, made him one of the real leaders of the expedition. Whenever we climbed together over the next few years,which we occasionally did, he would narrate exact text book descriptions of the anatomical and, occasionally, neurological changes that were shaking place inside, while he, finally, did — or more often didn't — move. Belaying him from above was like having a marlin on the line. Only rarely would I get slack, while all the time there'd be these reports in radio-crisp English, about his position: 'Relaxing left lat whilst abducting deltoid, presenting problems for thenar eminence in left hand;' and, once — which induced parasympathetic stimulation of my lachrymal glands: 'Hypothalamus: Are you receiving me?' But by the time he rose from the depths — sweat pouring off him — though my back ached, and my stomach too, from laughter and hunger, he knew he was in safe hands. As I did, intuitively, when I heard the Sherpas rocking as they rolled out of town.

Fego Locney. The less said the worse. Let's say he was in charge of food. We heard about him because he wrote to us, enclosing a clipping of his recent ascent of the Nose, which he'd told the world about in the local Santa Cruz paper. He also had strong connections with a health food store, and, apart from being able to pay full fare — for the expedition desperately needed fare-paying members — he would be able to 'get us a deal on the food'. Nevertheless, it had come as a shock to learn later that he hadn't — as the article seemed to suggest — in fact climbed the Nose alone; which was why I had favoured him when others, like Jeff and Dianne, had strong reservations.

Leaving the expedition on medical grounds, after returning to Katmandu, he soon discovered suitable employment for his talents on the black market. He even made one member of the expedition an offer he could have refused — after the expedition returned — and not spent eight months in jail: for picking up a packet for Locney that I was told contained thousands of dollars worth of contraband watches. Guilty of innocence at least, so are writers made. Locney escaped — via India — to, perhaps, Las Vegas, his true spiritual home: shooting crap; his name in lights at last: "King Con".

Which, to my shame, brings me to Margaret. Margaret was older, shy, stubborn — one of the first women to climb McKinley, she also flew her own plane — and lonely and rich. And because she was there, in California, able and willing to pay the last few thousand dollars the expedition needed in order to be able to take off — we, and she, were now here. Most of us hadn't had to find a dime since the expedition was principally being funded by a wealthy and generous Colorado oil man who needed a break . . .

And then there was Rodney, our manager. He had an extra-ordinary vicarious interest in the success of others. Though he didn't climb himself — and seemed to be barely tolerated by some who did — he was the one who would skip back and forth on the two week trek to and from Katmandu, whenever the expedition needed it: for food, to escort the sick and to accompany later climbers in. After Makalu I can imagine him having helped organise the last Rolling Stones tour, or be currently plotting Senator Hart's strategy for his attempt on a different throne from the stone one we had in mind.

Lanny and Lynada were from Fremont, right at the lobe of the great ear-shaped San Francisco Bay that Drake had passed by. Two of the most decent people I have ever known. I met Lanny in the Bugaboos. A cautious, courageous climber, honed on a hard work ethic that had barely been softened by the creature comforts of his wealthy, suburban parents. Below the youthful veneer of idealism and bright-eyed Christianity, there was a true photographer, mountain guide and all-time reliable person. Though he probably voted for Reagan in the last election, on the grandfather principle, don't get me wrong. Not given to abandoning ship for tempting tropical islands, apolitical as an oak, it is the likes of him who, after a crisis, clean up. He'll probably climb Everest. Lynada quickly became our Florence Nightingale. A tireless spirit, unaffected by altitude or anxiety, a potential astronaut. By the side of this pair of real people, when I broke down the next day, I felt as awkward as that Brobdingnagian, though, no doubt, nice Jewish boy, in Diane Arbus' famous photograph: the ceiling resting on his huge bent head, his little parents stand quietly by.

And who are you you ask? I was supposed to be one of the leaders: 'Mirror, Mirror'. Let's take a close look.

We all ate together. The meal was regal and lasted hours. It was like sitting in the middle of Chagal's palette as the various spiced delicacies and rice dishes swirled around the wooden tables. But I didn't like being called sahib.

That night, except for the two couples, we all slept in a long dormitory. The night was hot. Flies sizzled at the open window. I lay in my hammock with just my underpants on. Linda was a floor below me, down in the courtyard, in one of the rooms overlooking the central garden with its silent fountain. Tomorrow. 'I'll see you tomorrow,' she said as we went in to dinner.

The next day we had to buy the remainder of the food and do all our

[127]

packing for the following day's departure, when everything would be flown to Tumlingtar; eleven days away from Makalu. Early in the morning Fego Locney and I went searching for honey.

'Why aren't they giving us that one?' I pointed to a jar of thick brown honey as the boy hurried away. 'I won't be a minute.' I followed him around the corner, leaving Fego with the beaming shopkeeper who had apparently whispered something to his son.

The boy and another man were scooping honey out of a jar the size of a small beer barrel, using their hands . . . both hands. As soon as the offensive member oozed from the mouth of the jar, a squadron of flies fell on it, unbothered by its desultory flap. Several, like black raisins were suspended, or drowning, in the sweet trap.

'I think I'll pass on the honey.' Fego agreed:

'They'll prefer white sugar anyway.' That left rice, which was, flortunately, unflied.

After lunch we had the afternoon off. 'Pap-pap!' Taking the bicycle by the horn, I suggested a ride to her. 'Let's go to the Monkey Temple:' she pointed, to a hill above the city. A thin line of trees marked the road and clung to the several, tiered levels of the temple as if they were, year by year, scaling it. Flags flew in the breeze; it looked like they were expecting someone.

Inside the Boudhanath Stupa, the flags were more like gay pocket handkerchiefs; and, with the large, colourful sheets that were fluttering all around, it looked like washday. Except that everything was dirty, even the sheets. 'Prayer flags,' she said, that waved from saplings that had been thrust in the ground — like a dream of sailing — by the grubby, black-gowned monks. They scurried about the temple, ignored by its dozing crew of monkeys, sprawled in the sun, studying their navels, scratching their heads. Cranking prayer wheels and humming incantations, like so many harried engineers at the silent vents and orifices of a great liner that had run aground a long time ago, I felt sorry for them. Tiny green leaves spluttered from the tips of the improvised flag poles. Suddenly I hated it. The squat black tower with its maledictory slit eyes looking down on the people and surrounding countryside; the mechanical prayers, the priests oiling the squalor with their penitential patience; the pretty chains of poverty swaying in the wind, the stink of fear in the incense. The putrescent obeisance to custom and the past that reduced the sense of the holy to an ape shitting down the wall of a temple, photographed by snickering tourists.

'Christ!'

'What's wrong Edwin?'

'Nothing.'

'Come on, what's wrong!'

'This . . . all this fear, superstition. It's why I climb. I can't stand this inbred hopelessness, the feeling they have of a god watching them . . . I want

[128]

to live! Not be held down like that!' A German couple were looking at us.

She said nothing. I'd really put my foot in it. We clattered back, weaving in and out of the gawking crowds. Ah well. Back at the guest house she had got some mail. She turned to go to her room. Then stopped:

'Thank you.'

'For what?'

'For saying what you felt, up there.' I didn't know what to say.

'See you later?' What did she mean?

Was it that and the gentle smile that visited her face as we stood in silence for a second, before we went to our rooms? Five minutes later in the shower, with water streaming down my face, I started shaking — then weeping uncontrolledly, as if someone had just died.

'Take it easy,' said Jeff. He had his hand clasped on my arm. Tears were running down my face. Dianne had her arm around my shoulder. I could barely speak. The others had finished eating a long time ago, and left. We had been there for more than an hour. There was a small ring of white sugar on the table in front of me that I had assembled with one hand while the other shielded my eyes. 'Give yourself time.'

I wanted to leave — straightaway.

'It hit me in the shower-' I gulped 'Grace, Haworth — no one's' but the 'here' got lost. Dad. Grace. Haworth. Mom. I felt I was going mad.

'We're here for you,' said Di.

Rootless, carried along by the excitement of the others, drifting to Makalu, without any warning like a man who's fallen asleep in a canoe — waking when he hears the distant applause of Niagara. I swept the sugar from the table.

'I'm going out.'

And there was Linda. We walked around the city, circling beneath the high walls of the palace, for hours. I told her everything; nearly. It was dark when we neared the guest house. I still hadn't made up my mind, with less than a hundred yards to go. Then I did. Her hand was warm and soft. She left it there until we reached the lit porch. We looked vacantly around. The others weren't there. 'Do you want to come to the garden?'

Sitting in the jasmined darkness she held my hand. We heard the others come back. Lights, laughter. The generator stopped. Suddenly Lanny was there. He noticed.

'We went to the telegraph office. How're you doing?' Linda got up: 'See you.' Lanny lingered, his hand on my shoulder.

'What can I say?'

'You don't have to say anything.' Good.

I slipped out of the dormitory. The others were asleep. There was a faint jingle of crickets from the cloistered courtyard. I tapped on the door: 'It's Edwin.'

She let me in straightaway.

When I came back the flies had settled, braided black around the cords of the hammock. I fell asleep watched by millions of eyes.

We met in the lobby after breakfast. 'Why don't you come to Makalu?' I asked her back in the room. She played her flute for me and said she'd think about it. At lunch I mentioned it to Jeff. With a glance at Dianne: 'It should be okay; probably.' There was a letter from Grace.

The plane skimmed along the runway. I was relieved.

'I don't know what I feel. Maybe I'll go to base camp.' He was pleased. 'A Grace period,' he called it, smiling. She was still waving when I lost sight of her and the crowd withdrew to a red dot below me. The propellers drilling through thick cloud, I fastened my safety belt and opened the letter: 'Mon amour . . . .'

We erected our tents near the England-green airstrip. Before dinner I went for a walk. There was a skinny lamb that was bleating, and a sheep with a black bird on its back, pecking after ticks. I climbed a tree. Overhead, a bee as big as a black thumb hummed about its business. There were several strange insects, like small red shoehorns. As the wind rose and sank, the long feelers they held out in the air, as if they were fishing, tangled momentarily.

The sky above the dark-blue hills that ringed Tumlingtar had begun to clear. In the distance though, tremendous cumulo-nimbus were building; it looked like a mural of nuclear war.

'What?' It seemed hard to believe.

'Mountains, and in about eleven days Eddy m'boy you'll be standing below them,' whooped Jim. He handed me a plate: 'Pure poetry.' Christ he could be obnoxious!

The tent shook in the night. I woke with a cry. Grace had betrayed me in a dream. Steve and Fego were asleep. I lay awake composing the letter I had to write.

In the morning Fego and I ran down to the river, which, bifurcating several miles to the north, had cut out the long, table-shaped plateau, laid with its grass airstrip, rice and sunflower fields, and straw houses. We swam, and washed one another's backs. I was starting to like this easy-going west-coast demeanour.

A young Nepali boy silently approached, as if we weren't there. He cast his fishing net onto the river. It hissed, settling. While we sat speechless, he oozed through the water like a statue waking up, his feet ungluing from the river bed, until he was close enough to spear something in the net.

'Have you ever been married?' He hadn't. 'No children?' He didn't think so. Laughing, we set off at a run. When I glanced back the boy was watching. Back at the camp I wrote to Grace.

For the group photograph we all donned our sky-blue wind suits. We must have looked more like grounded navy pilots. Mike took me to one side. His former marriage and the catastrophic suddenness of the breakup; his new life with Debbie — how well it was going — and all he tried to do in the last few weeks before he left, to make it perfect; the chance he felt he was taking that she'd still be there when he returned. Perhaps I'd misjudged him. They were all trying. 'Then why did you come?'

'She knows I have to do my thing. And she does hers.' Why was I such a baby! What more did I want ? I started to wonder whether I should have written that letter after all. The breakdown in the shower, and in front of the others; weeping for two days; that I had not been able to tell her how much I'd wanted — needed — her to come: for us to do this together. And that I would, probably, return . . . Soon. I said nothing about anything from Dianne on. Nor that, in some inexplicable way I was glad that she hadn't come; it would have made it even harder to . . . What? No, it was too late. Glancing back as we prepared to move out, the plane took off; with my letter bomb on board. I had given it to our mail bearer that morning.

Topping the rise, for a second, on the plateau — against the oceanic jungle, the gorging rivers and coming rains that could disperse fields and families like a child stamping ants — that billiard-green airfield already looked like a long time ago. Lacking only a glass, a bottle of port and a bust of Queen Victoria.

I felt like I was on safari, or going to put down an uprising in the provinces in the nicest possible manner. 'Namastai,' called out the dark figures who had stepped from their houses, white teeth, wide smiles, as we trooped by their gardens, a blue-jeaned beggar's army, in big boots and tennies. One or two had staves and several, ice axes, gleaming from our packs like new-fangled crossbows. They looked happy to see us going. I felt a bit silly. Were they laughing at us? What did they really say when they went inside, out of the sun that some of us were already exposing pale parts of our anatomies to? The dogs didn't even bark. A few days, a few more villages, and the background titters would become twitters, simple animal interest, as natural as the branch-brown legs of the Sherpas bending beneath our loads. As if the trees themselves had decided to help us.

On Himalayan expeditions, an average of one in ten doesn't return. There were sixteen of us, with three or four others who were to join us from Aspen in a couple of weeks. Don't go eh? I must send her a postcard.

[131]

Khandbari: There I bought some scarlet cotton, handprinted with child-like flowers, that had been smuggled over from China, to make pillows with when I got back home. At Manibensun, I saw a young Nepali woman and walked more slowly between the stalls, stroking brocades and satins that in later Irans, men would start witch hunts with; while her lizard-green eyes flicked from my hand to my face. The length I bought hangs in my window today.

Just before Pangma the doctor exploded. He found Steve and Pete swigging chang — the local brew — from filthy glasses in one of the frequent wayside shacks.

'Parasites! You idiots! You can't do this! Typhoid, Cholera' — he slapped the table, glasses spilt, they started to get up — 'Hepatitis! you name it! Jardia if you're lucky!' Spinning on his heel he strode off. They looked into the murky liquid, shrugged; but didn't finish it.

At night, for as long as we could, we had meat with the rice and dahl. Usually a cockerel, *the* cockerel, of whatever sprinkling of huts we had camped near. The head of the Sherpas, Norbu, was dispatched to negotiate for the de-coronation rights — from the head of the village — to the head of that lower pecking order. A small crowd gathered, cameras loaded. I strolled over. Nema the cook had the shivering king cradled in his arms. He was stroking him, making soft clucking sounds. Everyone was silent. Then he — (the cameras saluted) — pulled — with a click — off his head, blood seeding over his toes from the feathered stump. They were laughing.

Somewhere between Pangma and Bodobas as I plodded the wide trade route early in the day, from a giggle of Sherpa girls swirling by in black skirts, rhododendroned and snowdropped with colour — one sprang, snatching at the pendant round my neck. It was a parting gift from Grace; three tiny stones from a local beach, held in a net of gold that she had designed. One for each year we'd been together.

I held on to the red beads slung at her dusky neck as we rocked and laughed, slithering on the trail, borne along by the jostling bodies. We let go — just as suddenly. Game over. A wave — and no more. I enjoyed that.

Looking back she was gone.

On the third night I won Lorry Driver of the Year Award. I had no idea that I could have even been considered for something that I didn't know existed. Keith, (who the hell was Keith? I asked myself), was driving a dumper truck — with me clinging to the yellow lip. He was yelling at me that I'd better be ready, (for what?), and that my recent behaviour, (who did he think he was to speak to me like this?), had really let him down. I was close to tears — but I didn't let him see. He hands me the award. Glaring at me is the red reflector off a bicycle.

'Stop, Ed, stop.' Someone was whispering in my ear. I forced my eyes open.

[132]

'What's wrong?' 'You were shouting.' It was dark.

'Sorry, sorry. It was a dream.' He grunted. Soon he was snoring. I didn't want to go back to sleep.

I woke to hear children chanting the thirty-six letter alphabet in a nearby schoolroom, the xylophonic phonemes reminding me I had done no Spanish since leaving. Would I always be a Sunday linguist, a tourist of other languages, able to buy food, ask where the train station was, but really remain in my compartment, first class English, for the rest of my life? It was time to get out; Fego had packed and breakfasted already.

Ururu, Mude — descending through sub-tropical forest, I thought I heard them. I sat and listened: nothing but a low, distant roar. Around me the magnolias had already flown. They looked like doves Matisse tore up. Maybe tomorrow the runner would return and there'd be a letter from G. After crossing the tiny terraces of rice, maize and sugar-cane patched onto the pitched hillsides, and reminding me of miners' gardens and hand-painted abstracts as the sun went to pieces of stained glass in the sheets of water on the fields, I finally caught them up.

There was a cry from below, Jeff I think, and either he or the river was getting a round of applause. 'It's here!' He was joyous. It was the fifth day and reaching the Arun — one the the Ganges' veins — evidently the bridge had not, as he'd feared, been swept away. I stopped: It looked like the local school's version of the Golden Gate done out of string.

One hundred and fifty feet wide, elephant-blue, rolling through the narrow gorge, the river was gangplanked by twenty narrow floorboards, slung between rusty lines of wire.

One at a time, with our packs in our hands, ready to drop in case the bridge snapped, we crossed. It felt like walking on an avalanche. After crossing, some of us sat in the sun watching Fego on the far side of the river, fidgeting with his toes at the edge of a house-high boulder. Below him the river was so deep, calm and slow, you had to look twice to be sure it was moving. Large, lazy eddies doodled downstream. He didn't dive.

Having heard the sahibs were coming, four children had run down from Sedua. They stood in the middle of the paunchy bridge. 'Aren't kids great?' said Jim. We walked along together a while. He was calling me Ed now. 'So tell me about Grace.'

Approaching the village, a flotilla of prayer flags came into view. The Nepalese on the white sheets looked algebraic, like Einstein's last equations or something.

'I wonder what they're asking for?'

'Rain, safe passage, sons,' he conjectured.

'More expeditions?' He didn't have an answer.

[133]

The next day we changed porters. It was to be a rest day. In the afternoon I went bouldering. Before long I had attracted a healthy crowd of locals. I didn't think it was my lama-like silences and propitiatory repetitions, nor my fits and spasms as I'd cling scratching and wrestling with invisible forces for possession of the stones, that made them start doing it. It just looked fun. I watched them from the entrance to the tent. By the light of the fire they'd lit near the rocks after the sun went down, they were still playing. It was getting hard to tell Sherpas from shadows. Someone added a branch, flushing the back of the last climber salmon-red as he slithered down. He was good, able to do everything I had done in EBs with his bare feet, even leaping onto holds he wasn't tall enough to reach. Quick, shy, sure, I felt heavy as a lion among these natural Daniels.

None of the villagers moved. The meeting had been ordered by the mayor of Sedua: 'In hour sahib!' after Jeff found some of the food from our portable hill of sacks and baskets was missing. The mayor ranted and waved his arms. Nothing materialised. 'Sorry sahib.'

The others left. On a knoll overlooking the village, I wrote, not to Grace this time, but Gene. He had been my first employer in the States. A former shipwright who'd had more than his fair share of union bashing in the thirties, he brought to everything he did the common touch; whether researching leukaemia, probing the toxic chemical pollution of drinking water or having fiduciary responsiblity for the apartment building I managed. With his grizzled beard and sunbeaten brow, a self-taught yachtsman who ploughed the big seas outside the Gate like a farmer on his tractor; conversant with congressmen, cleaners, cops, cosmologists and circumlocutious Englishmen, sturdy as a Spanish bull when it came to standing his ground in an argument — a woman could reduce him to tears. I missed him.

'We're all in the same boat,' he said to me, when, in the second year of my managing the apartment building, he had overridden the proposed rent increases the board of directors had imposed, while he still had the authority. Over coffee in a local cafe, when I had shown him the list of tenants who would leave if the rent went up by the thirty to fifty dollars the board were demanding, he vetoed the increases. I didn't tell him that it was me who had suggested to the devastated tenants — the Pleshakovs, Wongs, Mrs Sanchez, Chris, Bill, Elizabeth, Mel, Barbara and the bearded lady with the exercise bicycle, (who, between eight and nine every day, while others rode the buses, drove her elephantine thigh — she was an amputee — to work in her apartment) — that if they handed in their notices, 'Enough of you mind,' then perhaps . . . Gene got fired, the partnership broke up, the building was sold. Reagan began his weekly radio talks. The Pleshakovs hung on for a year.

Gene had been planning, after all that happened, to come to Makalu base camp in some fatherly role. I had encouraged him. Now I realised it would have been like having Thoreau as a marathon partner: he would have kept stopping to talk and I'd never be able to get away. 'Glad you're not here,' my letter began.

Then I prayed, for the first time with both feet on the ground, not the rocks. Up there I found praying as natural as sweating. And it didn't leave a bad smell.

I set off in a thin, bleaching wind. The others were at least two hours ahead; I'd be lucky if I caught Jim up today. On the outskirts of the village an old woman stopped me. She had something in her hand. It was a badge of a mountain; with a small green tree at its foot. And there was some French . . . I understood, it was from the French expedition that had climbed the South-West ridge, the one that divided the two faces like Madame G herself. She held up two fingers. I gave her five rupees. She looked me in the eyes, steadily: her face was brown as a walnut. She pointed at me, then in the direction of the huts, sipping, and at the same time, offering me an invisible cup in her small, brown hands.

We were heading for Tashigoan, the last village before the Barun La, or Shipton's Pass as Jeff termed it, perhaps in deference to my roving English eyes. The pass was the needle's eye into the kingdom of the Khumbu giants. Would we be able to get through? A lot of snow had fallen that winter.

I didn't really care, a letter from Grace had arrived and now the pleasure of yesterday only left me feeling more isolated, reminding me of warm Sunday mornings at Stinson beach, climbing our way over the boulders like large land crabs who forgot something. Swimming, eating oysters at the seashore cafe, I'd had a foot in both worlds.

Each day I left camp last — when I'd finished writing — long after the others had gone. 'In training!' I'd call out, panting past uphill, practising the rapid deep breathing that prevented altitude sickness and close conversation. I thought continually of Grace, at last at university. Her refusing to uproot. The struggles she was having with first semester French — the phrases she'd try out in her letters. Contemporary Literature, Psychology, and four hours at downtown Wells Fargo, from six thirty in the morning before going to school. Making a home for us in the flat we'd just moved into after the apartment building had been sold. Having to share, to do without meat and now, care for the six kittens that were born just after I left. In her letter she spoke of having to get a waitressing job at night and maybe drop psychology. How desperate she was to prove herself and, in her own words 'take a place in the world,' that I was walking away from.

And what for? To evade seracs, sneak across crevasses, and escape from

[135]

the wind, as efficient as the rip tides round Alcatraz. To defy ice and rock as perennially crisp as barbed wire; risk being shot, bombed, cut to pieces by terrorist minerals, casual gendarmes, a hail of stone-age bullets loosened by the sun; thousand-tank avalanches, rocks whirring in the air like falling choppers. No wonder Childs had such a gleam in his eye last night when they looked at the photograph! When I could have been taking on our overdraft, or making the bed I'd promised instead of that mattress on the floor. Cooking dinner for her to return to.

Was that it? Had I really come here in order to find out I didn't need to? Had I stuffed myself full of loneliness in order to make myself sick? Stuck my neck in the tunnel but retracted it in favour of candlelight, and not the gleam of star-struck ice at 28,000ft? To slip back to Ariadne's, pleading that I couldn't find the bull?

Not that there wasn't plenty of bullshit about. The only people with real experience were Matia and Boris, and they were as likely to climb with any of us as Barshnikov was to dance with Woody Allen.

Or was it something else that pulled me from the American nest we'd begun? Why was I still going on? Maybe I didn't want to settle down, rootless really as the winds and water that in time turn even the rocks their way; no more likely to bond with a person and place at this late hour in my life than Hamlet could marry Ophelia.

. . . I was sitting at dinner with some others. It was like the return meal in the film *Deliverance*, where Jon Voight eats with country folk after the river has finished with him. He was gulping back his tears — having been given a glimpse into a nature unrestrained by law or love. I start shaking uncontrollably, as if I am actually falling apart. Two women are trying to help me: the arms of one of them are far too small to contain me — although she's trying; the other's go right around me but they are so tight that I cannot breathe . . .

'Another bad night,' conferred Fego laconically as if passing me the milk. I almost laughed. His Californian equability was a relief, like sinking back into a well-upholstered Mercedes: it didn't matter where you were headed. No questions asked. Just relax.

I looked around at the other drivers. No matter what dreams they'd had, they all seemed to want to be somewhere else too, other than Utasay, Chinery, Darakaka, Unshesa, Kuma, Komila, Lakumu, Kikila or Mumbok, where the root-thick toes of the porters clung yesterday, under our packing cases, equipment, food, tents and sky-minded intentions. Places and faces passed like a roll call, names bounced off our miles covered like the rain on our anoraked backs and high-tech tents, circled together at night,

[136]

traffic-light-green and red after the lamps are lit, we've checked the guy ropes and made sure we've left nothing out. Kept at a distance, the chorus of chatter and coughing fitfully subsides into a jumble of damp, blanketed bodies. Daybreak sounds like an orchestra tuning: clattering pans, repacking, feeding sahibs and children. Then Jeff gives the signal: At Norbu, their leader, raising his stick, a hush descends; then, while their feet rise and fall into place for the next twelve hours, we stroll along admiring the spectacular scene changes.

Pemethang, Yangley, Neh, Ribapuk, Tadosa, Jaqweh, Langmali, Shershon; Camps 1, 2, 3, going going − all the way maybe to the summit pyramid, gasping like Cheop' slaves, waving our little flags at the universe. To turn around like ants, sensing at the tip of the horn of a bull slain in the ring, that there's nothing left − slipping away before our fingers turn black.

And were we serving a higher or lower purpose? Rustic astronauts, spores carried across the planet, seeding courage and humour in the bleakest, most inhuman places, the gray matter of granite, snow and ice? Or merely the e-coli of the human bowel, colonising the geological dead ends of the earth − where nothing grows − to pluck the flower fear and take a great human pride in not freezing our ass? Ends in ourselves, spiders whose only point of attachment was the end of the nylon rope we tied ourselves into? Or well-fed refugees of western society? Who need produce nothing more radical for the aid they receive, than a bunch of slides held up to the light of a projector − the natural crowns of other countries carefully trodden on − setting the sights of the folks back home, keeping them in line with the march of progress.

And while the real people ran out of firewood and washed their blue-grey rags in icy streams, one or two of us became legends in our own lifetimes: by giving away our jeans at the end of the expedition, and by raising a fund to bring a favourite Sherpa over to Yosemite, Disneyland and New York . . . Ah, Super-ego, whose unconscious soldier ants rear guard the imperial intellect, strong silent types, opening up the market for Coca Cola, Coors and colour TV, is that what we are?

Or was the only real parasite me − caught hitching a ride out of life, now struggling to find an alibi for not going after all? Children? Except for Margaret, none of them had any, and as for me, though I had a son, did he have me?

Entering Tashigoan, a young Sherpa lad and his mother rushed up to me, pushing blossoms into my belt and tossing them onto the packing case I was carrying. I had exchanged it a couple of hours previously, lower down the trail with the lad, for my backpack. I thought someone had left the case on a wooden chair. As I approached I realised the chair was moving. He was on all fours and his short legs were as thin as his arms. One of the new porters from Sedua, he couldn't have been more than twelve. 'Ramro sahib,' they repeated several times and picked up the blossoms that fell off, to throw them up again. 'It's Edwin, actually, but Ramro's fine.' It felt like my birthday. They were the same colour as Grace. For a moment I felt as happy as when she had taken me to meet her Grandmother Acebo in Oakland, long after Linda had gone back to England; who showed me the birds of paradise in her garden, orange and blue-beaked flowers, tall as bullrushes. Sleeping with them by the side of our bed I felt the olympic torch had been brought to us . . . They carried the chest off between them, beaming.

'Who is she Ed?' joshed Lynada, when I arrived at camp confettied with snow-white rhododendron. 'We were wondering what kept you today.' She was writing a letter. 'Should I mention it to Grace?'

'Oh yes,' brushing petals out of my hair in her direction, 'and tell her I've decided to become a Sherpa; oh, and to be sure to hire me when she comes on her women's expedition.'

Jim looked up, 'In search of the Abominable, um, Snow-woman, right?'

That night I helped Fego prepare dinner, stirring the dahl to prevent it sticking while he cut up the tiny, fiery peppers. Then, by headtorch, before I fell dreamlessly asleep, I read Coleridge's *Frost at Midnight*, written in contemplation of his new child:

'Silent icicles, quietly shining to the quiet moon.'

It was raining. The hills were veiled. We would not see Makalu today; our audience denied. The mug of tea was cool when the Sherpa handed it through the tent flap.

We were walking in a stream. 'This will bring the leeches out,' said Jeff. Clad in my old running shoes, my feet soon turned numb. Rather than sweat inside my cagoule under the heavy backpack, I ignored the drizzle. By the time we left the dripping forest, it was too late. Sodden, hungry, shovelling my legs along, I felt like a face worker trudging to the pit after a strike's been called off.

Out of the shelter afforded by the trees, the porters were having a hard time of it. It began to sleet, gathering on their sleeping blanket-covered shoulders with a mocking fleecy quality. None of them had shoes. A young woman's feet left red stains on the snow. For the first time I noticed that several of the young women had children shawled in front. I passed old men who were clearly unused to this kind of terrain, placing their feet on the icy slopes as gingerly as if they were beds of cooling hot coals. Large, useful, cracked, cheap feet, doing the expedition gig to keep their places by the fire? I gave one of them my Dachstein mitts. There was a sound coming out of him when he breathed, like gravel being walked on. His face a wind-written net in the spitting rain, the coconut-white circlets dangling from his ears growing a little icicle, he cracked a smile.

On the plateau where we were to camp, I crept inside my bivi-bag. Islanded in cloud, a number of us shivered in silence, waiting for the first Sherpas to arrive and put up our tents.

I closed my Shakespeare. I unzipped the door, letting a crowd of snowflakes rush inside. Jim looked up. Fego was asleep.

Closing the tent, I threaded between the gleaming domes, A-frames and pyramids that housed the expedition. Beneath a balcony of overhung rock below camp, the porters — more than fifty men, women and children — were huddled, swaying, waiting for dinner. After cooking for us, they had rebuilt the fire. Rice simmered in a blackened cauldron. Wet blankets steamed on their shoulders.

I sat down on a stone close to the fire. A little room was made. Someone handed me a sack. They went quiet as I opened my book. Flames licked the circle of dirty feet.

After a while my eyes were running. I screwed them shut and hung on as the wind, with a low roar, wrapped me in an acrid shroud of smoke that, at a distance, had smelt so good, bent on seasoning me, or driving me away from the orange-blue tongues chattering at the pot as if nature itself was licking its lips. It drifted over my bowed head, rubbing its spicey bitterness into my skin, brushing my hair with soft fingers, dropping a few crumbs of soot on the pages of my book. My lungs were bursting.

I looked up. Laughing, chattering, pushing one another, whispering, snuggling, tickling — it was like watching dolphins from a cliff. Someone chucked his soggy wool cap at someone and the fire — catching — sprang to its feet, flamenco-skirted, swirling around the naked brown legs of the Sherpas, scattering embers, red petals that were stamped on and kicked back. A natural salamander writhing on its back in the ashes now the pot was removed, someone threw it a branch.

Closing my book, I dived in with both hands. It tasted different, a bit bacony, but I was their guest. Two scooped handfuls in a donated copper bowl. It was the first time I had ever eaten with my fingers. The fire was devouring its branch; sap sizzled and spat. My feet were warm. 'Ramro, ramro,' it was — apart from 'good day' — all I knew. I couldn't even do the dishes, which were licked and finger-wiped clean by their owners. They began singing, chants that reminded me of blown bamboo or bone, the applause of pebbles when a wave collapses, and a choral one like a piano of icicles that I found impossible to hum; half whistle, half vowel, it melted away into silence; as if it was a memory they all shared, maybe a year when the rice failed, or some of them never came back.

[139]

It was quiet. I cleared my throat:

> 'In the bleak mid-winter,
> frosty wind made moan,
> Earth stood hard as ir-on,
> Wa-ter like a stone . . .'

My favourite carol, it had once earned me a whole pound. I was twelve years old. It was Christmas eve and standing on the front door step of a big house in Upper Penn, just before midnight, I could hear a row going on between the man and woman inside. Should I knock? Start singing? Or slink away down the crunchy gravelled drive?

They came to the door before the last verse. Holding hands. They broke into applause.

'How can you stand it?' It was Lanny. I opened my streaming eyes, and twisting backwards saw him standing at the edge of the plateau.

'I'm curing.' I turned back to the fire.

Jim and Fego were asleep. I didn't feel like reading, though there was only the last act left. I could hear the Sherpas coughing. It was snowing.

'A lot of them have tuberculosis you know.' I looked up: It was Jim in the doorway of the tent. 'It's endemic here.'

Snow had formed against the sides of the tents during the night, making them look like buoys that had drifted together in a swell. I popped my head back in, the porridge was coming. Sipping my second tea, I finished *The Winter's Tale*.

Still no sun. Wind from the north — we'd be walking right into it. Today we had to cross the pass. Stuff this . . . Reluctantly I left my sleeping bag and started to roll it up; Fego had already packed. Suddenly voices were being raised, I could hear Jeff's. I stuck my head out. He was facing some porters, sacks and boxes at their feet, children peeping between their mother's legs. Jim was walking over.

'They want the tennis shoes. But Long's worried once they get them, they'll run off;' he crawled in: 'Norbu thinks there'll be ice on the pass.' Apparently the new tennis shoes were to be awarded when the porters reached base camp with their loads. Only then did they receive their rubber pay cheque.

'Why would they do that? They've got a sense of honour,' I said as Fego squirmed past with his backpack. 'There's a long tradition.'

'Don't have pity for them,' — Jeff's voice rang — 'They're porters.'

'People first!' I roared. 'Porters second!' at the same moment as Lynada cried out. Jim said nothing.

I booted steps up the snow, twenty foot waves — frozen in mid-air. We

[140]

made human chains. Even in the new deck pumps the women and children slipped. 'I'm not going on if they don't get them,' I'd threatened. We reached a compromise. The men's feet turned blue. When I found the old man I gave him my old Nikes. I had new ones in my pack.

Silence. Frozen lakes like manhole-covers in a New York blizzard. Prayer flags, sun-bleached, blank. People like ghosts in my snow goggles.

I was the last in. Tempers had flared. A young woman had fallen. 'Just a little concussion, nothing serious.' Hearing that Jim stomped away to his tent. Lanny looked as if he was going to say something: Childs continued to unstrap his crampons. We got no first-aid lecture that night.

The trail wound through the rhododendrons like a fresh bandage. Buds, red-tipped, speared through the snow. We had swung westwards after the pass, and were now too low to see Makalu. We were aproaching the Barun Khola river that drains the glacier below Big Mak. Lanny in particular was suffering the fastfoodfast she was on, and had conferred the new name on her icy majesty's haute cuisine. 'So long as you don't eat it,' I added. We promised each other a yak steak when we got back to Katmandu. Getting closer, the river sounded like cavalry.

I stripped to bathe in a sidepool. Beneath the surface I could feel the current twitching. Bushes shook on the bank. Boulders surged like rolling ball-bearings in some unheard-of Himalayan engine where the river oiled around them, blue-green between the loose earth banks. Kneeling on a large, flat stone in the draught from the next fall, foam flying, was like shampooing my hair on deck. The others had gone on.

I was getting worried. It was like walking on a LA freeway. There seemed no way I could cross. The others had taken the left bank and I just assumed . . .

Above me on either side, soared ice-steepled towers and domes, for thousands of feet; vegetated castles where the sun set its ruby each night in the eyes of the ravens. Augustinian as the driven snow, not a soul in sight, a babel of winds portcullised by icicles, shrouded in mist. A fit setting for The Ancient Climber, if Coleridge had ever come here. Spindrift figures poured madly through a gap in the cloud.

For a moment I saw myself up there. Hiding, for a year or two in a madhouse of weather, while everyone thought I was dead. Scratching a living: berries, mice, roots, raven's eggs. Making my will and searching for the Abominable, long-lost Family.

Catching sight of the others on the far side of the river, I hurried up, and was able to cross quite easily where the river, unexpectedly, dived underground.

[141]

We stopped for lunch. Fruit and nuts, a candy bar, a nap . . . I woke to find the others moving on.

'I was just about to wake you Ed,' said Jim. I was so comfortable there in the sun, I didn't feel like going.

'It's Sleeping Beauty.' said Jeff. It was the first word he'd said to me since the plateau. Or beast? I scare myself sometimes.

'If you see any princesses . . .' He waved and I soon fell asleep.

I woke cold. The sun had set and the shadow of a mountain lay on me. There was a whisper — quick! — a roar I looked back — a tiger-striped boulder bounding down the hillside crashed into the ground in a cloud of dust. Dirt spurted at my feet. The river was so loud I hadn't heard it until it was almost too late. I brushed the dust from my hair and shouldered my pack.

The Valley had opened. The trees looked like something from Grimm, seaweeded with lank, damp moss. Margaret had draped herself with several lengths. She looked like an old mermaid, forlorn and mischievous. It was the only occasion that I ever saw her smile. She always seemed sad, as if she had been given some terrible news as a little girl, about tomorrow. Bewitched, in a way, Magdalene, 'Touch me' exuded from her pores; which sanity, compounded with other, natural odours, made her almost as distant a person as me. I think she had been attracted to me when I first went to see her, just after Grace had decided to stay. It was three weeks before we were hoping to leave: 'Provided we get the money,' Jeff emphasised. And, I suppose, looking back, the thought had crossed my mind, pandering as I was for our impecunious expedition. 'Shall we dance?'

I wish I had said that, there, right then, in that gloomy valley; for one magic second have entered her world, put my arms around her frail body that flew aeroplanes alone. I walked on.

Makalu tomorrow. We built a huge fire at Neh. It would be our last, firewood was extremely scarce from here on, rare as the bones of Red Indians around Kansas City today. We hatched a secret summit plan: to seal Lynada in a haul bag — she weighed little more and was not much taller than a large stork anyway; release her at 26,000ft and chase her to the summit. Which almost sounded like a wild goose chase, so we didn't tell the others. Lanny fanned the violet-primrose-daffodil-tall flames, that we stretched out our hands to. It was a warm, clear night. I decided to sleep outside, by the side of the jostling river. When I woke in the night it sounded like a crowd hurrying past after some government announcement. The fire a low, red glare.

At dawn there was a cradle of moon poised above the icy peaks. We scattered the ashes and headed out. 'Today then?' asked Dianne.

[142]

Last night I dreamed I was to play soccer for England in Mexico. Frantic — my special boots had not arrived — with an hour to go I rushed all over the teeming city. I was in the changing rooms and the others were about to run out without me when the manager hurried in with a sealed white silk bag. He handed it to me: Two, gleaming black, with lightning blue flashes. I wept on his shoulder. They were the Pumas I wore for the school team. Had my mind changed then?

Jeff nodded 'I can't wait,' she said, flinging her arm around his waist.

The half moon sinking. Wave upon wave — as if the Pacific had been parted and we stood on the ocean bed — white horses rearing above our green dome tent, bathyscaphe-tiny on the flat flood pain below the south face. We had arrived.

Scraping the ground clear of stones, I came across an old, bent, tent peg, left like a question mark by a previous party. We were regarded by silent, black birds, ravens or crows with thick, yellow beaks they scratched at the ground from time to time, as if making notes while we worked. Had they seen it all before, these featherless bipeds who come each Spring with their colourful materials, but produce no young? 'Kaahk! Kaahk!' they flapped off — shocked by Mullen's pebbles. They settled on the rocks, a little further off, a black circle of cackles, watching us.

'I wonder what they eat?' he said.

'You if you don't get a move on,' said Peter, still with his CAT cap on. He looked like the boss. Then, as if we were being advised, flurries of hail rataplanned against the tent. It was getting dark. I looked around: the porters who were staying on to help establish advance base, were building a wall to shelter behind for the night; until we could erect a tarpaulin or something for them tomorrow. Giving them a hand, then going back to the tent, I felt canine, a dog in the life of those real Denisoviches. What was I doing there? What had I done wrong? How could I get away?

'Tomorrow we have to repitch the tent.' Fego grunted. It was like sleeping in a box car next to the river. And, in a certain direction, the wind — when it hit the tent pole — went off like a siren.

'And the glacier snores!' But he was already asleep.

'There is this thief, an expert at breaking and entering and taking exactly what he wants.' Jeff looked away. I went on: 'It's dark. He enters. It's a trap — a steel shutter slams shut behind him. "Don't move" he cries, as if he is tracking the thief, as if he is up to some good.' Jeff looked back from the tiny blue figures of Mike, Geoff, Matia and Boris, who were threading a way through the river of boulders between the upper and lower glaciers. 'Is it too loud here?'

'No problem, carry on.'

[143]

I dipped my hand into the river. Clean, cold, clear green, silking off the mountain, a shuddering rope that stretched to the sea. I continued: 'Then, seeing stars reflected in a window at the top of a flight of stairs, he climbs up, believing that if he keeps up the pretence no one will know that he is the one. But, he doesn't know I'm following him. You with me?' Jeff nodded. 'He pushes the door: it's dark, slips inside — and the light crashes on! It's the office of the chief of police. Officers have him covered. Then — and this is incredible — everyone starts laughing! Including him. Because — and I think this is still in the dream — this is a true story of how they caught a cop.' Jeff was grinning now, 'for the thief, of course, went on to become an informer.

'Then I woke up,' I finished. Over at the tents, some of the others were loading their backpacks with food and equipment.

'What do you think it means?' he asked, picking a handful of gravel up.

'I've no idea — that I feel I'm some sort of fugitive '

'From the law?' I remembered us looking at one another in the manager's office in the Pyramid. 'Or love?' I laughed. He trickled the gravel into the water.

'Well, anyway I feel guilty, like I'm deserting you. I've already deserted Grace.' My voice trailed off.

'That's a bit much isn't it? I mean you could say she deserted you.'

He stood up. 'Why not wait at least until the Aspen lads get in? Or Rodney comes back? You haven't even seen the West Face yet.' The others had their packs on. 'But whatever you decide to do is fine.' As they headed out Mark waved.

Fine? That wasn't what I wanted to hear after telling him the dream. I felt naked, exposing myself in that way, hoping he would at least have dressed me in some bright idea, a real reason for staying: like the tickets couldn't be changed, or something. Ah well. He had a lot on his mind with Fego. I pulled my hand out of the river. It looked like a statue's.

He had come down in the night with something. Jim suspected cholera. He might have to be evacuated. 'Rodney will take him.' said Jeff. 'Okay:' I left it at that.

Although this was a rest day for some of us, the gang of four were going to scout out a place for advance base, as well as establish a dump site. After Mike's fatherly talk with me in Tumlingtar, I felt adolescent; hiking beside him up the Barun valley — ninety. He seemed made of indiarubber, pounding around day after day, climbing the nearest high points to spy out the lay of the land, bouncing out of bed every morning as if it was simply, a slow trampoline.

'He needs to be careful,' announced Jim, 'he's not allowing himself to acclimatise.'

That night before we went to sleep, Lanny and I stood outside for a while. He was making a photograph with a very long exposure, of the communal dome tent, glowing beneath the velvet snows of the majestic mountain. Figures were crawling about inside, there was a low buzz of conversation. Mike and the others had just got back. Inside they all looked like bees.

Suddenly the analogy got angry. Unwitting cohorts of an icy queen at whose feet we had gathered to make our sacrifices. Though I might be a drone compared to those workers, I wanted no part of the bloody honey.

'Beautiful!' Lanny said, 'It might make the catalogues.'

Next morning we hiked the moraine, following the red flags that the advance party had set the previous day, carrying loads to leave at the dump. And get a glimpse of our face if the clouds lifted.

I was aware, or should I say I had become aware, of something looking over my shoulder. 'What's that?' I pointed to a black face to the West, half obscured by cloud that looked like a leaning tower of Pisa two minutes after launch. 'Lhotse.' Between breaths I got: 'Messner's up there.' We both needed a rest. Slumping onto our packs against a boulder, he told me who he was. I felt nineteenth century. And in mountaineering terms I was still in the stone age. As if, in another rock epoch, I didn't know who The Boss was. Which I didn't.

Then we saw the West Face . . . Imagine the night with Marilyn Monroe: Are you awake? Slipping into bed, the unutterable plunge that made presidents of nations contemplate war; the slaughter of all your cautions, littlenesses; two thousand years of guilt gone in the twinkling of that long-lashed wet eye; breasts like falling down Everest at night, the black hole of the universe herself pulling you into the hot rhododendron-dark slit. Cut. Cold. Stiff. Lying in a pool of blood beneath icy sheets. You've made love to a corpse . . .

The sun was setting. Wine-dark streams trickled around our feet. 'God,' was all he could say. I shuddered. We dumped our loads.

'Ed —'

I'm in my parents house. My father isn't there. Suddenly I see the poplar tree, like a green wick going up in flames of wind, the one that carried me on rustling shoulders as a child, bearing me higher than the houses, showing me the blue hills of Shropshire, and — as I turn my head — the factories of the Black Country

'Ed —'

Out of nowhere, a kingfisher − the blue swoop of another − flash into the branches. My mother and I used to watch them over the Himley wall from the top of the Midland Red bus we rode to Gran's.

'Ed!'

My brother is shouting − deliberately scaring them − 'I'll give it you!' yelling, chasing him upstairs into the bathroom − forcing the door screaming − 'They'll go!' − 'What's so special about birds!' Mom! calling up from below 'Or you!' With a roar like I'm burning alive 'Can't you see what I mean? And the birds are so beautiful!'

'Ed! Ed!' − He was shaking me −

'Oh God' It was Fego.

'You sounded like someone was trying to kill you.' I could hear the river pounding.

'Terrible, terrible.' It was my heart. A grey light in the tent. He looked ghastly: two dark cuts, his eyes were hardly open. Sagged, yellow cheeks.

'Later' I closed my eyes.

Later that day I sat above the dump. The sun was hot. Rocks coughed in the distance. The cloud was lifting from the West Face. I considered what was facing me: Left of the centre, a spine of rock rose from the ice − 'My father' − (A nightmare, at some buried level I felt grave danger) − 'Which art in earth' − that led to a sloping plateau, beneath an immense corner like an inverted L − 'Thy name' − (something natural and deeply esteemed, warred on by a hostile female figure) − 'Thy will' − which it might be possible to avoid by moving further to the left − 'On earth as it was' − (although Grace hadn't come with me because I'd chosen what was hard and cold and far from the nest) − 'And give us this day' − which looked easier than going up the wall to the right − 'Trespasses' − that from where I was looked like frozen swans' wings − 'As we forgive' − (which called for putting my high-altitude-booted foot down, without a vengeance) − 'And lead me not' − equally hopeless really, the only possible way − 'The power' − (given our relative inexperience and youth) − seemed to be avoiding that Medusan prospect altogether: 'Amen.' It was getting dark as I set out for south face base. Running over the moraines, I felt like the Pony Express carrying a copy of the Gettysburg Address to my fellow slaves.

'I don't understand,' said Mike, 'run it by me again.' Dianne handed me a mug of tea. I sat down on a wooden crate of crampons.

'The face is impossible.' I took a sip. 'We have no oxygen for climbing; no fixed rope after 24,000ft and, after that, the most difficult rock wall in the Himalayas.' I finished my tea in silence. 'Like El Cap in winter, at 26,000ft.' Put that in your hash and smoke it: I'd smelt it several times over the last few days. Dianne passed me a bowl of steaming snowy rice, with a brushing of yellow dahl she'd wiped from the side of the pan.

'If the spine was taken, there is at least a chance that by zig-zagging, ice could be followed most of the way to the sloping plateau.' Nema had got some peppers from somewhere; they looked like tiny scorpions. They reminded me of Mexico.

'Then what?' asked Mike.

'From there, it looks as though an easy traverse leads to the North-West ridge. It might not be the directissima,' Jeff looked up, 'but it would still be an incredible achievement.' I popped a pepper into my mouth:

'There's also less avalanche danger.'

Lanny and Lynada had gone to bed. Jim wasn't there. When I first stepped in — after having got lost on my way down from the dump — they seemed surprised to see me.

'We thought you'd decided to spend the night out,' said Jeff casually. Was I already so distant?

I hadn't been able to find the red-flagged wands in the dark. The moon was obscured by cloud. Then I'd followed, apparently, the wrong stream, like a child hearing its name called in a crowd, unaware that there could be another with the same name.

Picking my way between ice-emeralded boulders, I had entered a dark alley where the stream hurried out of sight. After creeping around several enormous blocks, I went downhill too fast, as if the babbling stream was trying to get away. It felt more like Liverpool on a Saturday night, that labyrinthine silence. Even the wind was waiting. Ice gleamed . . . broken windows, a hint of steel where starlight shivered. The stream's voice lost, somewhere underground. When I turned the corner, for one awful glance I was in Communist China: Frozen lakes, concrete-grey, stretched for ever. I went numb. I was in the wrong valley.

It would take all night to haul myself to the trail. I couldn't stop now. I stepped onto the lake like I was going home after sledging, with the sleigh Dad made, the rope lashed to my hand, creaking across the ponds and fields like spilt milk frozen in the night, frightened of giving in; inventing the motor car, the electric blanket, a space suit — my feet amputated in the wet snow — dreading there'd be no light when I came round the bend; sitting on the step freezing, Mom not in.

The moon rose. I collapsed through the snow gasping 'Thank you!' soft, wet, hot on my cheeks, hurting like I'd just touched the oven, as I lay there, half-buried in a new mound of blown snow at the mouth of the lakes. For there, as if it had just landed on Mars, on the dreary, treeless plain in the

tunnelling dark at the end of the last ice-locked lake glowing, earthly-green
— was the dome.

I followed alongside the chattering river for a mile, then cut across the
no-man's-land of glacial debris and smouldering snow.

'I didn't know there were two rivers,' I said stepping in the door.

'God, that was good.' I handed Nema the bowl. 'Really, the best option
would be to forget the face altogether and take the North-West Ridge,
because . . .'

'Now wait a minute,' interrupted Jeff, 'I've already told you we don't have
permission. Besides it's the political border and if the liaison officer found out,
we'd never be able to come back to Nepal.'

Well that was no problem for me — at least as regarded climbing.

'Which may not bother you, but some of us want to climb here again.'
Matia, Boris, Geoff and Mike, stone lions in their bushy beards, didn't even
bother to yawn.

In 1984, Lanny told me we could have turned our attention to the
North-West Ridge without real opposition from our liaison officer and,
furthermore, that it wasn't the political boundary.

Jeff was the one: A last try. I chose my words with care: 'A cul-de-sac,' I
didn't want to say a dead end. 'It's a waste — all this money, effort, time,
people — and then taking that line.' It was a grave risk. Just a word together
— a glance at the photo — and I was theirs.

Friday April 1. Fego Locney leaves. Cholera.

'I wish I could,' said Jim.

'What?'

'Love someone as much as that.'

We were lying in the tent that we'd been sharing since Fego left. We were
discussing Jim's up-coming divorce and my feelings about (probably)
leaving, to go back to Grace. It came as a real surprise, hearing him speak
like that, since, in this rarefied world, where everyone hurt to some degree,
where dropping your trousers was as difficult as stepping outside an aircraft
at 20,000ft, my whining had begun to sound other worldly: like having to
do without television, or wondering what to feed the peacock you insisted
bringing . . . There was something I wanted to ask him:

'How did you feel about the body, you know,' — I was really thinking
about his wife — 'after you started to dissect cadavers?' I had heard of older
surgeons bowling their students over by wielding a newly-sawn leg and
asking: 'Cricket anyone?'

I remember his words exactly. When he was asleep I wrote them down, by
the light of my headtorch. And that did it.

There was a twister of spindrift high up on the French ridge, like a swirling pillar of salt, sarabanding my drudge up the moraine. It suggested another circle of hell that Dante may have pondered over long, a nether world of absolute, embodied pride, whirled to abstraction by the Icarus winds of the intellect, to the point at which the deepest passion becomes that of breathing. A frozen, ideal space, where the human figures I could see on the enormous sheet of ice above advance base were like mathematical points, dragging a blue, tear-shaped haulbag after them. An ultimate fatherland of grey stones, a platonic carbon, blue-printing my shadow on the snow.

Where to walk is like mining days underground bent-double, and climbing is learning to crawl all over again. Unsubordinated, clumsy, legs and arms like branches swaying vaguely in the same direction, feet rooted to the spot, as the wind strove for the mountain, its ferocious 'Ohhhhhhhhhhhhhh' overflowing the sides of the rocky cup that contained our lives, at that moment − in an ill wind on the hill − my will was written.

'No! No!' I yelled, smacking the echoes back and forth, while the bluebeards of the icicles hissed and my heart applauded.

I joined the Sherpas at the Dump. They were roasting potatoes: 'Sahib.' 'Edwin:' They grinned at one another every time I reminded them. Thendu peeled one for me with the black blade of his thumbnail, and dried out a mug with his wide shirt cuff. The tea was a transfusion. I felt at home, like after playing hide and seek on Cannock Chase, among the ferns for hours on a summer Sunday afternoon, then having a picnic with Mom and Dad on the warm grass; coming back once to find them asleep in one another's arms. Inspired I broke open one of the expedition's sealed food sacks; to commandeer a can of tuna for us to share. Thendu and I leaned against one another, mumbling, gesturing: 'Ramro,' and, his first 'Eeeengleeesh' word, 'Gahd.' Flakes of ash drifted onto our hair and clothes, a warm snow, as if nature − for a moment or two − made a mistake. They settled down for the night. I went up to the tent that a Japanese expedition had left. There by flashlight, I started *War and Peace*.

Advance Base was now the dome tent, transplanted to the highest cwm before the great bergschrunds that looked like toenails at the foot of the face. When I first saw the pale green dome tent up there, it looked like an apple left in the refrigerator.

Mike, Matia and Boris had already established Camp 1, above the glacier. No more had been said about the spine. The line they had chosen was the same straight one that had been favoured all along. But, since I had made up my mind and it was only a question of a day or two, I toed it.

From the cold comfort of the tent, Jeff directed operations, hunched over the journal where he kept the expedition's sanscrit-cryptic accounts. Or, like a lighthouse keeper, raised his glass to our smugglers, apparently fishing among the iceberg-size problems of a vertical Dead Sea that the chosen line so nicely parted, hoping to glimpse their landing, the spinnaker of tent pitched against that suspended world; while rocks went off in the distance. A gentler Qadhafi than most expedition leaders to his followers up front, I admired him. And, I've no doubt now, that if it came to the real thing, he'd join up.

'Lanny, I don't like this.' The crack had widened, in the two hours since we crossed it, to a trench. A faint Mediterranean light appeared at the bottom. 'It's really dangerous, if you consider how inexperienced most of us are.' He didn't disagree.

We had just carried loads up to the 20,000ft level, where the fixed lines began. The rope, a red and gold striped perlon that hung, twitching, over the icy bulge of the bergschrund, looked as inviting to jumar up as the tail of a Siberian tiger.

'I'll wait here.' He wanted to take a load up to the fixed pin, ice screw — I was chilling fast — Deadman, Deadboy, whatever. "Just to get the feel of it."

'Can you see the point?' I called up; but he was too far away.

'I'm going you know.' I had to raise my voice above the late afternoon wind scouring the ice.

'I thought you would,' he called from the other side of the crevasse as we adjusted the slack in the safety rope we were leaving. His parents had asked me to keep an eye on him.

'Just be careful. Don't forget we've got a few routes left to do at the Leap.' Dotted all over the world, our particular Lover's Leap was where we took Grace and Lynada climbing.

Back at camp there were two letters for me. My visa had been granted: 'I received your aerogramme . . . I almost went to the Student Health Centre for sleeping pills, but I was too afraid to have them round the house: I've been that bad . . . Why did I say no? Please don't hate me. Please Ed, please forgive me. Please . . .' Floods of self-abnegation, triggered by my avalanche.

I opened the next one. It began: 'Now I'm ashamed I mailed — even wrote — yesterday's maudlin weeping letter . . .' One bird with two stones. Neither here nor there. I had to move fast.

Jeff gave me some money. I felt like a mercenary. 'And my ticket.'

He came to the door of the tent. Dianne at his shoulder. I have not seen him since.

'Lowe fell in the crevasse we fixed a rope on. He not only ignores it, but removes it after.' Jim snorted. Meeting one another on the way down to the south face base, we walked along together. I hadn't been able to find him that morning, to say goodbye. 'I couldn't take it any longer,' he said, 'the hatred and aggression that's building up.' Matia had snarled over Mark bringing Peter down after he'd collapsed with hypothermia, instead of leaving him to wait on the ice; 'And going on alone to Camp 1 just so that Matia and Boris can push on with the line?!' So wrapped up in my own world, now I understood why everyone had been so quiet last night.

And Lanny had pulmonary oedema, and an embolism in his arm: 'He won't take it seriously,' said Jim. He hadn't even got to climb himself yet: 'I'll go back in a couple of days.'

That night in our tent we talked about infanticide. As possible fathers, we shared common ground: if something was born deformed we should kill it at birth: 'Just like in the wild.' I nodded. 'Or let it die.' 'Exactly,' he concurred. Though at the time I drew no connection, eight years later I feel that things had been wrong from the conception of the expedition. 'People second.' Sensing a sinking ship, I was, plainly and simply, a healthy rat.

While my guides, Thendu, Urkun and Norbu, were finishing their breakfast with Jim in the sun, I went back to the tent. There I put a lock of Grace's black hair, a stub of pencil, one of my Dad's war medals and a photograph that showed us laughing — in Yosemite, before we were married — in a small plastic box. With a note, vowing to return with her to climb Makalu in 1984.

I hear she lives in LA now, training to be a doctor; and plans to get remarried.

'Goodbye Jim.' Then I buried it, quickly — by the river. The people were waiting.

[151]

PART 3

Do They Reach?

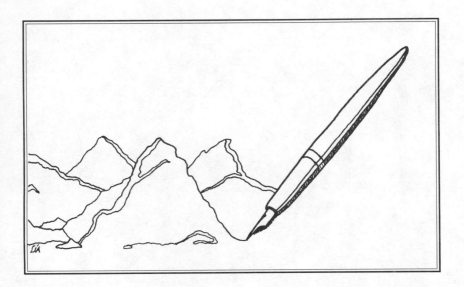

Between a Rock and a Soft Place

Light fading . . .

At the last rappel,
first one, then

another . . . mouse?
mouse!　　　　flick-
ers from a crack.

Grey, hungry-quick
— I shift my feet

in case they're like me.
Refugees of a world's high places,
gangs of ants
on half-demolished ledges,
rainy lean-to's of leaves
windowed with spider webs,
a tree, waving
handcuffed with slings,
natural warsaws of rubble and snow

where a few, blown grass seeds catch,
clawed into nests
that the wind, climbers might hear
— passing to higher things —

snatches at. Sowetos
of white dust
the rain washes off, dripping

on a long, dark descent
to the upturned faces
waiting for us
to come back.

The ropes are heavy, wet.
Do they

　　　　　　　　reach?

Nelson Mandela's Column

THE POLICEMAN had his back to South Africa House. He was looking straight at us, kernelled in the shadow cast by the huge block on which the Column stood, guarded by its four sleeping lions. I pinched the soldier's nose more tightly. An empty taxi sped past the National Gallery — the policeman glanced after it — just as my right foot, stemmed against the soldier's crotch — slipped towards Colin's pale, upturned face fifteen feet below. Wriggling a finger up his nostril, I sank onto my left foot, resting on the shiny black skull. I had no protection . . . Ian was sitting on the edge of the fountain, ready as a last resort should the policeman see us, to go and talk with him, to try to appeal to his conscience. Big Ben bonged 5a.m. Fingers sweating, I gripped the lightning conductor in my left hand, praying he wouldn't get his flashlight out. How did I get into this position?

'He's dead.' It was Deborah. 'The bastards murdered him.' She was crying.

'Oh God' I mumbled uselessly into the telephone. 'How did you find out?'

'Scott.' He was the leader of our local Amnesty Group in the Bay Area. 'Urgent Action Network.'

I'd never met José; none of us had. A young Nicaraguan, one of tens of thousands "disappeared" by . . . No one knew for sure how many there were since most of the jails and torture houses, *Casa Tortura*, the US supported Somoza regime had installed, were secret.

A month later, in December 1977, we held a commemorative protest outside the Nicaraguan Consulate in downtown San Francisco. On Christmas Eve, from noon to midnight. A candlelight vigil.

We had a large blackboard upon which was written, in Spanish as well, the details we had of José, along with a list of all those that Amnesty knew of who had died in custody, usually while being "interrogated" the government called it. It was a cold, cold day. I wore my duvet, the one I'd been given for Makalu.

Of the thousands who passed by in the twelve hours, of whom several hundred took Amnesty leaflets, around thirty stopped to talk. Four or five left their addresses to receive further information about joining. Throughout the vigil a police car was parked at the kerb. The officers were relaxed; sipping coffee from plastic beakers or reading the *Chronicle*, our presence like theirs a formality, since we had been granted a permit for our outrage.

At midnight they pulled away. We scraped the hardened tears of wax from the sidewalk where we had stamped our feet and hugged each other to keep warm. Then, as a last thought, I took Debbie's candle before she extinguished it, and climbed the inside of the mock Doric arch of the Flood Building that housed the consulate, placing the candle ahead of me until I could go no further. The group were amazed. We relit the candles and soon had more than a dozen tiny tongues of light nagging at the building over our heads, like strange baby birds from their improbable nest on a dusty inner city ledge.

'Brilliant,' said Debbie, her eyes shining. And indeed the lights were. It looked like a birthday we had just remembered.

In the following months, after articles appeared in *Newsweek*, an Italian magazine that I didn't understand, and an Australian one called *Pom*, that depicted me at strange angles to the pavements: 'Social climbing' as I termed it sometimes, to the amusement of many, the curiosity of some, and the consternation of a few, I was taken up by the local press. All around the city I worked out low-order levitations: like the Rate of Interest, a drainpipe-wide off-width sandwiched between a bank and an insurance company; The Heart of Stone, an obsidian sculpture, tiny as a rabbit-pill at the foot of the almost thousand-feet-high Bank of America, where I had a hand traverse that was so slick that if the air was misty, I found it no more possible to raise myself than I could have a loan from one of the marble-topped manager's desks inside the mountainous edifice. Twice TV crews filmed my private high-speed alpine purloins before the bank guards waved their arms at me and began shooing. There was the High-At, a pinch grip problem on the Hyatt Hotel. And Peeking, a concrete ceiling on a Chinatown public housing project that I termed 'An act of interracial co-operation' to the camera's blank eye. between the puzzled Oriental janitor who didn't understand English and probably thought I was the plumber, and myself. Before launching – *à la Sloth* – along a fat bathroom pipe that ran across the ceiling, from which I could swing for the chunky concrete front of the first floor balcony above. Holding my breath I'd scamper down the urine-splashed inside stairs.

And there were other vertical puns and plays on stones and words that I found among the concrete nooks and crannies of the city: 'It keeps me off the street,' I said more than once to a passing cop near Golden Gate Park – momentarily arrested by the sight of my feet in the corner of his eye – knowing I could probably disarm him with my charming English. In all I

[157]

found more than a score of these "buildering" problems around the city for which editors short of copy took up my cause: 'A Young Man On the Way Up,' read the headlines in one weekend colour supplement. On the pebble dash facade of a Cala Foods supermarket in the Haight, I rose above the crowd by means of pinching and sidepulling on the nose and ear-size sea pebbles that had been set in the concrete, and which I dubbed the Hunger climbs. This was in reference to the usual unemployed social engineers who dazed in the sun along the street, more flowers than power, panhandling for "spare change," who had even been known to waggle an unwashed arm between my wildly stemmed legs and ask for 'a dimebuddy,' unfazed by my evolutionary progress up the wall. On quiet Sunday afternoons, when I wasn't waiting for the telephone to be rung by some young woman I'd just jumped into after Grace and I — as we used to say — split, I would hang around these problems that I had managed to solve. I didn't go to the valley much then . . .

Unaware that within eighteen months I would be reduced as effortlessly as chewing gum by the media, through talk-show appearances and 'local personality' radio and T.V. programmes, to just another Californian product, like pet rocks or a rather slow yo-yo — sort of a yo-ho — six months after our solemn memorial I was headed for London armed with my climbing boots and a high ideal.

The policeman was walking on. 'Hold my foot!'

Colin sprang up to the scrolled stone step at the base of the bronze panel, cupping one hand under my quivering heel and supporting himself with the other. How strong he was! He lowered me down as gently as a wounded soldier from the still-life battle above our heads.

'Let's,' I gasped, not giving him a second to withdraw, 'wait until he turns the corner.' He seemed about to say something:

'You're standing on the rope,' I interrupted — 'Then I'll go for it.' We had at most ten minutes before the policeman returned.

'He's almost round the bend,' Colin looked at me: 'The policeman, Colin.' I manteled up.

'As soon as I'm on the ledge, I'll pull in the haul line.' I began laying off the turned cheek of the soldier at the bottom of the heap of figures.

I stood on his head; now I was warm I was going well.

'And Colin,' I had two fingertips behind the lightning conductor, 'It's going to be all right.' I reached down for a tape to thread behind the quarter-inch-thick, two-inch-wide copper strap: 'Okay?' 'Okay.' Was that a smile? I cinched the runner onto the bolts that held the conductor in place against the Portland stone, and clipped in an étrier. Is this the battle of Algeciras or Trafalgar? I wondered as I climbed through the grave black figures towards the naked form of the Column, towering above us like the monolith in *2001*.

I had only known Colin for five hours. I'd asked Ian first, an old friend from Avon Gorge days and Bristol University, where he'd also done some Philosophy, if he would like to accompany me 'on a political protest.' He stared at me for a long second: Is this Ed? He said nothing, just let me talk on until my ideas were accomodated by his natural avuncularity. Although Ian and I hadn't climbed together much, each time we had I'd never failed to be impressed by his aplomb. He didn't train; not for him sisyphean sessions of bouldering or penitential reps of rope climbing until the arms hung like tired pythons after their annual blow-out. For he had so much grace on rock that even when about to come off; his arms fading — for he is a big lad as they say — shaking under some overhang, he had looked more like a matador stamping his feet before the big rush, than I with my bull-in-a-china-shop displays in those early days. Spitting pitons from between my teeth, tangled up in blue and red No. 2 climbing ropes, I looked more like a calf being winched out of the passive backside of a huge cow when I backed down — bellowing like Oliver Hardy — compared to Ian's Olivier-like presence up in the air. So he was a perfect choice for the Column, where his sense of gravity would keep down inclinations to clown or to put ourselves on a pedestal, which was the danger: that the inevitable social highlight would dim the political spotlight focussed on Barclays Bank's support for South African slavery.

'Only if you feel strongly about it,' I concluded, no doubt with a *quod erat demonstrandum* beam to my face.

However, Ian's reliability in the realm of the vertical was coupled with a horizontal stability that ruled out aerial broadcasts. He had worked for one of the major airlines since university and was now a senior executive. His cool reserves of experience and judgement were as vital to its day to day success and financial viability, as the Nile to the building of the Pyramids. 'I might lose my job.' Nevertheless he fed me, housed me, gave me climbing equipment, advice and ideas. And Colin.

'Ed!' I sat up with a jolt. It was after midnight. Ian had someone with him. I'd given him until eleven p.m. of the 19th of October to find a partner for me. 'This is Colin.' He looked young.

'What do you know about Apartheid?' We talked until one: The part Barclays played as the major foreign bank; the encouragement our political climb could give, if enough of their customers withdrew their accounts, for non-violent change; that as a climber I was disgusted by our acceptance of financial support, without demur, 'by Bonington for instance,' from an organisation committing economic etc. 'Sleep well.' He rolled out Ian's

[159]

heavy, chicken feather ex-army sleeping bag on the floor of the tiny Notting Hill apartment. The alarm was set for three.

'We've got two hours. You watch, we won't wake until ten.'

The city was getting up. The first sparrow was at work, chirping like a bit and brace in a nearby linden; a red London bus trundled round the square, its learner driver happy at finding an open road where traffic usually snarled and crawled, swinging the wheel like a golfer driving off onto the fairway at dawn. The lions were glistening.

From my perch on top of the plinth I could see her majesty the sun approaching her loyal subject, a thin red line advancing from the east above the Thames. His fingers glued to the copper strap as it caught fire from the sky, Colin was trying not to use the étrier I had needed to climb out onto the ledge. Suddenly he looked like Midas, turned to gold as the sun rose over the Houses of Parliament. It was no time to invest: 'Use my ankle!' He grabbed it like a pint at 10.40 and pulled over.

We were clearly visible. Ian waved. Several people were standing at the railings, looking across at us. Did they realise what we were up to? Would they call the police? There was no time to lose. The constable would be back any minute. Quarter-to chimed.

'I'll climb halfway up.' I could see the policeman, about three hundred yards off, his dark figure steadily advancing. Unaware it would be a day that he would never forget.

'We can take a hanging belay.' Colin looked up: 'Don't worry, I'll use at least three bolts as well as the lightning conductor.' We moved around the Column so that we were out of line of sight of the Law, now strolling towards us and probably wondering what to have for breakfast.

'With a sling round this,' I started to thread up the next section of the conductor, 'it'll be like belaying to a railway line.'

'As long as it's not the third rail,' he added drolly. We laughed, not fancying our chances if lightning jumped to the wrong conclusion, our forms dribbling over the lip of the plinth like negro gargoyles in the sun. I clipped the et. into the first bolt and weighed in. It looked solid.

'The weather forecast was that the storm wouldn't break before noon. Slack.'

'That's why I left my umbrella at home,' he said without a pause. Good choice, Ian.

'Keep the sac on, then if they use a hydraulic platform they won't be able to grab it.'

In the rucksack was the banner I had made a week earlier, with its fiery accusation which I had spray painted in red, while staying with my Mom in

[160]

1   On an early ascent of Great Wall on Clogwyn Du'r
Arddu, 1967 – 'Seal cold in my shorts . . . a talisman
rurp hidden in my pocket.' *Photo: Ken Wilson*

2 The headwall of
The Long Hope Route,
St. John's Head, Orkney –
'The skyhooks winked twice
. . . perhaps fear is the
possibility of ecstasy.
Oh we warbled . . .
Impregnability perfected
by a single perfect flaw.'

3 Oliver Hill – 'like Churchill without the words.'

4 (above) Leading the second ascent of The Boldest, Clogwyn Dur Arddu, 1967 – 'my third day on that most audacious route, stuttering in the footsteps of Crew.'
Photo: Bob Llewellyn

5 With Dave Pearce during the first ascent of A Dream of White Horses, Anglesey, 1968 – 'his horse was light, mine dark – we made a good team.'
Photo: Leo Dickinson

6 7 The Troll Wall, Romsdal. 'If you ever go there and have it the way we
did, you'll know why we called it the alter. I went on it four times: three failed
attempts on the French Route and finally success on Arch Wall with Hugh.'
(The inset shows Ed Drummond and Hugh Drummond after their Arch Wall ascent.)

8 El Capitan – 'Saharan in the sun, Pacific when it rains.' The Nose is on the left with North America Wall (based on the slanting dihedral) on the right.

9   10   11   12   Scenes during the Nelson's Column protest
climb which Drummond made with Colin Rowe in 1978.
Photos: Mail Newspapers

'Do you take this man to
be your lawfully . . .'

Protest atop a Nob Hill steeple

Casting his protest banner to the breeze, Edwin Drummond, 34-year-old British-born poet and social climber, greets the day from the crowning cross of Grace Cathedral. He told groundlings he expected to spend the day there, reading and blowing up balloons to spread a protest letter to Gov. Brown demanding freedom for Black Panther leader Geronimo Pratt, now in prison for a Santa Monica murder. Drummond's ascent attracted police, fire trucks, an ambulance and a swarm of watchers. See story below.

San Francisco Examiner

Saturday, August 11, 1979

13 14 15   Protest Climbs in the United States: Grace Cathedral, 1979 (above); The Statue of Liberty, 1980; Embarcadero Building, San Francisco, 1981.

Liberty Island—By 2 PM, he had reached the small of her back and nestled there in the fold of her robe. His friend watched him from below, clinging to the back of her knee.

The two men from San Francisco, using mountain-climbing gear, inched up the outside of the Statue of Liberty yesterday to protest the FBI's activities in a California murder case. From the ground, they looked like Lilliputians exploring the body of a giant woman.

16 17 Poetry performance, National Mountaineering Conference, Buxton, 1985 – 'on his white tower sat the miser of air, the millionaire of pebbles who gave up everything to climb.'
Photos: Ian Smith

Wolverhampton. It had been over a year since I escaped — *en route* for Makalu — from the psychiatric wing as they call it. Whose only flights are stairs that lead to laboratories where the patients are connected with the body politic via electrodes, or liberal doses of psychotropic drugs, the wells of grief and fear — the waters of the soul — industrialised by the magical Nardils and Valiums, the chemical bromides family doctors have doled out for years. 'Work and sleep; work and sleep, I'm nothing but a bloody slave,' she'd say when money had run out or her relationship with my father ebbed even further. After we had had lunch, while she was asleep in the chair, her head twisted away from the side the stroke claimed after Dad died, I went up the garden with the white sailcloth I'd bought to do my letters to the bank. And I have to admit, finding them so deeply in debt as to be morally bankrupt, and then sending them a statement — in red — afforded me a satisfaction that only the poor, the overdrawn, or the chronic student can really appreciate.

I just hoped no one found out I'd once had an account with Barclays. It was in the late sixties, for an expedition that Dave and I were making to Norway. Nor had I closed it for reasons of principle. It became overdrawn. Had I in fact, I now wondered, ever paid it off? Or had Ed Ward Drummond, in whose name it was, simply disappeared?

'Hey! What are you doing?' Ian was walking across to the policeman.

'Quick Col, get out one of the letters and throw it down. But don't say anything.' He fumbled in the top of the pack for one of the half dozen letters I had typed out about the climb. As a last thought I'd put them in air mail envelopes. The wind delivered it to the feet of Neptune, straddled across a green dolphin heading towards the river. The policeman snatched it up. Ian, close behind, hovered while he read it.

BOOM! Ian was walking away. The policeman was talking into his radio. BOOM! I was at the third bolt. BOOM! There were at least thirty before the capitals at the top of the Column that, from where we were — BOOM! — looked like a vegetated cornice on some lost South American plateau in the Madre de Dios of Peru. BOOM! It was the imperial overhang at the top of the Column itself, where the great man stood with his back to the sun, that had me worried. BOOM! Big Ben's benevolent time bomb subsided into the growing hum around us. Climbing faster than I ever have in my life, I reached the tenth bolt just as the first police car arrived.

Within five minutes two more had lurched half onto the pavement, head to tail, blue lights pulsing. Then a fourth, miaowed to a halt on the paving stones directly below the Column. For a second I had the ridiculous image of all the portraits in the National Gallery blinking and rubbing their eyes. A police inspector with a flat cap got out of the squad car. Twelfth bolt. He looked up. Thirteenth. Studying us. Fourteenth. The constable came over and handed him the letter. He read it.

'The two men climbing Nelson's Column are engaged in a peaceful political protest, directed at the continued investment in South Aftrica and its immoral apartheid system, by — ' blah-blah-blah. He put it in his pocket. And there was an assurance that we were expert — though anonymous — climbers and were in no danger. Also we were taking care 'In our climbing methods and choice of equipment,' not to damage the Column. Sixteenth.

Damage the Column . . . I felt as safe as an ant on a giant tree. The fluted trunk of the Column, rising a hundred and eighty four feet, a sober cinnamon in the soft October light. But what a strange tree! Shorn of branches — connections — in most people's minds with anything but the pomp of society that thrusts dead men, from Christ to the latest astronaut, in the air for people to look up to — its roots ran the length of Britain: A belief in the power of the individual to change the course of history. Or was it simply a totem, without even the flexibility of one of Nelson's masts, unable to bend to the changing winds, a stiff, male thing, a reminder of the big stick of authority, on permanent erection? There seemed no David-like humanity in that heavy figure up there with London beneath his heels. Real leaders belong on the ground, not up in the air, fifty times life-size. So what was I doing there? Good question.

Traffic was being forced to crawl around the three parked police cars. Drivers were peering up as if something was about to drop. There was a five foot gap between the bolts. Standing in the top rung of my étrier, at full stretch I was just able to thread the next bolt. Then, with protection above my head: a quick layback, using a sidepull and a hand-pinch on the fluting while I smeared with my right foot and toe and heeled with my left, and I was able to go through the motions of free climbing, even taking one hand off to unclip my et. from the last bolt. A little fatuous perhaps, but at least I felt less like a dog on a lead, which the sight of a long chain of karabiners on an aid pitch always brings on.

A bus rumbled past. At my fingertips the Column mumbled and the Colin called up:

'What's that!?'

'Only a five-nine.' He grinned — I was in the middle of my quasi-free move — but for a second the thought of an earthquake had struck us both.

'Quite a way to get down,' I ventured, adding, a moment later: 'Just like the Himalayas,' where Nelson's-Column-sized seracs have crushed more than hopes. Had there ever been an earthquake in Britain, the kind that reminds us — surrounded by water as we are — that we're earthbound as well? A fire engine was being driven ponderously towards two of the lions. I signalled to Colin to get ready to jumar, then set about belaying. Napoleon?

Hitler? Only Gandhi, and rightly so, had invaded English hearts and minds with true success. I waved to Colin, then took in the 9mm rope to give him a belay while he jumared up the eleven. And what would Gandhi do today about South Africa? That was where he had begun to care publically and not just in the throne room of his own private conscience. The rope creaked familiarly under Colin's slowly ascending weight, like the dusty innards of a lofty greatgrandfather clock being wound up.

Two firemen were strapping the police inspector onto the end of the turntable ladder. He was about to be fired at us.

Colin and he arrived at the belay at the same time. We looked at each other. I was tempted to say, out loud: ''Ello 'ello 'ello. Wot's goin' on 'ere ven?' The inspector was very red in the face. His arms pinned to his sides he looked like the human cannonball, about to explode.

'I must ask you to come down.' I unclipped one of the ropes from my harness, motioning to Colin to do the same.

'Don't say anything,' I whispered as, with the second rope now changed over too and Colin anchored into the belay, I began to move on.

The inspector, sensing my thicker skin, turned his attention to Colin who looked like a nice lad. My unshaved scowl and long, lank hair, topped by a scarlet beret, must have been unsettling at that time in the morning; like finding a spider in the bath. What I was frightened of was being diverted, talked to a halt, forced into arguments about social responsibility: like tying up fire and police services while real needs went unmet. This had happened to me on the Transamerica Pyramid, after Makalu. Upon climbing in the window the policeman had said: 'I'll personally take you buddy, to explain' − to the hypothetical mother whose hypothetical child had died in the hypothetical fire that the real fire engine, parked at the bottom on the Pyramid had not been able to put out because of us − 'all about Prisoner of Conscience Week.' That was to have been the theme of the summit conference that my friend and I had planned to hold − via walkie talkie − on the translucent dunce's cap of the Pyramid.

Colin and the inspector were talking earnestly. 'Slack!' He gave me a yard. Were the police stalling for time, while − at that very moment − an S.A.S. helicopter was heading towards us with a crew of strong silent types? They would be dropped on top.

'He'll just try to talk you down,' I shouted down at Colin. A hundred feet up in the air, Colin was looking a bit ruffled, as if he'd been stood up. Images of commandos dangling around us like man-size marionettes; arrested in mid-air before our red flag could be waved at South Africa House; the protest aborted: 'Jail for Climbing Clowns' would read headlines. I couldn't imagine resisting with much enthusiasm, a bunch of slings in one hand, five or six karabiners − all I had left − in the other, as I looked into the third eye of a gun as well as the steely-blue ones of Her Majesty's finest.

[163]

A thick noose of vehicles had settled around the square. Nothing was moving. A posse of Press photographers were being cordoned off by the police. There was barely room for the pigeons; several had landed on one of the lions' heads and were making tentative stabs at the unresponsive cranium. The ladder had been withdrawn. They were, apparently, going to let us get it over with. Colin was leaning back in his harness.

When I'd reached the base of the Column proper, I'd run a loop of old rope around and re-tied it, to use as a running runner in case the bolts or lightning conductor zipped. It must have looked like a tourniquet I was applying to the arm of a giant, as I hugged it up the Column. Now, approaching the ornate acanthus that formed the jutting overhang of the final pedestal where the big man stood, I prepared to undo from it. It would be my final point of protection before I entered the den of rotting rococo plasterwork that all along I had been afraid would fall apart. I just can't find the words to tell you how I felt contemplating that flaky capital. Like trying to do the Times crossword in the pouring rain.

'Metal!' I yelled as if I'd got the last word in. Of course, nobody in their right mind would have used plaster if they'd wanted their work to last. But from the street, where I had surveyed the Column in the previous few days, the overhang had looked more like dirty cotton wool. I fed one hand over a four-foot plume of wrought iron, locking my fingers on unbendable black feathers. There was a cornucopia of holds, stanchions like yew boughs to hang from, leafy profusions I slipped my feet between, easing like a sloth among so many black bananas my hands didn't know where to stop.

From below, inching out I probably looked more like I was minueting with a formidable widow than having a ball, unless you heard, like Colin, my soft grunts of delight. I was aiming for a rose, or was it a sunflower? The size of a vulture, it guarded the exit to the ledge at Nelson's feet. Held by many black hand-size petals − plucked out of the void − as I pulled over, a roar went up like the sea breaking over the lions, crashing against the base of the Column.

I lay there, on my back for a moment, looking up to the still, royal-blue sky, like I was lying on deck on a fine day in the Sound, having returned from sailing alone round the world − not just setting out, which I was. For the real work had only begun. To most of those watching we were no more than entertainers, cock-a-snookers, not hangry young men. That is a middle-aged one getting a first head of steam and − glancing down I could see him chewing on a second nut crunch − a hungry younger one. Though it was hard to say about Colin. Not that I felt any need. There was a quiet freshness to his assent, his willingness to be in the wrong place at the right time (there was an International Anti-Apartheid demonstration taking place in London the next day), that next to my burning bush, like water in the desert, spoke for itself.

[164]

I became aware of someone standing over me. He looked as if he'd been in a fight. He had a black eye where rain seeped down his face from the cocked admiral's hat he wore. A good-looking man, his face was marred by disdain, cold-chiselled into the small lips. Invisible to those below, he really was looking down. The lush epaulettes of his uniform — longer than my hair — had been shat on by the pigeons. His jacket was starred with medals and he rested stiffly on a six-foot sword that the smog had blackened. One of his white silk stockings looked muddy, as if he'd fallen over playing rugby. A flat sleeve, where his arm had been, was pinned against his jacket.

Beneath his notice I clambered up the bell-shaped block he stood on and, holding on to his slim white thighs, I threaded a runner around the tip of the sword, for an anchor from above. It was part of the lightning conductor. Had he ever been struck? I looked again at the great face. Was it disdain? Or pain at being so isolated from the country he loved — and Lady Hamilton? Behind every great man . . . There was a tremendous rope coiled behind, the kind that ships are tied to the land with. Thick as an anaconda. For a second it looked like his guts, slinking, outside his uniform, that had petrified. A wind had sprung up and I soon cooled belaying Colin through the maze of metal foliage.

'I can't feel a thing!' he called up, after transferring from the jumars to his hands, the overhang gobbling the heat as his fingers wormed in its undergrowth. Suddenly he bobbed into view from the sea of heads that lay all around us like seals wondering what was up.

We stood up and — simultaneously tempted — our arms lightly round one another's waists, looked back at how far we'd come. A second, greater roar went up — a warm wave rolling over me from the upturned faces and open mouths . . . I knew, at that instant, where I'd come from: That I loved them and would always try to remind them of what they meant.

'What have you got to eat?' asked Colin, 'I'm starving.'

We had a bite, a bit of bread and cheese, seated at that lord's sized twenty feet, while we studied, as much as we could lay our eyes on, what heights the city reached.

There was St Paul's dome where the soul's Sunday climbers sauntered; St Martin's in the Fields like an untrodden aiguille in the Alps. Behind us we could see the gilded finials and spires of the Palace of Westminster, Patagonian in their aloofness those sunlight-iced peaks of power, and as removed from the lives of climbers like us as Cerro Torre was from Whymper.

Nine o'clock. It was time. The world was waiting to see if we had found anything wrong with Mallory's Law. Colin gently handed me the back pack. I peeked inside: white and soft, still peacefully tucked up. My first. Although there were some red stains and the sewing was crooked, to me it was beautiful.

[165]

'Obviously we've got to hang it below or no one will be able to read it.' I agreed. But the wind had other ideas and kept snatching at it as we lay on our stomachs — tied in with a figure of state behind us — attempting to thread the banner's cords through the evergreen root system of the pedestal. I had painted it to be read horizontally, hoping to have it flying from Nelson himself. But that would have required sitting on his shoulder or flinging my arms around his neck in such a way that I might be caught in some compromising position, in camera as it were, since I could see that at several points on the surrounding roofs press photographers had mounted tripods. I could well imagine "Give Us a Kiss" headlines in the Sin for sunstance, accompanying the picture of me as I searched Nelson's face for a point of attachment; always assuming that he didn't lose his head.

'Make sure it's not twisted upside down,' I called to Colin on the other side of the circle we had been forced to go half round, due to the long length of the banner. He looked over. Or everyone would think we were Turks when they tried to decipher what we were saying on our tiny island in the sky, 'It's all Greek to me' wisecracks going off from the almost-the-weekend crowd, who if we kept them waiting much longer, might decide we needed taking down a peg or two.

I peered over: 'It's too difficult to read.' Colin pulled a face. With the wind ruckling and pocketing the fabric it looked like a coffee ad., not a funeral notice. Even though I couldn't see it from the point of view of the people down there, I was sure that only "CLAY'S COFF" was clearly visible.

'We have to change it.'

Behind Nelson's back we rigged the rappels, looping the huge runner that Colin had untied before starting the overhang, around the plinth. Ten already! Colin went first, lowering himself out of sight like a caver; neither of us really knew where this was going to lead. The doubled climbing rope reached to the bottom of the fluted trunk of the Column . . . Just. He hovered, teetered, lightly landed, its casual Mercury. He was going to wait for me there while I re-hung the banner.

The police had erected barricades to stop the crowd from closing in. Were they afraid we'd get carried away? I studied what was coming up. The streets were solid steel, we had locked the great wheel of vehicles that turns in the heart of the capital of the world. The spanner in the works, not just a couple of grease monkeys. What an opportunity! I just hoped enough people saw it that way.

I stepped out, not knowing that at that very moment, according to the newspapers we read later, Prince Charles, forced to climb down from his Rolls and walk to work, (the Department of the Environment, where he had a meeting that morning), was watching. He turned up twenty minutes late. Did days on the Scottish hills come to mind as he studied our small figures on

[166]

the grey stone, or the scent of something that he seemed to seek, walking as
he did for miles over the heathered solitudes around Balmoral? Had he ever
known the joy of climbing, those quasi-archaeological days when the
petrified strata of the human brain yield such lovely Lucys up to our tired
hands, such rejuvenation that it is as if one's stone-age skeleton has been
exchanged for one of pure thought. When even your little finger thinks. And
what kind of king would he be? What mental Sowetos had he survived,
trying to forge an identity adequate to his own true nature, caught in the
class system as he was? What corpses of real ideals lay abandoned in the
royal closets he played hide-and-seek in as a child? Certainly he'd been to
university, but what had he studied in the school of humanity? Subjects or
people? Would he give us the same old line or, by example, raise the standard
of the greater dead? His own favourite monarch was George III, who —
though his own private decency and interest in science made him popular —
mistook rigidity for rightness and prejudice for principle when it came to
understanding the tremendous social changes that were blooming so
savagely in the French and American Revolutions; which may have been
why, in the end, he went mad. So why should Charles rock the boat when he
became its figurehead? Still, there was something different about him, that
came perhaps from the Greek side of his extended family. Insulated as he had
been for so long by so many willing hands, from cold, hunger, obvious
personal injustice, chances were his own natural anxieties would long ago
have dried up into a kind of academic snuff; something to sniff about but no
more. Still, maybe not.

After tying one end in to the plinth, I re-rolled the banner. Tucking it under
my arm like Sunday's *Observer*. I began to come back down to earth,
unfurling the sign that everyone had been waiting for during the past five
hours. By 'Barclays' I was level with the top of the trunk of the Column; with
"Profits" I'd sunk a further fathom. Turning in the wind, at 'Apartheid' I
was halfway down. Taking the bit of bamboo that held the end of the banner
between my teeth, I pendulumed in, slipping my fingers behind the lightning
conductor so that I could thread up a bolt in order to attach the end. I hung.
And looked up.

Not a word could be read. It had twisted as I turned and now it looked
more like a rope of tied bed sheets in a fairy tale, than a line of bankers' filthy
underwear.

Methodically I began to untwist. With the wind spinnakering behind it, it
suggested one of the prayer flags I had seen in the Himalayas, whose crude
equation, at that distance from the ground, hardly anyone would be patient
enough to solve. So there would be no mistake about those coffins, I hauled
down on it, tussling with the wind-powers that were, for the right to be
damned, with Big Ben tolling eleven in the distance. There . . . A murmur,

[167]

whisper, rumour, roar — as if the lions had suddenly woken up:- applause! Even the police. And Col was laughing, looking at me as I tip-toed down the Column. 'We've done it Ed!'

After we'd pulled down the ropes and set up the last rappel, while Colin went ahead, I sat and had a smoke. I'd noticed the van, its black doors flung wide. Some people on the fringes of the crowd were already drifting away. Suddenly I wished we'd planned to drop the gear and run for it — dash through the crowd like two good, if not terrorists, guys who'd taken a rise out of the cowers that be, one of the crowd to whom, in the end, we all answer. But Colin was there already, being amicably arrested. And they were waiting for me.

The police shook our hands. The Press made note from their corral. Smiles all round. They were allowing us to coil our own ropes. People were leaving, it was all over . . . For a second I thought they were going to let us go. Then a long black-clad arm locked itself to mine:

'This way Mr Drummond.' I tried to joke, mainly for Colin who was paling noticeably:

'May I have this dance?' But the honeymoon was over. Now for the marriage. A last try:

'Do you take this man to be your lawfully wedded-?' The policeman was not smiling. And before they slammed the doors I heard: 'What time's the next performance?' from someone who had just arrived.

Rounding the square, as we headed for a Bow Street police station I remembered as an integral part of the Monopoly games we unwittingly played as kids, as we swept past the National Gallery I got the picture, the mirror image of a thousand question marks, all those people with their heads bent to one side reading the vertical headlines of the home-made flag we'd raised to our shame:

BARCLAYS PROFITS FROM APARTHEID'S COFFINS.

'What!?'
'More than a thousand pounds.'
'But that's ridiculous!'
'Read it through please', said the inspector. Where was Colin?
'Where's my friend?'
'Mr Rowe has also been cautioned that anything he says,' —
What had he said? — 'may be taken down and used in evidence against him.' I read the Notice to Defendant: Proof by Written Statement, again:

That: "without lawful excuse, you did damage the lightning conductor attached to Nelson's Column, belonging to another, namely the Department of the Environment, intending to damage any such property or being

[168]

reckless as to whether such property would be damaged."

I couldn't believe it. They'd been so friendly. Had someone been on the phone to No. 10? I blustered: 'I thought it belonged to the nation anyway.' But he didn't seem to know what I meant.

'Don't ask me.'

After having the charges dismissed the following January in Crown court, we sang: 'For he's a jolly good fellow,' as the judge pounded his gavel and the jury blinked, Colin and I parted company. I returned to the United States. For another year or so my sudden appearances, on churches and skyscrapers about the city, had the quality of a pterodactyl or a rooster among the grey pigeons that lined the monumental buildings. I sketched in lines on most of the man-made mountains in the Bay Area. And elsewhere: The Statue of Liberty; The Kremlin; The Berlin Wall; The Voortrekker Monument, the very corner-stone of Apartheid. In a more Cristo than Christ-like vein I thought of spontaneous demonstrations − Orwell would have smiled − on The Parthenon and the Sphinx. I climbed on . . . But far from elevating the concerns of citizens to the wider world, apart from raising the eyebrows of the authorities, I slowly lowered myself to the level of an intellectual flea; something that made them scratch their heads. Then squash: With a five-thousand-dollar fine and a year in jail (suspended, provided I satisfied the three years probation they gave me instead). Upping the anti in too many places for too many causes, the climbs became antic; then antiquated. I went up and, politely, came down. The offending notice was removed − and sometimes returned − within hours. Everyone got excited; no one was really offended.

'What's your next protest climb going to be Ed?' called a young journalist from the crowd, as I signed (I see − the crowd had hushed: So. That's that.) − my last autograph.

It's Spring I am standing in Trafalgar Square, almost nine years later. Barclays have left South Africa. There, in 1961, the government imprisoned another Nelson, for trying to save his country from slavery. A quarter of a century ago. He's still there. How many times his eyes must have climbed the walls of his cell!

I am looking up. He is still there too, like one of Plato's forms, above it all − the crawling traffic, unemployment, the riots, the rise and fall of government. A blind eye turned to the Houses of Parliament, the other on the rising sun. Aloof, alone, confined to his island of stone as well. And I see that notices − signs of our times − specifically forbidding climbing on any of the structures in the square, have been erected . . .

Fine name, fine British name, Nelson. I wonder what the *next* sentence will be?

[169]

The Black Lake

(Llyn Du'r Arddu)

From the cliff
the lake waits in the cwm
for the crumbs of scree.

Holding back the monarchy of rock,
she gathers the cadiss
in her lap, hikers on the skyline,
purple ravens' wine.

She does the washing when it rains.
Hanging up the clouds for days,
swilling piss-yellow out of the peat,
pelting the sheep,
rinsing the mountain's dusty feet.

Our local black hole, a bowl of plums
when the night wind comes
softly.

A choppy day: snappy
as a collie, running all over the place
splattering foam. My teeth chatter.
Skin and bone and stone and stars.

After sunset
she bites. The man in the moon
shivers all night.

The buttery look of the sun.
Lukecool by summer, there are Septembers
water won't melt in her mouth.
Around November
 − organpiping icicles −
she runs aground,
a thick, blue porthole
the rain rivets and the wind pounds . . .

[170]

Shut.
The sun rusts
away. Days like icebergs

stuck.
Whistling gleaming creaking
cracks, grass bending
wind winching
— a deep, blue roar —
reopening the colliery of the sky,
making the mountains soar

and tremble . . . Where I look down,
her wavy, young hair, blown
across his cold, bare stone.

Snowdon

(for P.C.)

The mountain, nude,
facing the gales off the Irish Sea, whose
craggy, grey breasts
brood clouds . . .

Easter: she takes visitors.
Men with quiet wives
and two children
— scolded off the snow
as if it was carpet
they'd be charged for marking;
noon's hugging couples,
chess-pieced on the polished rocks;
striding, whippet-kneed climbers
with ropes, boots and thick woollen socks,
here to tick off some classic routes.
And there, turning

[171]

slowly, to see what I might be,
one of those rare, elderly gentlemen.
Sticked, piped, steady as a clock,
he knows when to wind down

the rock.
I gangplank the ridge.
Lakes, ink drops,
a little cloud of sheep
— not lost or happy —
a thousand feet beneath.

The wind licks the pinnacles,
juggling gulls;
cooling masses of hot air rising
from the valleys . . .

The train puffs past, Britain's
last rack railway, squeaking
into the one track station.

People leak about,
looking for the toilet, someone,
the place you go
to see what you came for.
Camera and card-carrying fellow travellers,
we meet in the concrete bunker
of the restaurant,
while nature waits outside.
Soft apples, hard cheese
sandwiches, hot sweet teas.

The last supper, a good-sized crowd,
and company before the cloud.

The black train chinks down,
brandy windows gleaming;
they'll make Llanberis
for drinks all round.

I walk out.
A smithering wind's

detaching things — trash, birds —
flinging rice-light rain in my face
not words.

The sun stokes the ocean for the night.

Stars come on like pinpricks.
What is it?
Ledges, plants, walls, roofs;
draughty, rent-free,
a certain stage
where I played out my slack.
A few jars on the way back
home. Gulped down joy.
Broken cars, ties, the poems of a boy.

Under my nose for twenty years,
might it be
the tip of the iceberg, where
— after really only looking away —

I'll see what was beneath me?
Clean water, ore, bones,
abandoned machinery, homes
that grew out of the stones we climbed
— a mountain of time,
riddled with tunnels
the sheep blunder in.

Up to my eyes
too — at the end —
digging in or buried,
I might fall through — into underground skies.

And bump into you.

El Capitan

Saharan in the sun,
there are those
who, to cross its burning plain,
left home, jobs, wives.
Some of them had the time

of their lives.
A Pacific-grey wave
when it rains – capsized by overhangs
and falls – blown
apparitional across the walls'
blood-orange granite.
Dark alleys of diorite.
Bad jazz in the night
the sound of pounding hammers.

Where the swifts lay
– all the way from Africa –
fitting the slits
like slippers at the end of the day.
Where fern, falcon and wingless human flies
share air space,
hammock oases that sway
on the sienna-Dawn wall, the N.A's cool Cape Horn.

His tongue a wad of dried saliva,
prizefighter hands, taped and scarred,
savvy as a surgeon
tying off: for Homo Climber
with fingers, pins, nuts and bolts,
there are no holds barred
except, maybe, ladders.

Inching on or standing in its shadow,
the revolution seems over,

a tale — told by a summer ranger —
full of sound and fury
that made the Sierras tear
their bushy, evergreen hair,
down to the snowgold bones
round El Cap's polished throne.

For older climbers crossing the planet's foam,
the village store,
the wooden tables in Camp Four's
Atlantis, Lhasa, home . . .
A carpet of pines,
a river that winds
across the floor;
star-sparkled falls
combing, combing down the walls.

Like tanks advancing,
thunder booms
send glances round the lounge: Who's up?
Who's down?

In the clouds for days.
A breath of wind brings out the ropes
— with scores of tailors overhead —
stitching up the sun-patched slopes
with green, blue, red and orange thread.
Like a kite line — in a telescope's

eye — held, so another can fly,
little did I think that's what I'd get up to.
Or be a zookeeper
when I grew up . . .
Friend to a wild, white elephant,
a lifetime climbing up there
— chimneying the Ear, clinging to the Nose,
swaying up the headwall —
lifted into the air
from England, all those years ago.

Haulbag-hunchbacked on a narrow ledge;
oozing over the rim

like fingers from jam
– pausing at a frog enshrined in rain,
quiet and green . . .
Does it wonder what I am,
talking back to an expanding flake,
eating raisins, salami, sardines
– for breakfast, trusting the rusting pin
of the sun will hold till I break

out the deckchair?
To watch the young elephants
holding one another's tails,
and feel the eagle in my shoulder blades
as they round a roof.
Remembering I rode the rhino too,
compounding a line of half-in pins
– my leading rein –
with a hook or two
on a horn, a wart of quartz, an aplite vein.

The night on Sickle frightening mice
I did not invite to breakfast;
the fears like fleas I never quite tamed,
the feeling of falling head
over heels each time I look up
to wave.

How slowly this local colour, Happiness,
goes . . . From my spot on the shelf,
the taller the trees,
the longer the shadows,
the younger the self.
Warm trunk of light, reaching
to the meadows from the rain-battered height,
picking up the eyes of a truck driver,
or anyone down on their luck
in the night.

But be sure and take enough water.

The Competition

They crossed the snow like toreadors
to the bull-quiet place,
behind the village, between the tors.

Puffing — pygmied on the massive jowls —
they prised, poking
at the rain-shined brows,
weighing up a problem's size.
Clambering on their backs,
sticking fingers in damp cracks
— taking a running jump
to grasp a horn — for a second
like an angel torn

out of the overcast sky.
They try, tire, try,
panting, cursing, wrestle-
nestling a jam, pestling a finger
in a fossil-toothed hole.
Their shoulders ache
as if they've dragged a dead stag
through brush for fifteen miles.

Heaving up the earth,
fingers sniffing — feet pecking,
the clashing of those stones
and trembling bones, again and again
above the unlit heather, made them fit,
weathered men.

Wondering how the women were,
they headed home
red-handed, hungry, grown
tired.

Behind them garlanded with moss,
washed by the sun,
a line of limestone oxen.

Snow drips from their stony lips.
On unbent knees
— tossing the trees!

The Accident

While she was at dance,
I hopped around the house
with a crutch:
wading the rugs
like a heron — one leg to stand on —
jabbing the television
on and off.

Or sank in a chair,
gnawing my fingers
— feathers of doubtful worth.

The cat purred in my lap,
the sun stared,
reddening my leg once again;
now a snow-plastered stump . . .

It had split
— a twelve inch slit —
when I slipped
and blood poured over my climbing boot.
Which squelched.

I tried to smother it.
Then a friend dragged me off.
The fangs of broken glass glaring in the grass
at the foot of the boulder.

In hospital she watched them scrub,
picking out the dirty bits of fat,
making me laugh — shot with Lidocaine —
'We're vegetarian.'

Then they tacked a hundred stitches in.
Like lightning.
The cut's throat gulping
the bitten — apple — grin.

She made dinner and washed my hair.
Then went dancing.

Still I sat here, in the window
looking out, a suburb
of decisions taken somewhere else
on a sunny afternoon.

Listening to the wind
brushing off the glass
house all around, again

I jumped
out of my skin,
slashing the wrists of facts
that let me down,
twitching on the ground.
For there is that.

She comes in.
'I decided not to stay.'
Sweating, in the doorway
with fruit, flowers, kids.

I'm famous it seems
as they tip-toe close:
though my leg — propped on the bed
like a present — they don't know how to take.
As if their parents have bought
a bit of statue.

They — I might break — touch it and run

[179]

off to play.
She ambles through the house
sprinkling plants,
patting my foot
like a lamb
this first, long day
I cannot move. Lion-shadowed sunlight
gathers in the room . . .

The minutes flinch.
The typewriter sits like a seismograph.

The Question

In South Africa now
schoolchildren set the examinations,
finals being one question
in black and white.

And taking it
— at funerals for example,
where a police captain
cocks his wrist, looks
at his watch and says
— as if starting a race,
backed by the judges —
"I'm giving you two minutes"

the students are awarded
— on the face, the genitals —
the sjambok's full marks.
And though it may not be recorded,
they pass, with highest honours
from the class of the eighties,

to the prides of eyes of natives
waiting outside the jails.

Those who cannot stand examination
fail — heads bowed
for the wheel of fire
come full circle, a rubber tyre
filled with petrol.
For telling white lies
to the ones who give out the passes,

and sell the black-blue grapes
that look to us
— so ready to burst —
like eyes without whites,
pupils of the night.

The free, gold coin of the sun
— over Robben Island a rose star,
now a blood drop on the horizon.

And the answer?

JimLove Menwords

— a review of "Menlove" by Jim Perrin

I was asked by the Editors of the *Alpine Journal* to write a review of the book *Menlove*, by Jim Perrin. When they read what I had written, they decided not to publish it. Or speak to me. When I called them on this, they declined to discuss. In the course of time I became informed that certain of my remarks were just not cricket: as if playing with myself — even though I was only practising — *ipso facto* ruled out playing with the reader. One scholar, critic and confidant of my publisher wrote: 'Who in his, (overlooking the reality that women do too) right mind would start an AJ article with a reflection on wanking?'

Sadly, not Edwards, who also, probably, thought of it as — in his own words — 'a dirty miserable hystericalised ecstasy of slime production.' And so, since shame is not sanity — semen after all is milky life — unBritish as it may be, I have. Candour is the midwife of the mind.

THE EDITOR OF MOUNTAIN once said to me: 'Maybe you're like Edwards . . .' The diet, shorts, red-faced reticence among the farting hard men in the Padarn and my iconoclastic spasms in print, were not what came to my mind. Did he suspect that I did it then? For hadn't I once — glancing at Samson — read that Edwards was "an onanist", imagining the stiff upper lip of the writer as he dotted the "i"? Shame on me, an — apparently — married man . . .

That was seventeen years ago. Bog-trotting down from Moel Siabod in North Wales, where I'd gone for an early morning run before starting work on this review of a book I'd read twice during the previous three months, while driving round Britain performing and reading poems to audiences of climbers — I realised that Edwards and I were a world apart. As I returned to the Plas Y Brenin Mountain Centre, where I'd given a presentation the previous night, I found the winter mirror of the twin lakes of Llynnau Mymbyr at my feet. It was an upside-down world of frosty mountains and Easter-Island-blue sky. With not a soul in sight, I got the picture of Edwards diving in — clear, pure (water with the illusion of heat) — cutting through that petrifying element to emerge, flame-red on the far shore, having run the gauntlet of the cold gods again. Where maybe Jim Perrin would have run up with a big bath towel to give him a hug.

But not me: cold feet. Though maybe Ed Ward — someone I was close to once, would have given Edwards a swim for his money. And isn't there that in all of us who continue to take our lives into our hands climbing, which in Edwards drove him to take his life out of the hands of those around him? And I do respect Jim Perrin undertaking a lonely, ten-year journey deep into the labyrinth of Edwards' remains. A great effort.

But I think he got lost in the ancient maze of the suicide. And stopped just short of the bull. Perhaps because of the reappraisal of what we may be doing to ourselves if we climb too hard — take too great a risk too often — a reappraisal that I feel a close reading of Edwards' life and writings enjoins us to take, Jim Perrin, regrettably, leaves us with a legend rather than the life. As the jacket cover proclaims: ". . . his story has the force and intensity of Promethean myth . . ." — Edwards as the titanic benevolent being held down by the gods, the light at the end of the tunnel, Perrin would make us believe. Not the tunnel at the end of the light.

"Force and intensity." You can almost see the biro bulge as he presses the point; as if, in the absence of another quality, it needed saying twice. An unconscious recognition that he forgot something? Epimetheus perhaps, whose name means "Afterthought" in Greek — Prometheus' brother. In the myth, Epimetheus gives animals all the best qualitites — wild animals that is — leaving nothing for Man to defend and shelter himself with in a cold and dangerous world, in which, up till that point, Woman had not been created. Because he cannot look ahead and see what the consequences of his actions might be. So Prometheus — Forethought — steps in. The rest is History: Fire, followed swiftly by Women and Kids.

It is my claim that both Edwards and Perrin, giving the animal-physical-male qualities such due — courage, endurance, a fierce refusal of pain — have too little to say for our personal-social-love needs, in what is still a cold and dangerous world: Clough, Estcourt, Burke, Tasker, Boardman, McIntyre. and now Rouse . . . I may be out of step with the climbate of our times, nevertheless, I think that in misunderstanding the nature of Edwards' destructiveness, in utilising him as a peg to hang an ideology on, Perrin has not only rendered Edwards further injustice, but us — and especially younger climbers — as well: by depicting Edwards as some kind of guru. Clearly these are large claims. I shall endeavour to substantiate them and show that, *contra* Perrin, Edwards' life really serves as a warning: 'Climb down,' not an invitation to follow. Anyone doubting that Perrin is conceptualising Edwards as a role model, could read his own evaluation of what he believes the significance of Edwards' life is: In *Crags* (March 1980) after quoting from Edwards' last letter: 'How anyone can pretend that there is any friendship or indeed any other quality worth having in the dirty, sadistic idiocy that all of you and England in general has put up towards me . . . a miserable, hystericalised ecstasy of slime production.' Perrin writes of the whole delusional passage:

'. . . Much of what he had to say . . . is borne out . . . by reflecting on his life and the tributes . . . of people so adept at compromise that they could not embrace his massive honesty . . . rock climbers owe more to him than any other figure . . . for the mental release which he gave . . . Razor to the argument of climbing . . . (he) pulled it clear of the mists . . . into the honesty

[183]

it possesses today . . . No one possessed the same integrity, intellectual grasp.'

I wonder if John Syrett grasped that before he made his own hystericalised slime production by throwing himself off Malham Cove last year? (Read Perrin's obituary in *High*, August 1985). In a similar vein Perrin puts his arm around Edwards' shoulder when commenting upon the manner of his suicide, (swallowing potassium cyanide): 'What an appalling way to have to die.' Perrin is a fatalist, denying to Edwards the knowledge of his own failure — depicting him as a victim of what Perrin calls "Society," thereby adding to Edward's burden his own considerable chip. And this is in spite of the fact that Edwards twice in the same letter asserts that he's not 'talking about background principles of politics and thought, and such more important things,' but about, '. . . false propaganda set up around me.' Edwards, even in his madness, could draw a distinction between the social and the personal that Perrin appears to have abandoned.

Hence this essay's title. Since neither Edwards nor Syrett is here to voice objection to the Menwords written about them by Perrin, I shall play devil's advocate to his angel of death.

In the introduction to the book, Menlove's brother Stephen expresses his gratitude to Perrin for his 'deep understanding of Menlove,' unaware of the vitriolic comment about 'people so adept at compromise,' from which Perrin only excluded Edwards' sister, which is lacking in the toned-down book. Stephen goes on to refer to Edwards' increasing difficulties 'in communicating any real feeling or meaning,' for the last fifteen years of his life. Which sounds to me more like evidence of Edwards' disintegration, than of 'integrity and intellectual grasp'.

One of the main ways in which Perrin attempts to giantise Edwards, is to gloss over his lack of genuine intellectual achievement by associating his name with more than one indisputable intellectual pioneer. When, for example, he refers to Edwards' putative "theoretical" writings, he claims to be comparing them to Freud's, and others'. Quite apart from the — it seems to me vital — question of the destructive impetus given to Edwards by certain aspects of Freud's work (the "Thanatos — Death — principle", as well as what has become recognised as Freud's disability to conceive of a more fundamental security figure in his own childhood than his father — his mother is never mentioned) it is paramount to recognise that there are no "theoretical writings" of Edwards to compare at all.

It is not enough to say that others destroyed them. They did not destroy them in his lifetime. Had Edwards been willing to communicate with his colleagues, to show, share, discuss and defend as he did to a degree with his climbing stories, to evaluate his own thought by having it scrutinised in journals, articles, letters and other forms of public, interpersonal discourse, then we today really could assess the worth of his work. There is no point in blaming him, which I'm not, he was obviously terribly unwell to shut his mind away like that in crypticindecipherablescript, a kind of linguistic babbling. Hafod Owen, Kirkus' cottage where he lived alone for a year during the war, (for which Kirkus falsified medical documents in order to be able to participate in), must have been Babel as far as genuine work was concerned, not a white-washed ivory tower where a great mind broke down the walls of ignorance — while all around him the ignorant were at their wits' end trying to break down Hitler. He was probably climbing the walls himself: 'Climbing, climbing up the back of my mind trying to find a way out.' Publish. Or be damned.

However I do wonder if his lonely shell might not have grown a pearl or two in the field of human psychology, had he been more willing to acquaint himself with the work of others in the field apart from the founding father Freud. Jung for instance, with his recognition of the male and female aspects in all of us; Otto Rank, with his understanding of the connection between art and healing, who spoke of 'the courage of having a real illness;' an hour with him changed Henry Miller for life. Or his own contemporary Ian Suttie, who in his book *The Origins of Love and Hate* (Pelican), rediscovered the crucial, primal role of the mother — not the father; and the awesome part played by separation anxiety (something which climbing by its nature plays with all the time), in post-natal character formation.

We meet the compulsion to make Edwards out to be what he was not, at its most strained where Perrin compares him to the young Czech philosophy student Jan Palak. Jan Palak, after having drawn the short straw from among his twelve fellow philosophy students, then immolated himself in the main square in Prague, in a Kafka-Gregor-like protest at the Russian invasion after the Prague Spring of Dubcek, in 1968. A totally social and Socratic sacrifice. Coincidentally, I happened to have asked many people in various European countries during 1985, whether they remember who the Czech philosophy student was who made that supreme sacrifice. Young and old, almost without fail, have not forgotten. But I rather doubt — apart from the odd climber — whether any of them would have heard of Edwards, the taciturn conscientious objector of the Second World War. The principled pacifists such as Bertrand Russell — another big name Perrin dangles — felt it was a person's duty to oppose Nazism-Fascism. Now while I think Perrin is wrong to concur with Edwards' blanket pacifism, he is to be applauded for daring to raise the possibility — at least by implication — that there might be a connection between the freedom of climbing and that of society, between the freedom of movement we grunt and grasp after on rock, and that of speech when we have our feet on the ground or the street.

Why didn't Edwards want to fight? Perrin doesn't look at this at all, other

[185]

than to assume it was a noble stand of conscience, making I believe the same solipsistic mistake as Edwards did in assuming that ethical terms, like "rights," refer solely to whatever individuals want them to, irrespective of the fact that language — by its very nature — is interpersonal, intersubjective. Thus he credits Edwards with 'a massively principled silent stand ... in a society bent on war.' Could it have been that Edwards, in cultivating his muscles, imposing a regime of hardening himself to pain through such physically punishing exploits as rowing the Minch alone, rowing home from Conway to Liverpool alone, swimming the Linn of Dee (the liquid equivalent of a chain saw), training, climbing in the rain, climbing out of the sea by means of the waves throwing him onto the rocks — the list is long; his arms were strong — was actually sick of war because that was what he had been making on his own feelings for so long? Which, as we shall see, his public-school childhood had prepared him amply for.

In *Little Fishes*, the 'fine bike' — which Edwards says is 'destined,' 'breaks down and dies long before we reach the warm, soft southland.' This is not only a geographical metaphor of schizophrenia but an admission of the failure of Mechanism — or scentific materialism — as a philososphy, to restore the individual to their origins and sense of home (the warm and soft). Most of Edwards' exploits take place in the North. They are punitive, alone, cold and chosen. He could have gone south, learned to sit at bars and outdoor cafés by the Med — what a challenge! To make friends, to discover that those indubitable muscles love to relax sometimes; to open that lighthouse mind to the public. So that when the terrible social schizophrenia — war — took place, the murders of millions of women, children and brothers, the breakdown of civilisation, he might have felt more and been more able to respond. Is there a connection between his muscular materialism, his atheism and his inability to feel positively (for there is more than a touch of *schadenfreude* in him) for most things, from mountains on down to women?

Edwards wrote of the muscular system that it 'is always the easiest to bring under conscious control.' Perrin, following Samson, requotes 'that if a brilliant, physician-friend had been allowed' — (raising the possibility that Edwards refused) — 'to take electromyograph readings of his muscles, accumulated tension — associated with high graph rises — would have been shown.'

The point of this is that such muscular tension numbs the sensitivity of the afferent sensory receptors. These are responsible for informing the person of their internal-external environment, of the changes in feeling and sensation and perception, that are continually taking place both inside and out. One has only to read *Rowing Across the Minch* for instance, to learn of the kind of damage to himself that Edwards frequently ignored, his wrists virtually slashed by the flagellative rowing.

Edwards was aware of this, he knew he was turning himself to stone inside. It's in his writing all along. And the core of my disagreement with Jim Perrin, is that he has misread Edwards, turning a deaf ear to what doesn't fit in with his thesis of Edwards being a man's man, perhaps because he is too much in awe of Edwards' massive displays of animal force. 'I can never bring myself to be hurt, yet I must, I must. Life will go on like this till I can' *(False Gods)*. Now that sounds almost Promethean.

However it was cold, which isolates, not fire which warms by sharing its nature, that he chose. So it is that, unable to tolerate or express fear himself, he is arrogant when it comes to understanding other people's, pouring Menwords on their inability to repress their fear as efficiently as he got away with doing for a time. Nevertheless, at times during the war, he longed to be a part of it: 'Wish very much that I too could be in on things. Damn it. It would be grand to try.' And what a commando he might have become! Imagine him on cliff assaults. And he might have made a bit of peace inside himself as well. And been with us today. Revealingly he says he has, 'No objection as a matter of feeling to killing people . . .' (a strange pacifism, no?). Does he mean by this that he would feel nothing if he killed someone? Which would support the idea that he knows this because he has been killing someone (himself), for a long time. Or does he mean that he does sometimes feels like killing people? Both I think.

I have spent time on this issue of struggle with and against other people, (of which war is one form), since I think it is deeply connected with Edwards' miscomprehension about the nature of love. In *Scenery for a Murder*, he tells us, 'there's nothing I've hated so much in my time and so reasonably' — identifying reason with negation and hatred — 'as love . . .' Although the literal context of this remark is love for the mountains, the spirit of the story is clearly about the inability (learned or innate being the crucial point), to express personal love for anything, or anyone.

Perrin dismisses Edwards' recognition of the self-destructiveness of his passive-pacifism (which came to him after his first suicide attempt), by calling it 'an antidote, looking for company.' Here's Edwards on Edwards: 'I want to withdraw the exaggerated statements I made last year about myself; also about my pacifism and about being alone. And wish you could help me in any way to get out of this mess I am in.' Can we still not hear him? Unconsciously perhaps — in spite of his own contempt — as if there was something wrong with wanting company, Perrin has perhaps caught the sad strain of Edwards' music: by using the word "antidote" is he not acknowledging that it was Edwards' ideals themselves that were the real poison?

And Perrin is not able to avoid getting into a similar mess himself, when he writes of Edwards "surviving this," (i.e. his own!) suicide attempt, still

haunted by "values" (pacifism and self-sufficiency), that others had betrayed
— according to Perrin, if, likewise, one assumes that people can be said to
have betrayed values they never in fact held. As if, in other words, suicide
was altruistic murder; and, in a way, selfless. It's clear to me that as far as
Perrin is concerned, it was because other people didn't hold those values
(unquestionably good he presupposes) that Edwards almost died. Whereas in
fact was it not other people who saved him from dying? And the values
themselves that — had other people not intervened — would have killed him?

Which was what Edwards felt and said: that, in a way, his "values" were
really disvalues. After all, isn't suicide the final solution to a terrible
compulsion to be alone? And isn't it also the most literal form of pacifism
there could be? — both an admission of the self-cancelling nature of absolute
pacifism (that is a rejection of the right of self defence in its most basic form,)
and, at the same time, an act of total war, on oneself.

But by brushing over the often contradictory things that Edwards says,
with sweeping statements, Perrin's big picture emerges: "Society," not
Edwards himself — killed him. A new kind of murder — by abstract idea
(Ideotide) — one neither the Greeks nor Jews had any idea of, other than,
perhaps, divine intervention. Since "Society", for Perrin, functions much as
"God" does in the Old Testament — as an apostrophe of our fear of what we
are in ignorance of — perhaps this should be capitalised.

By not seeing that Edwards no longer believed in pacifism and self-
sufficiency, Perrin allows himself to become Edwards' *superego*, paranoically
generalising an 'intolerant, insane society which persecuted, cast out,
judged and warred' (p.270). "Value" is a human concept, philosophically
incomprehensible apart from the concept of good-for-something, or
someone. Since we cannot understand the concept of good, apart from good
in, or for, Life-on-earth — which is all we can really be said to know, wasn't
Edwards' suicide the recognition of his failure to value other people, i.e.
company, 'Society,' someone else, enough? This killed him, not other people.
I hope this isn't too painful for Jim Perrin to see, in spite of his
paradoxically Hobbesian view of life IN society, as 'nasty, brutish,' and in
Edwards' and Syrett's cases, 'short'. Were the war tribunal so far from the
truth when they said of Edwards that, 'We think his aim in life is to be left
alone and undisturbed' — ? Again, the horse's mouth: 'He pretended,
forgetting his duty to his fellow' *(False Gods)*.

The denial of feeling was inculcated from the earliest days. The mother,
whom Edwards clearly identified with, was — as Edwards saw — dominated
by the father: 'Mother always walked off her feet . . . Mother used to weep
sometimes in despair.' It's an anti-type *Sons and Lovers:* 'weak' mother,
patriarchal father who can never be satisfied. To see, hear and probably feel
the hot, salty, soft helplessness of his mother, must have made a deep,

drowning impression on the gentle helpful little boy that Edwards was. And just as the mother was literally force-marched, brow-beaten by the hectoring father, so also were the children. They were made to go off alone, away from their mother at a very young age, in order to fulfill the incredibly demanding trials of endurance — out in the wilderness, not the local park — initiated by the father; which they were not allowed to refuse. Edwards, it appears, hardened himself to these Laius-like separations from the primary female, with such force and will and inner hatred, that later he would not budge: 'The rock, it knows what I feel . . . some great force, a force partly of its own making, has trodden on it, scarred it, planted heavy grass to wave on it, and left it there to carry on and forge more of the same force *(False Gods)*.

Rowing Across the Minch was unpublished and unfinished; and, according to his companions who watched his swim of the Linn of Dee: 'We somehow had a terrible sense of anti-climax. Perhaps because he chose to say so little about it.' Perhaps because he had not learnt — or been taught — how, since maybe the appallingly lonely physical exploits he made, and of which he had so little to tell, were the psychic replays of what occurred so often as a feature of his early lonely life. But it is vital that we recognise that — as far as we can judge in these matters of the human heart — the other children in the same family circumstances, were not, as Edwards evidently was, devastated. If this speculation is anywhere near the truth, is it little wonder that deep down a part of him — crudely, the part connected with the expression of feeling and speech — petrified? If, like Suttie, we regard the larynx as the primary organ of Love expression, it is quite possible that Edwards' hyperthyroid condition in later life may have had some connection with this willed refusal to express and speak. Clearly a vicious circle — 'In a family like ours you could keep away easily and there was no need to try to say anything,' — Edwards, on the inside looking in.

So, evidently a much more sensitive child than his brothers and sisters, he set great store upon controlling fear and any signs of affectional needs — not giving himself away as we say. The price was awful. To fear fear is to fear a real feeling: one thing may lead to another . . . Ultimately, in Edwards' life, it seems to have contributed to his inability to communicate other than through his cryptic climbing stories. Conversation became impossible, body-language limited increasingly to those silent soliloquies on rock.

Is this refusal of expression why his stories and poems are so often lacking in registered, felt detail, painterly strokes of attention to Nature (including his own) through language — as something vibrantly present; alive? After all, a hypersensitive child who's been forced to separate from his mother is not going to have much interest in — and thus will have little to say about — either the natural world around or his own experience, dragging off — gulping down the tears, under the great Male's standard.

[189]

Noyce, who was perhaps Edwards' only lover, tells us that 'What Menlove disapproved (of) was . . . affection or repugnance for (mountains) . . .' The whole spectrum of feeling ruled out by this surly Liverpudlian, a skinhead of silence at his worst. Edwards' tragedy, ('I must never let myself want affection. − *False Gods* again), projected onto the mountains. But by denying all feeling − either for or against − mountains, *ipso facto* we deny to the earth herself, of which mountains are a part − perhaps the oldest breasts − our love. And the earth is after all our true home. So wasn't it inevitable that for Edwards mountains could only be 'lumps of rock or grass or snow'? A pretty lumpen proletarian view I might add, and the materialist's pathetic fallacy, not Nature's. To me it is tragic that Perrin makes the same mistake as Edwards, by failing to see that his legacy − the denial of feeling and especially feeling for − (which Perrin denigrates as 'romantic self applause,' thereby scorning, in true Edwards' fashion, both the notion of praise, and also the self that needs praise) − is no more than fear of fear. And certainly not the 'honesty, integrity, and intellectual grasp' he proclaims it to be. Edwards was phobo-phobic.

To deny the worth of any feeling is to become numbed to differences, the vital changes that make all the difference between life and death: hot/cold; food/hunger: ('Food was not important to me now . . . I threw the last bit overboard' − *Rowing Across the Minch)*; to love and hate, to good and bad, to self and other: ('Are you hurt? he said. Me, no me? Not me, no, I said. He said nothing.' − *Scenery for a Murder)*. And this psychic numbing, this loss of vitality and purpose in the individual − is always manifested in their loss of self expression (meaning-creation), and this is most fundamentally shown in the absence, or denial, of language. Our choice of words is the mirror of our soul, and of our society. When Edwards wrote of 'the mirror in the cliffs,' he was aware of the fact that somehow we legislate, or create, meaning. And perhaps the primary way we do this is through our choice of words. Shakespeare knew that: 'Mend thy speech lest ye mar thy thoughts.' If we denigrate, deny and rule out as "irrational", meaningless and absurd, any words, we thereby − in effect − numb at best, destroy at worst, our capacity to know, feel and live. To respect language is to respect what was alive long before oneself, or any of us. It is to respect the independent existence of the world as the world of other people, plants, animals, stars, etceteras . . . In other words, a spade is a spade not a word. So when Edwards rules out, as Noyce tells us he did − influencing a generation in the process? − "affection" and "repugnance", the whole spectrum with all the fine shades of feeling between − from giggles to grief, he is ruling out being human − the final act of which was his suicide.

Hence, I feel that Perrin's eulogisation of Edwards' denial of language and feeling, in the name of suffering in silence as he ran his soul back and forth over a razor's edge of risk for most of his life, is hubris. Perrin writes: 'The feats of the grown man were extraordinary' and, at another point, he speaks of 'unrestrained childhood experience encouraged by the Father' — biblically capitalising the particularly oppressive patriarchal male parent Edwards got stuck with. Perrin's adulation of sheer physicality in so much of the book, is tantamount to idolisation: 'He taught me the lesson' (what Perrin calls a 'humorously ironic' outlook), 'that . . . serves as a model for the wider conduct of life.' Has Perrin really read Edwards? Edwards would have laughed. If he could. As I read the stories and poems they are the written equivalent of Münch's painting *The Scream;* without the scream.

On page 45 Perrin quotes Edwards evoking a memory of school: 'The wind moved over the brow of the hill and the stones nestled closer down among the grass.' He mistakenly calls this "sensuality", claiming it to be 'characteristic of Menlove throughout his life.' If only it had been! Such passionate longing might have saved him. But what could be further from the truth?

'If I'd wanted company, why hadn't I seen to it? Well, I'm as much at sea there as you are, and anyhow, as I've said before, I did not want company.' *(Rowing Across the Minch).* And, contradictorily: 'I wanted a friend, not this. I wanted understanding, not this. I hoped we might help each-other pierce the partitions: how can one do that while one holds oneself so, clenching the muscles of the jaw, getting blunted;' *(False Gods).*

Menlove wanted Love Jim, not Menwords, this secret of life you claim you've found in what you call his "detachment". Maybe the secret is gravity — attachment. Which as Syrett found out the hard way, becomes terribly attractive if you get too high.

On the theme of poetry Edwards said, in keeping perhaps with what most of the climbers of the fifties, sixties and seventies would have said if asked: 'I've really very little feeling for poetry in most ways.' He also equated the writing of poetry with illness: 'With any luck, I'll not feel neurotic enough to turn out any good poetry for ages.' Unfortunately, much of Perrin's discussion of the poems seems influenced by Edwards' low self-esteem and is crudely reductionistic. He assumes — *à la* Freud — that the "real" meaning of a work of art lies in repressed-sublimated sexual needs. So, according to Perrin, a 'dirty puff of smoke' is flatulence and trees are pubic. Should this make me wonder whether he wrote this book using his pen . . . with a rubber on the end? Furthermore, the pedantic and technical language he is prone to employ — rather than trusting his own raw impressions and feelings when it comes to appreciating the poems — often obscures them. See for instance the lovely snowflake passage in the poem *Now Here We Are, My Sister.* where, unnoticed by Perrin, the clipped syntax and spaced repetition of "down" and "came" and three "she's", lofts and drops

[191]

mimetically through the one, long, un-full-stopped, fifty-word sentence, capturing exquisitely hesitant descent.

Perrin also name-drops, using Wilfred Owen, the war poet of all people, to suggest depths and feeling for others, that do not exist in Edwards' work. No wonder Perrin never actually compares texts. If you do though compare the work of a poet such as D.H. Lawrence with Edwards, you realise that it's not just another world: it's *the* world — present, quick, alive, redgoldgreenhotcoldsoftloudspicedwet — friended, that is almost always missing in Edwards' poems and stories. Edwards could not be light. His colour is black, the tone stone: 'You rock, you heaviness, a man . . .' As Perrin suddenly sees 'The tragic resonance lies . . . identifying the poet . . . with the rock'. But this vital insight is not developed.

In fact only rarely is Perrin able to step out of the shadow of Edwards, and allow his own natural lyrical gifts — which might be the snowdrops of his true growth as a writer — to show. For instance, on pages 53 and 54, he crisply evokes the first meet of the newly founded Liverpool University Rock Climbing Club, in language that is personal, tense and visual. And on pages 89 and 90, there is his piercing insight — all the stronger because delicately suggested — into Edwards' condition, where he connects the state of Edwards' self respect with his obsession with the ossiferous, decaying rocks of the Devil's Kitchen, that seem to have functioned for Edwards' mind as a kind of brothel. And Perrin is at his best when allowing his own tender regard for nature to emerge as in the kinaesthetic, felt, soaked, quality of the "November was wet" passage on page 267. If only this pen-light quality of intellect and feeling, focussing quietly, detail by detail upon its subjects, allowing the shadows to be cast by implication, had guided more of this book!

Much of the time Perrin blazes away. Look again at Edwards' description of someone climbing for the first time on the slabs. Gently parodying the self-defending process of fear that prevents people from getting into situations that they haven't learned to cope with, Edwards then perversely identifies the power of choice, 'the right direction of effort,' with self deception. Phobophobia, the scorning of the process of learning from one's mistakes, from the earliest days had made Edwards a person who would despise. 'What a fat margin of safety the coward body must wrap around itself!' (*Young Climber*, 1934). Granted that Edwards recognised that fear inhibits learning, we still have to see that he confused social embarrassment and organic, life-preserving fear, not to mention guilt and shame. And, to relate this back to my charges of intemperance on Perrin's part, the same kind of lack of distinction between the self and society, between the individual and others, mars his reading of Edwards.

His gloss, that this passage of Edwards' about a beginner climbing, is really about the individual against society, and that 'Society' according to Perrin, is 'myth, taboo and clutter' (three different concepts just picked up like stones and thrown at one another in one headstrong outburst that adds up to an act of war on words) — is nihilistic and dictatorial. It prevents him for instance understanding that true poetry does not control emotion — in the way he assumes that Edwards' poems do — but defines it, realising it by playing feeling and observation — as language. In much the same way that musicians play music, well or badly, with feeling or not.

Assuming as he does that poetry is essentially disguise (repression) — and holding that climbing is, just is, total self control, Perrin effectually obliterates the difference. Clearly there are analogies: one trusts for example that the line is there to be discovered/created; and there is much in common between the negative uncertainty engendered by a blank sheet of rock and that of paper. But there are vital differences: rarely is the writing of poetry life-threatening, even for poison pen wielders. In climbing, one's life and often those of other people is always in one's hands. Only when the state intervenes to prevent freedom of speech and thought, is it a real danger to be a writer. Mandelstaam is a classic Twentieth Century case of a poet witnessing History and its makers so memorably that he was murdered by the state: his poem on "The Kremlin's mountaineer" was more than Stalin could bear. Rarely does poets' work rise to such depths of understanding of their lives and times, notwithstanding Plato's disquiet about them.

Unless you believe that poetry is feeling alone, that need have — unlike music — no instrument, no reference among a shared world of listeners (the verbal equivalent of silent, Caged music), then most of Edwards' poems will disappoint. They are inherently amniotic cries for help, poems aborted upon the fear of needing people. Which life-long fear condemned Edwards to be, at times, inhumanly and pathetically literal: see page 117 and his account of a loose block he encounters on a climb. The block 'comes alive as if it was loved' and then hurts the one who pulled it to them. The wilful denial of love also, at times, could make him pathetically and literally inhuman: 'We found that amusement could be provided, even with the rock. One cleared the whole upper face from people . . . Good.' Trundling as bombing, no wonder people felt uncomfortable around him.

To consider what factors shaped his development will help to make clearer the differences between Perrin's interpretation of Edwards and my own. Edwards being forced to go away to school, his sister told later, would during the first two years put him in misery: 'For three days before he went back . . . the tears would trickle down his face throughout the day." This is what Perrin calls: 'unrestrained childhood experience.' As a practising psychiatrist Edwards wrote (False Gods), after seeing his mother's old dictionary thrown around and damaged by the other boys at the school to which he was sent,

'They're so hard at school, I must never let myself want affection.' This was the point of no return and we should note well: that he wrote this more than ten years after the event; that he uses the present tense — as if he is still there at the school and this has only just happened; that he's a practising psychiatrist entrapped in his past; that the incident itself is a searing instance of language being severed from its female and affectional bonds with Edwards, for it was his mother's dictionary and one of his most treasured links to her, from whom — just as on the father-forced marches of his childhood — he had again been made to separate. And finally, that his vow never to want affection, is perverse because one cannot not want, one can only pretend — to oneself and others — that one doesn't: a want is a want, not a wish. We need to recognise this for what it is: a decision to be mentally ill, which if pursued as consistently and powerfully as Edwards did — in silence, solitude and the pursuit of suffering — does not lead one home.

The facts are not in dispute. Where Perrin and I disagree is over the degree to which the family, school, friends, military tribunal, Noyce etc. are to be held responsible for Edwards' madness and suicide. Why should Noyce not have tired of being Edwards' lover? Is there no distinction to be drawn between love and infatuation, especially when the public schools of the times were such cold beds of what we glibly call sex? Is it *ipso facto* wrong for a military tribunal to refuse to designate anyone as a conscientious objector? Is absolute pacifism absolutely right in absolutely all circumstances? Only if you believe there's nothing worth fighting for — not even an argument. Were Edwards' fellow psychiatrists to be held responsible for his professional isolation because they couldn't understand what he wrote and he wouldn't discuss his 'thoughts' anyway?

In a nutshell, Perrin blames 'Society' for 'what happened' to Edwards. Basically, I hold that it was Edwards who allowed various things to happen — he could have smacked a few faces among the brats at his school, for he had the physical force — when they threw his satchel around; and it was Edwards who made the decisions, the furtive, secret, silent decisions, that, as a result isolated him from the mainstream of life at such a terrible cost. He did not have to make those decisions: 'With the right direction of effort the mind of man can accomplish almost anything.'

But he did: 'I must never let myself want affection.' If he had written *for* affection, he might have paid Paris or New York a visit, which were both well known for their thriving (if that's the right word), homosexual communities. Perhaps he didn't know what he wanted. When his friend complained of the unintelligibility of his 'notes', he could have explained or discussed them — if he understood them himself. Instead, he retreated behind saying that they weren't intended to be a form of communication. As if he was just wiping his mouth or something with the pieces of paper.

[194]

Perrin however suggests that there, but for the disgrace of 'Society' (monoatheism writ large), went the mind's Einstein. But isn't this whole quest on Edwards' — or anyone's — part — to find some single mental law through which all personal actions, decisions, feelings and thoughts, could be predicted and ultimately controlled — just dreadfully mistaken? Fascist? An expression of that infantile desire for omnipotence that Freud recognised in the infant child before it realises the mother's separate existence?

Referring to his work as a psychiatrist, Edwards was to write later: 'I don't know that there's much honest work about me.' He even insisted that: 'I'm better at theoretical psychology than practical psychology, certainly than with words.' How on earth theoretical psychology could be done apart from language — the interpersonal articulation of personal enquiry — was clearly beyond Edwards too, since he produced none to speak of. This particular passage is linked by Perrin in a powerful but unexplored allusion to Edwards' description of the beginner's self-induced inability to balance, in *Young Climber*.

However, most of the time Perrin is intent upon convincing us that Edwards was a highly successful psychiatrist. Several letters from former patients are quoted — far from favourably, but by now Perrin's thesis is set and, presumably, we're not supposed to notice. The proof of Edwards' success is assumed to be provided, principally by Ada's letter. This is quoted without comment — as if it was self-evident that she has been helped in some life-enhancing way. Is this because her concept of self-value is also close to the author's? 'Some day I will learn my lesson, and never give in, but lock everything in my heart.' That sounds desperately like Edwards to me: 'I can do with very little appreciation . . . affection, and long since realised that if one,' (notice the lapse into the formal), 'cannot do without what one wants, one had better go hang.' (Although it wasn't hanging but another method that he chose, the innate destructiveness of his decision to deny is clear). In the same passage from *Rowing Across the Minch* from which this quotation comes, Edwards says that he wants to: 'have another look at oneself.' Sadly he didn't and the piece remained for ever unfinished.

Of these life-threatening situations Edwards threw himself into during his life, Perrin writes: 'Perhaps his feelings of isolation were such that only by placing himself in these situations, could he gain any sense of integration into the natural world.' Let us consider more closely the import of these remarks. Surely Edwards needed to be more integrated not into what Perrin calls the natural world — (a distinction that reinforces his own subconscious assumption that the social-interhuman world is somehow unnatural) — but the personal one? By assuming that such solitary exploits were the only way of integration, Perrin is begging the answer to what went wrong with Edwards, since he never once considers whether it was doing such things as

[195]

crossing the Minch alone, that helped to disintegrate him. But we must ask whether this kind of "integration" — literally, at-one-ment — crossing the open sea for forty miles alone in a rowing boat for twenty-eight hours, might not so very easily have led to drowning, the self swallowed up, dissolved, disintegrated, into that huge, heaving, salty body . . . Which sounds more like atonement.

Indeed, I — as Ed. Ward-(Drummond) — used to think that the pursuit of calmness, that vital need to suppress anxiety in the high risk situations of climbing, would help me to become a better, steadier, person. It no longer seems so simple. Can't the capacity not to feel threatened become a tranquiliser, debilitating our awareness of what is actually happening, in just those situations where we most need to know, that is, in personal relationships with others, situations in which it is vital to express, not to suppress, feeling? From tenderness to anger, praise to blame. In order to become unto others what we are to ourselves. One of the results of which is that we do in fact become more — not less — ourselves. This is a kind of integration without which integrity — one of the words Perrin bestows so naively on Edwards — is impossible. It is the offshoot of a Latin root, *tango* — 'I touch,' which always, as we know, takes two.

How strange to spend so much of our time as climbers hugging, holding, stroking and leaving with such reluctance — stone: 'I wanted a friend.' Does the large number of failed marriages among climbers — my own included — have anything to do with this trained indifference to anxiety, coming as it does in the case of soldiers, from long exposure to hardship, deprivation and fear? In the context of this I found revealing Perrin's recent review of Greig's book *Summit Fever*, in *High*, where he denigrates Greig's recognition of human persistence in a non-climbing context, apparently because the only area of human freedom (volition) that he, Perrin, tolerates, is the climber's.

Though Edwards grew increasingly suspicious of what climbing might be, calling climbs 'the brief symptoms of some psychoneurotic tendency,' Perrin ignores such doubts. They neither fit the legend he is fashioning for Edwards, nor his espousal of climbing as a way of life. His use of such phrases as 'established top performer,' as if climbers were rock stars and not strange starfish, (or even fallen angels showing the young how to hold on), is the language of the ad. man, and caters to a notion of society in keeping with his own crude concept of the body politic. It is a step back — not forward — from Mallory's brilliant 'Because it's there', which succeeds in being both a high class 'Piss off!' — a warning to "Mind your own business!" — as well as an admission of agnostic reverence that still inspires climber and non-climber alike. Perrin's philosophy of climbing is in danger of becoming a script for making means, not ends: Business as usual.

At best noble savages, to imply that climbers, by virtue of climbing function as critics of un-free, immoral societies, is grandiose, self-serving and false. If Bonatti had said nothing about his Dru solo, it would have been but a climb on the scrap heap of history as far as most of us were concerned, rather than the figure of human faith that it has become. For the dances that Nijinsky performed in his madness we care not, knowing nothing . . . Mere movement, across the Minch, up the Dru, round the bend, amounts to nothing until it is received, remembered, talked over or read, in the kitchens and living rooms of those others who were not there. If we are unwilling to find a place for climbing within the larger society of home bodies – humanity that is – and insist upon regarding it as by its very nature anti-social, and then equate the social with the unnatural, arguing that only those who move (apparently fearlessly) exemplify true human feedom and in so doing criticise the lack of it in their societies, then we must be forced to uphold the South African Rugby team as a formidable critic of apartheid. Or the Bolshoi Ballet of the Gulag . . . The truth is that as climbers, most of us are about as political as snails.

A sub-textual Marxism in Perrin's writing here, that 'the thrust of Western civilised society in industrial and political terms lies in the accumulation of wealth and the defence of property,' even if it were true, in no way justifies Perrin's implied claim that Edwards – or for that matter any of us – was, or would be, in any way right to go mad. The history of civilisation is the story of the determination of small numbers of people to remain sane in the most difficult of circumstances.

Perrin quotes at length from Edwards' address to the Liverpool Mens' Institute. As with most of the things that he wrote, the piece affords insight – even in the most self-condoming passages – into what Edwards was doing to his own awareness. Edwards equates the attempt to gain self-confidence, (something which he describes as 'stupid' – one of his punch words), with the practise of self-criticism. The error is compounded by then equating self-criticism with the chronic, morbid state of having doubts and fears of and for the self, the unpredictable, libidinous, unknowable self of Freud. It is the dead end of Cartesianism: I fear, therefore I am not, which was itself the death of God, long before Nietzsche was born; that is of personal veridicality, which climbing – standing as it must on the very compass needle of true and false decision-making about balance and sensation for example, is in a unique position to look into. The mirror in the ifs.

Edwards in a telling phrase says: 'Left to itself, the mind is stupid' and, 'it doesn't see the nature of its own feelings' – intellectually cutting his own throat by denying – ipso facto – the insight he has also just expressed. How sad for Edwards, and for Perrin, offering this self-stultification as a guide to our lives and times. Edwards again: 'Nowadays it is almost usual not to turn

[197]

(the mind), into a more useful, healthy thing as one grows, but simply into a mess.' A self-cancelling prophecy. The loco men must have got pretty ugly-drunk that night. Though not so drunk as Syrett did with Livesey on the night he threw himself over Malham Cove, which Livesey described with such abandon in his obituary as, 'Syrett doing what he had to.' Had to? Doesn't that sound familiar? Free climbers? You make me cry — and quote Messner:

'I've often thought how it would be if I just remained sitting on an eight thousander. Is it not a mountaineer's secret wish to stay up there? Not to return to the world that has only just been left behind with such effort.' That sounds like the scenery for a murder.

The most violent of Edwards' portrayals is *Scenery for a Murder.* 'There's nothing I've hated so much in my time and so reasonably as love of the mountains.' It is, I believe, this hatred of love that is the real murder that Edwards was trying to inform us about. I quoted earlier from Noyce's acknowledgement of Edwards' influence upon his generation, through his disapproval (commonly regarded not as a feeling but a principle by those who refuse to praise) of affection or repugnance — i.e. of any kind of feeling in general — for mountains, as being 'irrational'. Reason equated with restraint, the prefect of the soul, not Plato's wild horse rider. In the story, very early on, Edwards accepts responsiblity for just this state of affairs, for having convinced the young man Toni — by his sickly analogy of the chestnut stewed in sugar — that tender feeling was to be scorned, and — reflecting on the chestnut that he chose to symbolise the experience of rock — that climbers had better be thick skinned. The I, Edwards, of the story says, when recognising what a cold and distant figure Toni has become to him, 'What have I done Toni? And as I came up towards him I almost began to speak of my feelings; but I stopped halfway, he was already thinking more of the cliff again than me.'

Noyce it seems agreed with Edwards about feeling, at least as regards the mountains, since he quotes approvingly that Edwards' 'real self knew them for what they were'. That is, 'lumps of rocks,' etc. Eventually Toni, who throughout the story remains a cold, distant, affectionless, almost inhuman figure to Edwards — who says of him at another point, 'You have come here welded . . . your one object is to climb' — dies. Revealingly perhaps, Edwards supports the head, but makes no attempt to restart the heart of Toni. The identity of who killed who, or indeed of what died, is left in doubt: 'Did he die? Or I? Or was I alone?'

For Perrin the story is a parable about society, notwithstanding that very early on we are told of the other people in the cabane that 'the crowd did not count'. Toni's inability to appreciate natural beauty, 'her . . . red . . . Truth, naked' and to 'come down,' is due to the fact that, 'It was all he knew. It was so he had been taught'. Here, Perrin, Edwards and I share some agreement. Where we differ — and this is crucial — is regarding just exactly who the teacher of Toni was.

Hasn't Edwards already told us? 'So when a fellow produces a thick syrup whenever he sees a hill, he may protest any fine origin for it that he likes, but most of us consider it simply sickening. We are right? Yes, he said. So I went on talking; for he did not understand: he had less experience of having other people's feelings himself than a child of ten.' I take this as Edwards' oblique acceptance of at least some responsibility for having influenced Toni-Noyce to be incapable of showing feeling for anything and — as he felt — anyone, especially himself — so young and impressionable was Noyce when he first met the older Edwards. Furthermore, the period of the climb in the story, is the same as that during which Edwards kept vigil by Noyce's bed, after his almost fatal climbing accident with Edwards. It was an accident for which Edwards may have felt some responsibility because Noyce was clearly inspired by Edwards' disdain — as he tells us — for 'everyone herded up like sheep' with 'a large number of unclimbed faces still staring down upon a pretty stiff-necked generation.' Noyce may well have felt himself pushed by a desire to please Edwards, into situations that were too difficult for him to cope with. It may well have been true that after the accident something in Noyce had died to Edwards, perhaps from some obscure recognition of the impossibility, on many levels, of love for or from Edwards. Or he may just have grown out of it. Noyce or Sutton in their book Samson said that Edwards 'often encouraged those less expert than himself to lead him up climbs he thought they could do.'

At the end of his life, Edwards in his last letter lost most of any sense of authority for his life, paranoically blaming Noyce and everyone else (i.e. 'Society') for 'the destruction of my life and work'. The frangible lament of responsibility in Scenery for a Murder (1939), in which it is my belief he comes closest to acknowledging what he had done to himself and To-Noy — Youthanasia? — was to remain a cri de coeur. In passing it may be worth noting that Edwards both felt and looked old, as a young man, to himself and to his peers. As for murder, we cannot ask Noyce and all the others who lie beneath the lumps of rock and snow and ice they chose to climb with such passion, since they are not here.

With regard to Edwards' putative homosexuality, I found the psychiatrist's letter relevant in so far as he recognised how much of Edwards' life was focussed on not-wanting, not-accepting. Perrin's scorning of this insight is a further instance of his unwillingness to examine his ideological assumptions about Edwards. He could certainly act in ways that used to be described as inverted. He could be coy: see for example his 'Lord of the universe" remarks on page 28 of Samson, where he describes a ladies' day

[199]

outing that he had climbing. He could be subservient — as some of his letters to Noyce show, and, further, he was clearly at times an exceptionally compassionate person. I don't think that homosexuality — whether genetically or culturally acquired — is the central problem. What killed Edwards, in my opinion, was his determination not to communicate his feelings, to take emotional risks, to venture into the sea of humanity with anything approaching the humility, the sense of offering he must have had, that enabled him to go to sea as he did, to dive into the Linn of Dee, or climb the dangerous long layback at Helsby. It seems that these tremendous feats of "I will" power only hardened and isolated him further.

He took to sea in his troubled times like drink as Perrin understands. Rowing across the Minch, he must have felt like a real life Ancient Mariner: 'Water, water everywhere'. By the time that he understood what he had done to himself, which understanding came after the failure of his first suicide attempt, he felt it was too late to change. If there had been a woman whom he could have loved, he would in all likelihood never have known since he would have been too afraid to take the chance of being rejected. In this connection, it's interesting as well as saddening to speculate about his great anger in Cornwall, after the war, when, having arranged to go climbing with a woman friend, he charged off by himself when she brought a (male) friend of hers along too.

He could have gone into the army, where he might have met other men in a safer environment for a homosexual — although that would, I think, have been too much like a replay of school days for him, actually joining up: 'A large part of me would like to be in on this war.'

Most of all he could have said more, could have embraced his demon by — as Lawrence enjoined that frozen generation — opening his mouth: 'Within a year or so I may begin to think about starting (to write)', he wrote, which seems like the linguistic-mental equivalent of running, or being out climbing alone and too frightened to make the next move, and about which he had written, 'It is difficult to describe what it feels like to be so, to describe that extreme desolation that may be left behind in the human brain when it is without anything working in it to spur it on.' This sounds like brain death in a way: 'The brain occupied sick and stiff with its fears', and a warning surely against treating ourselves as if we were climbing mechanisms. This extraordinarily honest and clear account of the inherent mental conflict of climbing is ignored by Perrin. It hardly fits into the Promethean mould. 'It is schizophrenia, the split mind', Edwards himself says (*A Great Effort*), seeing in his mind's eye what he was doing to himself, putting up routes, not putting down roots.

Alas, Perrin's blindness to the incipient sense of responsibility that Edwards did have for his breakdown, leads him in the closing pages of the book to echo Edwards at his most paranoiac: 'I would be quite willing to take on trust, several of the social criticisms voiced in this letter', he writes. Apparently, he totally accepts the 1957 reply to Noyce too, with its insistence that it was everyone else, Noyce and They, who were to blame for: 'the dirty set up around myself', for his insanity as, 'an illness induced artificially by your set up to me' and for his coming suicide when he writes of: 'your and their destruction of my . . . work and life'. It is pathetic and reprehensible that Perrin has no comment to offer on such madness. So hugely has he identified with Edwards, that it becomes hard at times to know whose voice is whose. It is his own tragic thesis, altruistic suicide, painfully clear. Thus to him, 'there is a weight of truth in this letter'.

Edwards knew that he had followed false gods. In a passage that echoes Christ's temptations (to self-sufficiency) in the wilderness, he wrote, 'So he sang to his own god . . . like a sound in the wilderness . . . it was so beautiful that it was some weeks before he began to realise he had been stupid again'. In my book, Jim Perrin is a false prophet, whose doctrine, *Dulce et decorum est scandendo mori*, the new lie, I hope attracts no (more?) followers.

That is too hard. Perhaps I have read into his book dangers that exist only in my own vision, as I claim he has in part, into Edwards. And, and . . . Perhaps I have not appreciated sufficiently just how much Edwards managed to achieve, what he hinted at, if and if . . . the vision of human confidence in appallingly hard — though principally physical — circumstances, that glimmers from his life and climbs sometimes. Though set alongside someone like Panagoulis, of Oriana Fallaci's book *A Man*, the idea seems fanciful. But who knows, you say? But then I say who can this who who knows be, but you, but I, sticking our noses in where they belong, in wondering about this turbulent nature we find in and around us from dawn to dusk everyday of our lives.

Make no mistake, this is an important book, one you should judge for yourselves and not take my word for. It is a letter home from the front line of the mind in our times and, in the end, the real hero may well be Jim Perrin for daring to try to understand. It may well prove to be the scenery for a birth of writing about climbers as people, instead of the other way round. Which may not change the stony face of mountaineering literature, but might knock it off its pedestal. And that would make Edwards happy. In fact, if there is a place where climbers who have killed themselves go, some long, flat, black, beach where they are condemned to build sandcastles in perpetuity for small children to knock down, I can imagine you know who giving Edwards a copy of Jim's book and a day off to stroll to the top of the distant dunes and read, the sea breeze ruffling his hair and the strong, green sea grass tugging back and forth while the grains of sand shiver down closer as he writes some comments in the margin . . .

[201]

Let the last words be his: 'This climbing. Perhaps, really, one was never made for it. I have a conceit that I was made for even more than that: more than to satisfy extremely one's own pride. It would be nice to feel that one could have the possibilities of interacting in an expansile manner, contacting with life beyond and outside of ourselves.'

Syrett

A charcoalgold face, peering
up; a dusty, David-torso
hunched over a beer, in the Valley
twelve years ago . . .

The serpentine eye looked
down – away –
back, blinking
like an owl at the hot light of day.

And soon took off.

I'd heard of his routes:
that swallow-glide at Almscliff,
nesting nuts with fingers like feathers
of leather, cresting
where the gritstone juts at the wind.
Mercurial, knuckles unskinned
he skimmed the edges of England.

A trembling branch of climbs.
Where the golden egg of the mind
must be pushed to the brink
of cliffs even plants gave up,
when the last ice age
stiffened over Europe.

He hadn't washed for weeks.
An oniony smell arose

that made me wonder.
Close up
he was English,
a pale face
behind the coalman's grimace.

A touch of thunder
— he exclaimed — 'I'
glancing away — 'am
climbing badly.'
I listened like a doctor
to his shame

at feeling grounded — I had felt the same —
by those big names: the brain-dark N.A.
the hawk-picked Nose.
But the way he drummed his fingers
on the flat surface of the table,
made me feel composed.

Next day he skipped out
with two birds from L.A.
Years after, I heard
he was drinking — back in Leeds.
The hard stuff they said:
words that hold nothing back;
like sex, drugs; like the miners and police
— left/right thugs of a state on the rack.
And the crags black for months.

Past first snow,
heaped, behind the drystone walls,
like salt against summer;
and sheep, chewing gummy grass,
with crude red stains
they never even felt
brushing their thick-skinned pelts,

I drove the one-track road to Malham Cove.
There, Earth, the first mother,
pushes the climbers away from the cliff.

Bright threads hang
from their waists as they tread
the deep air,
fingers sticky with gravity
— honey of despair
to a climber tamping a nut in a crack.
Woodpeckering a peg, yelling
for slack they crawl the great wave
of limestone forestalled
in the head of the dale.

It was dark when he made his way round.
Taking the walker's trail,
that ladder of boards
sunk in the ground
— or the pale path —
to these tables
of rock, polished and set
for the next
glacier to knock

over. Nice spot
for a picnic, thinking;
the blue-green dale
— church spire sinking in the mist —
Aegean when you get this high.
Trees like sea anemones . . .

And did he stop in this cave,
with a tiny blue flower like a low, gas flame,
and wonder what else he might save?

A dog barks — Cerberean —
cutting the ground beneath my feet
like a tin can kicked
down a long, empty street,
past silent factories.

Here too, once,
a waterfall's white beard practised,
woolly rhinoceros guzzled lush moss,
pterodactyls took off . . .

Rabbit pills like oily
piles of ball bearings
— I must be careful;
slick stone, like bones
in surgery.
And there — an airstrip of turf
where he sat,
perhaps for something to dawn;
a free country
— a hundred metres beneath
his cold, wet feet.

I heard — an hour ago —
'It's the finest limestone crag:'
and someone coming up the road.
Tall and willowy, a climber perhaps,
with a small daughter
clinging to his rucksack straps.

'Is that what you woke me up to see?'
his wife, alongside puffed,
bulging from a dark blue suit.
'It's just a piece of bloody rock.
Do you mind if I go back to sleep!'

Was it that?
Were they too heavy
for his new extremes?
Or had he
— who flew so fast at the lime light glancing off
tall walls — got fat?
Was he drunk?
Without a mate to climb down to
when the holds shrunk,
and the dole queues got too long to wait?

Too long to wait.
River like tarmac, sheep
maggot-white in the fields

— the wind feathering his heels . . .

The sun bursts
out, setting a red
sheet on the hills.
The eyelets of beer cans gleam.

Malham Cove, a black hole
dreams ahead of me,
the last step
I cannot see . . .

Unless I'm pushed.
So I must feel my way
like child coming backwards
downstairs, mud sucking
my bootsoles where the underground
river bleeds, looking towards
the bright lights of Leeds
and Manchester.

He threw himself at her.
She snatched him back.

A few sheep stared.

Stone

I'M TRAPPED. Roofs, running into space, like a tank backing up over me. Entrenched in four inches of water, half a mile up. I smell like a tramp and next year I would have been forty —

Stop it. I was growing all right, sprouting a couple of hundred feet a day with my plum-blue and cherry-red haulbags, for the last two weeks. And after looking up to the North America Wall like a gigantic x-ray for seventeen years, since I first saw a picture of it in *The Alpine Journal,* and the thought that I would one day cross it alone began to bother me, I was about to be released, cured — just two pitches short of easy ground — when a storm out of Canada slammed down the west coast. Washing El Capitan with icy rain that has fixed on the summit like a coma; its bitter east winds are stropping back and forth like gigantic razors across the wall. And I feel as if some horrible operation is about to be performed . . .

It is the first October snow on the valley floor in twenty years, they told me over the radio two hours ago. Now the meadow has the faint yellow look of a polar bear rug and I can see the rescue team like bright red ants crossing back and forth. The cloud drops. I can hear cars and snarling snow plows. Waiting to be rescued, at first I'd felt like an important patient at the head of the queue. Now as the light lowers and the haze grows thicker, I find myself thinking of the swifts, deep inside the cracks, the feathers of the fathers cupping the shitty blue eggs. It's time.

And when the toy-red and white helicopter that's been eddying back and forth between the summit and the meadow — Christ knows why — stands like a dragon fly, about two hundred feet out, scrutinising yet again, I gesticulate like a football supporter — but stop immediately, resulting in a movement that must look as if I'm hitting myself on the head, since they might think I was waving good day, and was not halfway to my eyeballs in self pity. Better try mouthing. So, like a red-faced goldfish blowing bubbles of help, hoping they have binoculars trained on my bulging cheeks and are, at this moment, reeling out the line they will shoot in to me — I've heard of it being done — I'll backrope myself down and out (mustn't forget the camera).

'Come back you bastards!' As I blink the helicopter flicks five hundred feet sideways. They hover about the Nose, apparently studying something, which from here looks like a flame, playing at the lip. Then they slip over the top. Sightseeing I suppose, as I sink back into the clam that my hanging tent has become since the snow began melting a day or two previous. Or was it an hour?

But I can't get back to sleep, so I turn to the valley floor, the rash of hikers, gawkers and climbers (drawn from the warm hotel lounges by the prospect of fast money on a rescue). There's hardly anyone . . . Where's Lia? Three days ago she was sitting on a red blanket in the meadow, playing with Carie our god-daughter, while Stephen and I were discussing technology over the walkie talkie that I've clutched like a babbling baby each day talking to her, and friends like Gerald and Irwin who've come up at the weekends to see how I'm doing and keep her company. Then, today, for the first time since the storm broke two days ago — I guess around noon — her voice came in, astronomically-tiny. 'Edwin, where are you?'

A good question I think now, noticing the radio on the floor of the tent, like the black box of a flight recorder. And it comes to me that, if I have to, I can cut loose the hanging tent, with me still inside, since it might — if I clip myself into the aluminium frame of the ledge upside down as a counterweight — act like a parachute or a windsock and, since pigs can't fly, land me gently at the foot of the wall. Better than freezing to —

Go on. (Say it.) I can't. (You have to) . . . Peering into the void where the wind is smashing sheets of plate glass rain against the wall and tearing at my fly . . . Yes. True. I do . . . The polite, tight-lipped hymen of my platonic self-sufficiency, intact these thirty-nine years, starts to give . . . Silently, slowly, shamefully, savagely playing with the idea — all of a sudden: 'Help! Help! Help! Help! Language spurts from my mouth in a helpless coming of age.

The wind mmms, buffeting the haul bags fastened in below the tent, so that the slings creak, briefly sharing my wet dream of rescue. Let me introduce my family: Mom, the bulging blue bag that held all the water, and the softwear, my down sleeping bag, polyprop sweater, clean green underpants, red stockings and orange turtle neck for the summit day, along with my coffee and toiletries, is half full of icy fluid. I'd left it open, outside the hanging tent two nights ago after flopping around like a triple amputee for several hours in the dark trying to fit the Porter ledge together. Now the aluminium skeleton is showing through the fabric, where the tent's been grinding against the rock. Haworth, the smaller red haulsac I've named after my son who lives in England, and which carried the cheese, muésli, carrot cake, curried chicken, canned tomato and clam chowder soup as well as around a quarter of a million raisins and an apple a day, my provisions for the entire climb, is empty. Dad, the burgundy, tear-shaped haul, I specially made for carrying the hardware, bangs into the tent with each gust of wind, as if kicking me out of bed. I noticed this morning the first freckles of rust

[208]

forming on the pitons, when I made the last radio call. Four hours ago.

If only I could sleep, lie, a cool snow-white in my glassy plastic bed until the first rescuer arrived and shook me, then — about to kiss my hirsute, tomato-soup-fringed lips, give him the shock of his life by hissing 'Darlink, vhere av yoo beeeeen', instead of becoming this terrorist of myself, making yet another pathetic last stand against growing up. I might then live to become a bus driver — remembering again the test I took in Sheffield in 1974, when, on my way back to the bus station, I'd overtaken another double decker bus and left the test inspector speechless, beetroot, banging on the window behind me. Or I could be a teacher again. Even a businessman . . . Like Mr. Robbins.

Ah he's led me on more than one wild goose chase over the last seventeen years, with that stare. It transfixed me in 1968 when I first noticed it, branding my back as I fumbled at an off-width near Bridalveil Falls, and it confuses me still, breathing over my shoulder long after the fun has gone and all I really want to do is go home, whether he would stick it out or not. And did he always know I'd have to show my face in his den? Sprawled like an old wino in my hammock in the Black Cave, singing sunday school songs I'd forgotten I knew, I made my self behave sensibly when I got frightened . . . Just like him. Guzzling water I had no right to when my second's back was turned in the past; sawing through the laces on the boots he lent to me sixteen years ago, and then throwing them off from Sickle Ledge in the night, to give me an excuse to retreat from the Nose that was looking down at me looking down. That's me. No wonder we could never be friends, no wonder I ended up like this. How on earth did I ever climb anything? And what is it that makes me write like this, gnawing away at my own fragile security when I should be gracious and patient, garnering my resources — like him — so that I can get back to —

'Lía . . . LÍA!' I bay her name, but it's like shouting into a bottle. The thick cloud smothers my voice. I wiggle the aerial. A crackle like cellophane as the last electrons jostle for the poles.

It will be dark in a couple of hours. I lift the fly. Over to my right the great gouge of the Cyclops' Eye seeps. There, two nights ago — or was it three? — the full moon set, a white pupil, illuminating the cavity scratched out of the face so long ago by the glacier. I felt wonderful lying on my back looking up, and the next morning I wrote a postcard to Carol, resisting a temptation to send it airmail. Doing the A4 pitch across the eye was like hanging the washing on a windless day, free but for a peg or two; I felt young, happy, hard-working as a bee in my bright yellow climbing pants and black balaclava. It's my son's birthday in a month. He'll be eighteen. How old will I be? I listen again to the hiss of the departing traffic, the angry horns. What if war has been declared, if Livermore, the nuclear weapons centre a hundred

A DREAM OF WHITE HORSES

miles away, has gone up, and I manage to make it off? A nuclear winter in Yosemite, with a pack of climbers, hikers, weekend skiers and rangers. The disputes over food; how many could be crammed into the fall-out shelter beneath the Ahwahnee Hotel. And who? Madness, riots, executions . . . I wonder if there's any liquorice in the bottom of the haul? All I find is a couple of raisins, soggy as bogies.

Over the public address system five hours ago, I heard that there were two other climbers in grave trouble on the Zodiac wall. Now I know, just know, as my eyes get heavier, that the rescue team's decided that two are worth more than the one they can't even get their hands on, it is so overhung. And I remember Birtles saying once in Norway, at the end of the sixties, how a climber up in the mountains was, in real terms, above the law. He could, he said, have committed a murder and no one would know, or be able to get him. And, worming into my sleeping bag I turn on myself again, like a cheap dentist pulling his own teeth: 'Get what I deserve', poking in childhood cavities I'd forgotten I still had, living for the last nine years in sunny California: The shame in the police cell a month previous, caught shoplifting three rurps, after having spent ninety dollars on gear for this climb. My heart pounding as the policeman approached the cell door . . . Had it turned up on the computer that I was on probation, after the climb for the nuclear freeze campaign? Terror that the year's sentence in jail (suspended), would be re-invoked. That I would be deported. And what would Lia do? I think of her trying to survive in a damp council flat in Britain while I draw unemployment.

I pull the bag over my head. An awful thought is forming. Have I really been trying − in all this climbing − to get away? To get myself into a position where life itself will vomit me out. A bloody mess.

Unless it is that climbers are actually students of the theological college of the galaxy, training to be angels after life, guardians for the young, high on being gods . . . Now that brings a smile to my face! So, once again, I pull off the bag from my head and start rowing back and forth to warm up.

Six hours since you called. The cracks that I'm bivied in, running with ice melt for two days now, are getting louder by the hour. That's all I need, a waterfall in my lap. The web of nylon straps inside the tent that suspend the artificial ledge, has turned into an eight chained instrument of torture. Every interstice of clothing is being invaded, each drop of water, a smooth, pear-shaped seed, blossoming innocuously against the sleeping bag, is instantly transformed into a deadly chemical, a cold napalm seeping into the nerve centre of my life to steal its secret: Heat. The inner, stellar furnace is being turned off. I am now hypothermic.

Frantic, I start doing sit-ups, thrashing back and forth in my blubbery bag as if I was a human washing machine in some impoverished bachelor flat.

Like a fish out of water, gasping at the analogies I've lost control of, I see my heart like a red snapper slammed on the ribs of a rowing boat, empurpling with rage. Wringing and wringing my hands, reptile-white, wrinkled, ancient, almost gooey, as if I'd been living half-submerged for decades in a gutted spaceship, trying to get back from Venus.

Pulling myself up with a burst of fearful energy I wobble onto the support bars of the ledge like a bewildered orang, and straddled across them I let down one of the corners by releasing the friction buckle, so that the obscene liquid drains out. When I look, the ground, twenty-five hundred feet down, is like a black and white photograph appearing in the developing fluid.

Seven hours. I'm draining the water every ten minutes. Each time I lift the fly, a gust of freezing air rasps my face. I could cry; what little heat I have vanishes as quickly as . . . What? I try to think of something to keep my mind from thinking of — A snowflake in Hell — No we've had that one. A personinafurnace — SHUT UP! The lighter . . . Even though I ran out of gas for the butane stove days ago, I do still have a lighter. Three inches high, of blue plastic, I flick the tiny knurled wheel and a violet flame dances. Olympic. I hold it to my open mouth and breath in the hot air, happy for the next two minutes as a kid with a straw sunk deep in a milkshake. I drop the lighter, hissing into the water, when I smell the singed whiskers. Stupid prick! I mean my moustache of course. But that reminds me. I haven't seen it for ages. Blue, crocus tip in a patch of damp, brown humus-like hair and dirty, green underpants. And, because it's there — now I know it's there — I feel obscurely reassurred, my end in sight. The faint, vinegary smell — like the fish and chip shop on a windy night — Food!

I've eaten all my food. Karrimat . . . Appalling to think of such a thing, even if I succeed in getting any down, won't the vomit, for I'm sure to ejaculate it out like some ectoplasmic egg yolk, just suck up my vital core heat? Perhaps I could see the yellow mat as freeze-dried female Chinese feet, pressed and packed centuries ago? Well, that, along with envisioning the headlines in the Reader's Digest: "Man Saves Life by Eating Bed" with a tawdry photograph of me holding up a ragged piece of closed-cell foam, makes me think. Meticulously I start portioning out the six pieces I have with me. First one for my back, jammed down my shirt where it sticks out like Clark Kent's Superman cape after a heavy starching; then I puff out my chest with another and add a roll inside each trouser leg. In the faint blue glow of the last rays of the sun through the tent fabric, I must look as if I've just landed. Then, threading a spare bootlace through holes I dig out with my Swiss Army knife, I make a funny hat. Glancing in the mirror — the stainless steel lid of my cooking pot — I'm a coolie, waiting in the rain in Shanghai for some tourists. I buff the lid against my balaclava and look again. Bloodhound-eyed from no sleep for more than forty-eight hours, with

[211]

my long, drawn out limbs I look like J.K. Galbraith in the shower, waiting to be gassed — flash of a young man out in Reagan country, sleeping beneath the freeway in San Francisco in broad daylight last winter, as I was on my way to court, with a sheet of cardboard over him while trucks thundered past, inches from his head. Why do I do this?

Something flutters in my trousers. Greasy, bubbly as a snail coming out of its shell. A fart . . . And cold! Now that frightens me, the hot snake of my intestine turning grey. I writhe, hugging and hugging myself — I feel like a bag of bones — curling up, small, making myself so small maybe I won't be noticed by the grey forms prowling and howling outside my hole. Remembering the bullies who used to corner me in childhood: Ormerod, Gordon Evans whose mouth was as sharp as a dog's, the Jeremy Bentlys of Hilston Avenue I lived in terror of, whom I once really believed were just a temporary aberration of Wolverhampton, where the Wolves came from . . . in their black and gold strip on alternate Saturday afternoons, sprinting onto the pitch to the guttural cataract of applause that roared down from the terraces on the North and South Banks, to explode out of the stadium and turn heads as far away as Wellington, as if the sea had just entered the Midlands. And Bert Williams, "The Cat" as he was known all over the world, tigering his line while a fat little boy behind the goal flung his school cap in the air: 'One day I'll play for England,' he vowed. They're in the Fourth Division now.

Feebly I begin squeezing each muscle I can think of, from my sphincter to my scalp: abs, calves, lats, I even try wiggling my ears, to get that hot flush that makes my finger-ends feel as if an elephant's been stood on them when the blood comes back. It makes about as much difference as closing the gate in a field. So I don't start thinking about what it would be like living in El Salvador, waiting for a knock on the door in the night, nor about being held in that football stadium in Chile, when they stopped playing games. I have enough to do feeling sorry for myself in the freezing water, like when I was a boy waiting and waiting for my mother to come, trying to fall asleep, my boats motionless in a sea of scum, my knees two ice caps.

Until she got me out, rubbing and patting me down to my smothered protests, before wrapping me up in the orange bath towel 'Keep still!' while she grabbed at one foot with her pliar-like fingers, pinning my big toe between her forefinger and thumb, and cutting my nails as if there was money in it. Twisting, wriggling, yelling that my toe was broken. The clippings flew.

Remember when you had her out of New Cross? You were thirty-five, and as a surprise, just before you went on Nelson's Column, you had her from the psychiatric ward. And Mad told you she wouldn't, after, watch the TV news that showed you climbing it, because in her mind, since she saw you actually moving, it must be live — and she couldn't bear to see you fall. And

[212]

you took her back to the flat that had been bought after your Dad died. For a week. 'You are a good boy.'

You had to sign for her. It was after the stroke, and the left corner of her mouth dragged, as if a fish hook was attached by a fine line to her left foot, so that every time she shuffled, her lip tugged down in time with her step. And there she stood, dripping, in front of you, in the bathtub. Finally, you had your chance. Like an ancient mermaid, her vast, whiskery breasts, with those short legs dwarfed by the wrinkled, baby-white elephant bum, and which she pressed together, so that it looked as if she was only balanced on one, that ended in something under the surface . . . Her left arm hung.

You began sponging her down, working the wash cloth like a potter around the folds of her slippery stomach like some fragile vase, and as you whisked it over her overflowing thighs (you were trembling), she leaked on your hand, giggling and squealing like a little girl. It was one of the happiest moments of your lives, like sitting down at a piano and suddenly discovering you can, after all, play.

The light is gone . . . I lift the flap for the last time. A star is sparkling, like the tip of a scalpel, piercing the deep water-blue night. Cars have their lights on, a stream of vehicles driving past El Cap before the next storm. Due tomorrow. The air gnaws my shoulder. I can see my hat, snatched by the wind as I climbed the pitch above in the dark three days previous. Deposited back on the ledge I slept so well on at the Cyclops' Eye, now, with a crust of frozen snow on it, it looks like a fresh loaf of bread left on the doorstep in a supernaturally early delivery.

I take a deep breath, a tremendous effort then to get warm enough to fall asleep. Go! − running on the spot, up stairs with someone after me, one step behind, clawing − leaping, twisting, kicking, punching − I stay ahead, the tent walls flapping like an accordion. Now I can barely move, my legs felled, flat on my back, the next step so enormous, sheer, my fingers can't quite reach the lip. Why am I so little and why am I crawling up here? Where's the door? − the handle quick − don't look down − there's the bed − I dive, tearing at the sheets. A cave, and it's warm . . .

I can hear her heavy breathing outside, running her hands over the bed, pinching, pressing − 'I can't breathe!' She lets me go. I pop up like a seal. 'Again!' Time for my story. 'Once up . . .' And she reads. And reads, until, eyes drooping, she tucks me in. Kissing me: 'Sweet dreams' she opens the door − a shaft of light − 'God bless' she whispers. "God" sounds nice . . . Funny, warmy wordy . . . whatey doey meany,

'Otway ooday ooyay eanmay Iway underway, ooway areway ooyay'

'Get to sleep!' Her voice from behind the door.

I fall slowly

asleep . . .

Everest

Tread softly
— like Beirut —
through the icefall's snout.
Nature shoots without

asking why . . .
Fleas on the sheeted ice,
when they stepped out of our telescopes
Mallory and Irving were giants.
Such high hopes the rope

would come full circle, a birth cord
of hemp — Earth's first —
to present to the king.

Fifty years ago.
Now more peer
from their bunkers
in the snow, hearing
the missiles; an avalanche
clearing its throat in the night.

Down and in,
the only way out

is up . . . 29,000 feet,
crawling like infants
in the teeth of seracs,
Reason's ice axe

gripped. Stone-aged hands,
ten strange sticks
we rubbed together
so long ago
in the ice caves.
And made fire, wine, Rembrandt's mind . . .

Such Humanity left behind,
they vanish, beneath
the star-eyed ice . . .
Or maybe they fall through
— hair on end in the sun's cold stare,
like a rusty halo —

because there's nothing there.

Hubris

An Open Letter to Royal Robbins

Royal,

FOURTEEN YEARS AGO, a letter from you fell onto the floor, almost at my feet, in the house where I lived then in England. I had written inviting you to be a reporter of my solo attempt on the North America Wall.

Certain of your lines were memorable: 'It sounds more like hubris than love of the warm rock beneath your hand . . . I want nothing to do with it. R.R.'

Branded. Hid it. Swallowed it. Never said a word. It was what I expected. And, perhaps, needed.

I still came to the valley that spring. Ostensibly to solo the NA — or die trying — the real reason, if I can speak of reason here, was I think to reach another point of no return. And turn.

Lying at the foot of the wall that April, watching the raptors turning, soaring over my head and the clutch of haul bags that I'd bullied to the top of the first pitch the day before, I knew — like a kick in the face — I didn't belong there. The quick-clean strike of your letter had pricked the bubble I thought was balls. So I went home — well, back to that house — with my tail between my legs; though all too soon I was to grip it between my teeth. Grateful?

Hell no! Having assumed you were of the devil's party, I hated you for your righteousness, that zen-like refusal to play my game. I wasn't looking

[215]

for a father, the figure would have done. Unable to follow in your own lean footsteps, I had to make do with putting my feet where they belonged: in my mouth. Telephoning the newspaper back in Sheffield to tell them that I couldn't go on, was as easy as falling out of bed from a nightmare of jumping off a building. Yet there was a magic in your silence and still, peregrine eyes, that followed me back to England. Love?

For, leaving Yosemite, I had looked back through the windows of the bus as it gathered speed: grey-headed, El Cap waited; an April shower washing the valley, ointment of light spreading across the face.

Not until 1984 though, sometime after the waters in my head had broken — with the nurse left holding a beautiful-but-still-life-baby, the picture of my love — was I ready to grow up there.

November, heading across the States for Europe, after fourteen days alone on the N A — a day for each year before I came back — I'm finally leaving it behind.

I told you a lot up there Royal, if you were listening, your turned back always just ahead. When I slunk up the confined chimney of the fifth, I heard you cough around the lip of the roof as you knocked some stones out of the crack to make me think twice. On the pendulum at the end of the eighth — on my twelfth or thirteenth attempt — just the picture of you sitting on an old pin, arms folded like Brando leaning against a wall between takes, was all I needed to make me feel you were on my side, not the angels'. Sitting in my hammock in the Black Cave, when I yodelled to Lía I heard your laughter echoing after. When I reached the Cyclops' Eye after ten days and sank thankfully asleep, it was your snoring that woke me to see the moon like a cigar being pushed into the horrible pupil. A warning of the storm being on its way had I but known it.

And you'd give me marks up the entire route. A single bolt at a belay, where I'd have put in two or more. It looked punitive, a concession to those like me who steal by holding their breath. And those traverses of yours, like tightropes that ended in mid-air. Along which I'd wobble, juggling nuts, holds, hooks, pins, more out of my mind than in. The odd, spartan ledge, flat and factual as a raft on the ocean, at the end of another gulping day.

Examining the granite, calculating the specific gravity of a move, weighing a crystal, checking the spectral line I recalled against the knucklebashing rock, the haulbag-slashing, gnawing actuality of cracks, flakes and slits that digested my lines, twisting them intestinally, so that I had to perform the most delicate obstetrical manoeuvres in order not to lose those vital inches . . . I passed my days. Nights were another question.

In fact, the whole climb, an obvious blind alley, a kind of myth, weaving between the daylight granite and the nightdark diorite, the plain and the gothic, slashed by aplite's white lightning — visual and mental — was a brain wave. Who knew what lay hidden? Somedays I danced, swung on the horns, slapped that warm backside and got a move on; sometimes, late in the day with the clouds closing in, I rappelled into hell for my haul bags. Couched in my hammock talking out loud in the Black Dihedral, I would have made Freud's hair stand on end.

Reading the bold prose of your story after the first ascent, when I was twenty-two, in 1967, having just finished my first degree suffering in Philosophy, was like having the church walls fall down in the middle of the service and realising, though everyone else was still singing Beatles' songs, that I was free to leave. The four of you: Tom, Chuck, Yvon and yourself, were more like astronauts, opening the space age after the Kennedy promise, than climbers.

Twenty years later the moon is crowded. Scruffy, slow, muttering to myself, I must have looked like a Vet to you, like one of the street people I've observed over the last decade living in the Haight, as you free-souled ahead of me in your shorts and white hat between Calaveras and Big Sur. Having heard of the legend, a kind of freedom, they potter around in the sun, panhandling, looking down. But though I may — to a tourist with a telescope — have looked high, most of the time I was on my knees. All around me the South East Face bristled with modern new routes, high rises put up by the yuppies of Camp 4 with computer-designed bits and pieces with which to get even more attached . . . One-grand-a-day pull-up boys, with Liddy-like wills, washboard abs and birdy ribs; bankrolled with lats, biceps, triceps and quadraceps — alongside them I felt like a septuagenarian tramp, a cheap monocep, a head on legs, shufflingalong, wondering what could be free. Cool hot shots with upper class grading systems and air-splitting refinements, had they reduced El Cap to a big chip? Though as much a prisoner of my times I suppose, playing truant in my hammock, reading a book or writing a letter long after respectable climbers had gone to work, when I was winched to the top by the class of 84, a deep, woad-blue in the freezing twilight, I probably looked Middle Aged.

Sitting on Calaveras Ledges, wide-awake in the dark from a dream I'd had of my brother and sister having died; at Big Sur, with one of the pendulums done, of a tiger slipping silently into the black lake I was swimming across; again in the dark beneath the box-car of blocks above the Cyclops' Eye, trying to get the octopus of poles and slings that my porter ledge had become to cooperate; and, finally, like a lifer, trying not to see how narrow the view was from the confines of the Black Cave — if you had deigned to put a hand on my shoulder at any of these moments, I would have been crushed. Or at least felt guilty, if you'd suddenly appeared on rappel — like noticing a cop on a bike in the rear view mirror.

[217]

Not that you'd have arrested me. More likely you'd have just handed me a warning about going too slowly in the fast lane: the British equivalent of Harding's whacky anarchy, your felon climber . . . For some days I just loved sitting there like an old bum, scratching myself with my pen, keeping half an ear on the roundheads all around me who'd been hammering since dawn. A royalist really, like you, not quite fitting into the businessman's suit and Modesto mountain shop. As though a shop could be that big! Or vision that short-sighted. You who revered the walls like that old Italian his marble, for the true form within, not the cost; and made a mountain out of a piece of paper and a pen, engraving the minds of men and women who climb, with a look like the David, as they face themselves . . . Quite right — damn right in fact! I did get angry Royal: your witty thrift with the bolts; stretching the truth about those so-called rubber band pendulums — they were no more than home runs — wasn't what was biting me though . . .

Now the Black Cave was elsewhere some — I mean it was out there. When I meet Chuck again, probably in Berkeley, sitting on a bench in the sun with an icecream, or waiting in the rain at a bus stop, humming some Pratt Vivaldi would have liked, I'll prostrate, right there on the sidewalk — provided I don't get walked all over — saying: 'Master.' For not since the first slither onto *terra*, has such a lead been given; though, knowing Chuck, he'll probably say it was because you were giving him one of your looks . . . Sinking past my Friends, hidden deep in the crack, when I eased my head around the corner and looked up at the hanging shards of aplite, the rusted, half-in pins, the gaping roof, I felt like a dentist starting work on Hitler's teeth after the assassination attempt. Anything could happen. I stuttered at the bristling lip, the wind making my ropes stand on end — as if the natural laws had been inverted and I might at any moment hurtle upwards feet first. A Bosch world, where etriers float sideways; where my red hand — scuttling after a placement — hung from a hook, while the crack looked the other way.

Working my way back down into that sepulchre, my heart-bomb ticking faster . . . I burst into tears: There was no one there. No wife, son, friend . . . No Horror of Nothing. Not even a note. Just a maidenhair fern I noticed, green in the dark at the back of the cave; and the cave, whistling to itself.

When I launched my old haul bags into space from the back of the cave on the ropes I'd suspended from the jutting lip, I hollered like a boy discovering his testicles.

For there was, after all, nothing to be afraid of. And that is why I was angry with you. For from some grim, unfathered part of your self, you tried to scare me. Once by daring to describe me as a little Madson, just after he'd gone off his own deep end, on the Dihedral in 1968; and then in your letter three years later, in cold ink, again you made me more — not less — afraid of myself. Dangerous medicine Royal. But I forgive you, and must admit to a blush of respect — why not call it love? — for your hard-hearted heart. After all there is still the North America Wall for other Egyptologists to dig. The valley of the kings . . . And the queens? We do see some women nowadays. A lighter breed you say? Are there no Cassandras in the Gunks? And all those Electras and Sibils in LA, surely some will climb the walls?

For me, climbing until I couldn't move, poised three pitches above the Cyclops' Eye at the start of what you called the hardest lead of your life — hanging like meat in that storm-freezer but still kicking — was a theological experience akin to having a baby. After the first October snow in twenty years anaesthetised the tan valley floor to a white sheet in minutes; when, after two days in the acid bath that my hammock had become, my hands pickled, my feet — floating on the surface — fishy, my farts gluey, my heart like an operation was about to start: to be delivered from that oppressive igloo of self-sufficiency — Descarte's bunker — was the high point of my life.

Even though you rarely replied to my letters, I had hoped that if you got wind of me up on the NA after all those years, you'd meet me off. Ah well, a moment of strength, I'll soon feel normal. But maybe, passing through Modesto sometime, I'll see if you're up for chess, or a burger. We could discuss your latest river or line in shirts, what's not been written. And you would tell me off for being an ass, expecting one of the sons of God to climb on my back. There, that made you laugh too.

A nice picture. Somehow though I don't think it will happen. People — in general — don't seem too interested in remembering what passed, let alone putting the record straight. I might be wrong — it has been known — but even if I am, about us, by the time I get back I bet you'll have moved on, up some creek, around some bend where no one's been before, paddling your own kayak. Mark my words: one of these days I may be there, waiting for you for once — sitting on the bank mind, not quite as crazy as you once thought I was, out there in your own deep water, showing us, immaculately, how.

Dear Royal,

In the school of hard knocks there are no teachers. Thank you for refusing to pretend.

A Dream of White Horses

Palomino in the morning,
as the sun rose higher

they dashed, their manes on fire,
pounding their hooves on the rocks.

And smashed — we were climbing —
sank, broken, foaming . . .

The wind lashed them back,
combing their matted hair,

swollen green sea mares twenty hands high,
surrounded by herds

of nervous blue stallions,
snorting and champing and trampling

us under, given the chance.
We stood by — a pitch apart —

watching the rein of our rope,
that led between the last grey overhang,

redden like a vein in the sinking sun.
And breathed again.

Their fire gone,
the black horses were drinking,

and we were thinking of a name . . .
Nothing had been forced — Then the tide

turned, they surged, rearing
— manes smoking white —

running, running
in the night towards us.

[220]

Addendum

Notes about the articles

TO CLIMB OR NOT TO CLIMB Written after a day on the rocks at Sugarloaf, North California, just before returning to Britain to present my poetry performance. *Between a Rock and a Soft Place*.

BETWEEN THE LINES Stanage, 1985. Returning to Britain − after a nine year absence − with twelve poems and a portable mountain, I find myself on trial, charged with being a 'publicity seeker'. I decide to tell the truth, the whole truth . . . and some more.

THE HERETIC Yugoslavia, 1985. Written after a year of visiting cathedrals and famous buildings; in longing for the sacred pagan places.

PROUD . . . Italy, 1986. Awoken by a nightmare I recalled my adolescent religious nervous breakdown and a 1963 ascent of Tower Ridge, Ben Nevis, with a heavy man of God.

I FELL A reflection on a fall from Pontesbury Needle, Shropshire, in the early sixties, with which was revealed my life's direction. This and the following eleven poems comprised the text of the performance I gave in Britain during the winter of 1985-86 along with my portable 7000mm mountain.

A DAWN WALK Yugoslavia, 1985. In 1964 I went to Bristol University to study Philosophy, Psychology and English and I soon discovered climbing. The article describes my first climb in the Avon Gorge with Oliver Hill (who knew how to do it properly), my arm still in plaster after my near fatal fall in Shropshire.

WHY? Written over the last twenty years; it probably began when I first put hand on rock. A realisation that words are holds. Published in *Mountain* (1981).

GREAT WALL 1972. Having met the electric Pete Crew in 1967 I made the fifth ascent of his famous climb. A shorts-clad, doubt and date-eating upstart, on tip-toe among the hard rock gods. Published in *Hard Rock* and *The Games Climbers Play*.

SUGARLOAF Written whilst belaying on a winter's day at Sugarloaf, North California. Published in *Mountain* (1981) and *The Climber* (1986).

WHITE ELEPHANT − WHITE WHALE On my first visit to Yosemite in 1968, as the metaphysician of the self-styled "British North America Wall Expedition", I couldn't even complete the first pitch. Leaving Yosemite I felt like Adam cast out of Paradise. Published in *Ascent* (1971).

THE GHOST The ghost of my warmer self tapped me on the shoulder. Makalu, 1977.

OUT OF THE MIDDAY SUN 1968. A near free ascent of the Lost Arrow Chimney in 1968, when I had my first bivouac. Published in *The Alpine Journal* (1969) and *Mirrors in the Cliffs*.

ON MT. DIABLO 1977-1984. Written during visits to the mountain that overlooks the Bay Area and has a splendid panoramic view. On a rare clear day you can see Half Dome, and almost any day the nuclear weapons factory at Livermore.

THE INCUBUS HILLS With Oliver Hill, my first successful biggish wall climb. The Long Hope Route was named in memory of the crew of the Orkney Lifeboat, all of whom were lost at sea just before we arrived. St John's Head, Hoy, is the tallest vertical cliff in Britain. The climb took nine days and is unrepeated. It was my baptism by air. Published in *Ascent* (1971). *Incubus Hills* became the name of a Californian wine.

THE WAY DOWN   Yosemite, 1983. Written after a descent in the dark from Arch Rock.

MIRROR MIRROR   An account of the first ascent of the Arch Wall on Trolltind, Norway. This was my third attempt to climb the route without resorting to seige tactics. My baptism by water. The climb took 21 days and is unrepeated. Published in *Ascent* (1973) and *The Games Climbers Play*.

STARTING UP   1983. Making the bed one morning, I get a surprise.

EASTER ISLAND   Yugoslavia, 1985. A first ascent on Ilam Rock, Dovedale with Hamish Green-Armytage in 1973, prior to leaving for a year in the United States. Published in *Extreme Rock*.

NIGHT FALL   1983. A nightmare, followed by a down-climb and breakfast in bed.

END'S LAND   Mexico, 1974 (while ill). This unhappy piece is included for historical interest. Perhaps it was an attempt to jump the bergschrund between climbing and living that widened after the ascent of Arch Wall. A story of two (or was it three?) wearying failures to climb a 900ft turdstone cliff on the north-west extremity of Scotland in 1973. With Tom Proctor and − at sea − Linda. Published in *Mountain Gazette* (1975).

DEER TO ME   Yosemite, 1983. Written while eating breakfast alone in the forest.

FRANKENSTEIN AND LINDA   Italy, 1986. Whilst living in America, having left teaching to write more, I just about made a solo ascent of The Nose of El Capitan over nine days in 1973 (possibly the first by a non American). The rise of a self-made man . . .

THE CLIMB   1982. Remembering an ascent of Tensor, Tremadog with my son. Published in *Mountain* (1982).

CHILD, WOMAN, MAN   I fell (again) and stayed on in the States. A 1974 ascent of Snake Dike, Half Dome, with three children of varying ages. Published in *Climbing* (1986).

GOD   Written on the summit of Las Tetas de Cabra, a volcanic mountain in northern Mexico, after finding a summit bottle. Published in *Mountain* (1982).

A GRACE PERIOD   Italy, 1986. In 1977, while living and climbing in San Francisco, I got called up to the Himalayas by an international . . .pedition to climb the West Face of Makalu. The story of my ex . . .

BETWEEN A ROCK AND A SOFT PLACE   The title poem of the performance; written in Yosemite at the last rappel in the dark from Rixon's pinnacle. Published in *High* (1984).

NELSON MANDELA'S COLUMN   Italy, 1986. In 1978, Colin Rowe and I climbed Nelson's Column − with one enforced bivouac in Bow Street police station − to protest the involvement of Barclay's Bank in South Africa, and, ipso facto, that of the BMC which banks with them. Barclays have now left South Africa, but Nelson Mandela, imprisoned immorally for the past twenty-four years, is still inside. Perhaps it's time to take up the story again . . .

THE BLACK LAKE   1975-1986. The lake at the foot of Cloggy: the cliffs in the mirror . . . I keep returning to it. Published in *The Games Climbers Play* and *Mountain* (1982).

SNOWDON   1975-1986. This still feels unfinished, in the way perhaps the mountain is making up its mines. Pete Crew, to whom the poem is dedicated, is now a working archaeologist in North Wales. Published in *The Games Climbers Play* and *Mountain* (1982).

EL CAPITAN   1968-1986. Written in the presence of this natural stonehenge.

THE COMPETITION   1985. After a winter bouldering session with David Craig, the flint-tongued poet who lives near Carnforth, Lancashire.

THE ACCIDENT   1983. A three-foot fall whilst reversing a boulder problem in Glen Park, San Francisco, resulted in more than a hundred stitches.

THE QUESTION   1985-86. To free or not to free: that is the question. Whether to suffer the tear gas and nightsticks of outrageous fortune, or take arms . . . .

ADDENDUM

JIMLOVE MENWORDS   Italy, 1985. Climbing as a way of living? Or Dying? A critical response to the story of the life of Menlove Edwards by Jim Perrin.

SYRETT   1986. Written after he killed himself by leaping from the main overhang at Malham Cove. Contrary to popular opinion — *à la* Livesey — he did not have to.

STONE   Cambridge 1985. The first chapter of a novel — "Stone, Water, Flame". Trapped by an unseasonable storm on the North America Wall of El Capitan, with incipient hypothermia, after two weeks alone an ego starts to cave in . . .

EVEREST   1984. The perennial fascination with that point at which the climber is closest to leaving earth.

HUBRIS   An open letter to Royal Robbins, one of the founding fathers of modern rock climbing and writing.

A DREAM OF WHITE HORSES   Yugoslavia, 1985. Watching a sea storm brought back the day in Wen Zawn seventeen years earlier, when Dave Pearce and I had a dream. The name was Dave's suggestion for the route we had just discovered during a charge-of-the-light-brigade day of waves. Published in *The Climber* (1986).